CONCEPTUAL ENCOUNTER

A Method for the Exploration of Human Experience

Edited by
Joseph de Rivera

UNIVERSITY
PRESS OF
AMERICA

To

Is Chein
(1912-1981)

-- whose insistence on the scholarly legitimacy
of qualitative methods
-- whose advocacy of an integration of the
scientific and the humanistic
-- whose presence as a teacher
supported our work.

CONTENTS

v

PREFACE

Many of us are committed to the formation of a
more humanistic psychology, a psychology that pays
respect to the freedom as well as the necessity in
our lives, to the fact that persons are the creators
of themselves and their culture as well as the
created products. We have both the hope that a
humanistic psychology may aid us in the art of
living our life, and the belief it may encourage us
to honestly and systematically look at the full
range of human phenomena and, hence, prove to be a
worthwhile scientific endeavor.

But humanistic psychology is in a position
that is dangerous as well as promising. Our awareness of human freedom and of the fact that our
subject matter involves human experience prevents
us from completely relying on the traditional
scientific generalization prevents us from relying
on the methodology developed by history, art
criticism, or the other humanities. Left without
the balancing influence of a disciplined method,
humanistic psychology runs the danger of being
self-indulgent rather than creative, of succumbing
to the excesses of romanticism rather than quietly
aiding the lyrical development of human life. We
must work to develop our own discipline, to develop
methodologies that will be true to the spirit of
our inquiry.

To the extent that we can view ourselves as
objects -- our behavior conditioned by past events,
determined by natural selection in the course of
evolution, controlled by gestalt principles --
traditional psychology and scientific method help
us understand ourselves. But to the extent that we
view ourselves as subjects -- as creating art or
science or our own behavior, making choices,

responding to values -- traditional psychology has
little to say and traditional method is inappropriate.
There are aspects of psychoanalytic thought, and
related developments such as Jungian analysis and
gestalt therapy, which provide conceptualizations
that are often useful to us as subjects leading our
lives, but there is no established way to test the
general truthfulness of these ideas. These conceptualizations, derived from clinical work, are often
primarily designed to be helpful rather than
systematically true in a scientific sense. Such a
pragmatic endeavor is complementary to but not
identical with the search for the truth of our human
position and needs to be balanced by and to draw
upon a broader humanistic psychology. One can conceive of such a psychology, a psychology that would
have a different approach to persons, that would
recognize human beings as subjects as well as
objects. Giorgi (1970) has articulated some of the
features of such an approach, suggesting that it be
termed "human science," in contrast to the "natural
science" approach to persons as objects. He, and
Fischer (1977), have shown that such an approach is
not simply a new "third force" psychology, but one
that has really been present throughout psychology's
formal existence.

In this book we want to share a method that has
gradually evolved from our attempts to study the
emotional dimension of human experience and that
should be useful in studying a wide range of
problems in a humanistically conceived psychology.
In the first chapter we will sketch the overall
features of this method which may be called "conceptual encounter." Then, in successive chapters, the
five of us will each present the studies that were
generated when each of us used the method to investigate a different type of experience. We
believe that each of these studies is of interest
in its own right. Together, they suggest that
human experience may be described in much the same
way that a land may be mapped by a geographer.
There is an incredible richness to experience. The
English language has over 400 names for different

emotions -- yet our method enables us to describe such moments of experience in ways that lead us to both appreciate their uniqueness and see the relationships that exist between them. Thus, conceptual encounter makes it possible for us to systematically explore the new psychological continent which it reveals.

Most of the studies in this book were originally Master's Theses or Doctoral Dissertations and we would like to encourage the use of conceptual encounter as a method for such scholarly investigations in the future. The method may be particularly useful for students in clinical, social, or humanistic psychology who want to work on meaningful and relevant dissertations in areas that are not easily amenable to experimental investigation. If the reader finds our results to be of value we hope he or she will support and encourage the use of conceptual encounter as an alternative methodology.

In the production of this book, we especially want to thank Becky Clark, who typed the first version of the manuscript, Eric de Rivera, who drew the "maps" of experience, and Sadie Kreilkamp, whose trenchant editorial assistance improved some of our thinking as well as our grammer. Finally, we want to express our appreciation to Elizabeth Spencer, for understanding the manuscript at the same time she was typing, and for the dedicated care with which she typed this work in its final form.

References

Fischer, C. Collaborative psychological assessment. In C. Fischer & S.L. Brodsky (Eds.), Client participation in human services. New Brunswick, New Jersey: Transaction, 1978.

Giorgi, A. Psychology as human science. New York: Harper and Row, Inc., 1970.

About the Authors

Joseph de Rivera is Professor of Psychology at Clark University. He graduated from Yale in 1953 and, after working as a research psychologist in Naval Aviation, took his doctorate at Stanford in 1961. After teaching for a number of years at both Dartmouth and New York University, he came to Clark in 1970. He is the author of The Psychological Dimension of Foreign Policy (Charles Merrill, 1968), Field Theory as Human-Science (Gardner Press, 1976), and A Structural Theory of the Emotions (International Universities Press, 1977).

Joel Funk is Associate Professor of Psychology at Plymouth State College in New Hampshire. Initially a chemistry major (B.A., Rutgers, 1967), he became interested in humanistic/transpersonal psychology and in the work of Wilhelm Reich. A songwriter by avocation, he began working in musical perception, earning his Ph.D. in this area from Clark University in 1977. He is currently applying to developmental theory to such topics as religion and music, and has published a number of articles in these areas.

Susan Goodman is a psychologist with a private psychotherapy practice in New York City. She graduated from Bard College and worked in a number of New York's hospitals, colleges and clinics, as well as teaching at the First Street School and the Lower Eastside Action Project. She was also a staff reporter on the Village Voice and a contributor to Dissent before earning her Ph.D. in clinical psychology from New York University in 1975.

Thomas Kreilkamp is a Staff Psychologist at the Harvard Community Health Plan in Cambridge; a Senior Counselor at the Bureau of Study Counsel of Harvard University; and Instructor in Psychology in the Department of Psychiatry of the Harvard Medical School. He graduated from Harvard College in 1963, and then studied social psychology at New York University, obtaining his Ph.D. there in 1970. After

xi

teaching at the University of Massachusetts-Boston, he moved into clinical work, training in clinical child psychology at McLean Hospital. He is the author of The Corrosion of the Self (New York University Press, 1976); a chapter on 'Social Maladjustment' in Volume VII of the American Handbook of Psychiatry, edited by Silvano Arieti (Basic Books, 1981); and an essay in Men in the Middle, edited by Peter Filene (Prentice-Hall, 1981).

Janice Lindsay-Hartz is a psychologist working at a psychiatric hospital for children and adolescents and engaged in private practice in Miami, Florida. She began her career in biology (B.S., Brown University, 1970), worked as a research assistant in physiological psychology and taught at the Germantown Friends School in Philadelphia. She earned her Ph.D. in clinical psychology from Clark University in 1980 and trained in family therapy at the Nathan Ackerman Institute in New York. The works of Martin Buber have influenced her understanding of persons and relationships.

I

CONCEPTUAL ENCOUNTER

Joseph de Rivera and Thomas Kreilkamp

Whenever we attend to a person's life, whether it be our own or another's, we find a person who is existing in the world in a certain way. We may catch ourselves, or the other, involved in some project, or in the midst of anger, or falling in love, or simply disinterested. Persons may always be seen as having some way of being in the world. We shall use the term "personal experience" to refer to a person's awareness of how he, she, or some other, is in the world, of the awareness of involvement, anger, love, disinterest.

It might be objected that a person may be in the world in many ways at the same time, that terms such as anger or love mean different things to different persons, that it would be fruitless and unprofitable to study anything as nebulous as a way-of-being or meanings as imprecise as those of love. In this book we shall show that, in fact, it is possible to describe precise structures for different ways of being, structures that may be profitably used to map our personal experience and that enable us to share our experience with others. We shall describe the method of research we use to create structures which reveal important aspects of different ways of being. Our findings are mere beginnings, our method is still being developed, but we are excited by a glimpse of new worlds to explore. We want to share what we have found thus far and the method that has enabled us to find it. We want others to join with us in mapping personal experience.

The knowledge generated by conceptual encounter, together with the skills involved in using the method, is useful both in the art of leading one's personal life and the practice of helping others.

First, it helps sensitize us so that we see choices, ways of being that we were previously unaware of.

Second, we begin to appreciate the functional value of ways of being that may have previously seemed alien. Given our ideals, it becomes clearer what we are called upon to do, that there is a necessity to certain choices.

Third, knowledge of the structures of different ways of being leads us to be aware of specific relationships so that if one aspect of experience is known we have a set of "looking rules" that lead us to ask questions about other aspects of the experience. This is especially useful to the clinical practitioner who may have to be sensitive to a nuance of behavior and infer aspects of experience of which the other is unaware.

Fourth, simply having a clear description of a way of being helps us recognize the experience. In the case of negative experiences, the mere fact of recognition, together with the knowledge that others have suffered the same experience, may be relieving. Further, a knowledge of the parameters of the experience may aid a person in managing the experience in him or her self. Likewise, one is equipped to recognize how an other is being and to respond in an appropriate way rather than thoughtlessly reacting. And one may have to recognize the existence of experiences which one has never personally experienced, whole ways of being in which the self has never engaged.

Because knowledge of the structures of personal experience helps us to recognize an experience, see how it relates to the way we are being in the world, what choices we have and how

2

different choices will lead to different experiences, such structures are analogous to maps, though
they are maps of personal experience rather than
physical terrain. And just as knowledge of the natural world helps us notice and appreciate a plant in
the woods and instructs us in the building of a
house, our knowledge of personal experience helps us
to appreciate and accept the psychological events of
ordinary life and enables us to transform our personal lives, to help others, and to make our relations with others more comfortable.

                *   *   *   *   *

     Conceptual encounter refers to an encounter
between the investigator and a person who has agreed
to act as a research partner. The investigator is
studying some aspect of human experience, such as
getting angry or falling in love, or making a
decision. He or she is trying to fully comprehend
this experience -- to understand the way in which
our lives are structured when we are angry or in
love, to grasp what alternatives are available, to
be able to articulate an abstract description of the
general phenomena that will illuminate our specific
experiences and enrich our appreciation of life.
But to achieve an abstract conceptualization that
really comprehends experience and is not a mere
intellectualization, the investigation must be
solidly grounded in the concrete experience of
actual events in the lives of persons. Accordingly,
the investigator asks each of his or her partners
to give a specific, concrete example of anger, love
or whatever is being studied, and to faithfully
describe the actual events that occurred in as much
detail as possible. Carefully listening, skillfully
questioning, the investigator allows the partner to
recall, and to some extent to relive, a concrete
expreience. After this is achieved (perhaps 15
minutes, perhaps an hour or two has lapsed) the
investigator shares his or her abstract ideas about
the essential characteristics of anger, love, or
whatever is the general type of experience under
discussion. Now, the inquiry shifts its focus from

3

the concrete experience of the other to the abstract
ideas of the investigator. She or he attempts to get
the partner to comprehend these general ideas and
asks the partner to what extent they fit the specific
reality of his or her concrete experience. Thus, the
abstract conceptualization that has been created by
the investigator encounters the concrete experience
as comprehended by the partner.[1] Is there an en-
lightening "fit" between ideas and experienced reality or is something wrong?

Some of these encounters are mild affairs where
there is an easy fit between concept and experience,
others are complete misses, cases of mistaken identity where the experience is not really relevant to
the conceptualization. Often, however, the encounter is highly interesting, the impact of the
experience forcing the investigator to create a new
conceptualization, or the power of the conceptualization leading the partner to a new comprehension
of his or her experience. Thus, in the course of a
series of encounters with different partners, the
conceptualization becomes more precise and acquired
depth and generality so that it can illuminate some
aspect of human experience.

* * * * *

The topic of inquiry may involve any experience,
behavioral pattern, or psychological phenomenon for
which the investigator and research partners have a
common name. The investigations considered here
include various emotional states such as "anger,"
"joy," and "anxiety," the behavioral pattern of
"laughter," and the interpersonal phenomenon of
"distance" between persons. By using the name of
the topic, the investigator can ask the research
partners for examples of the topic, thus generating
an unlimited number of experiences of whatever he
or she is interested in. Such experiences should
always be personal in the sense of being the person's own experience, rather than hearsay, and
should be a concrete instance (e.g., "last night
when I was angry at Sally I got hot," rather than

4

"when I'm angry I get hot," or "people get hot when
they're angry"). However, the experience may be
the person's own experience of someone else's behavior (e.g., "he was so angry he turned red"). At
first the partner's awareness of the experience may
be rather sketchy. However, if the investigator
quietly listens to the experience and is sincerely
interested in finding out exactly how the event was
experienced, amazingly detailed accounts may unfold.
After this spontaneous account of the experience,
the investigator may ask about important details.

Often, the investigator prepares a list of
questions about general aspects of experience, and
inquires into whatever aspects are not spontaneously
mentioned. Thus, if the research partner has not
mentioned how she or he experienced time, or bodily
sensations, or psychological space, the investigator
may ask how time, the body, or space, was experienced, and the extent of what is recalled may be
expanded, in whatever areas seem to warrent
attention.

The concrete experience of the partner's
individual case provides the raw data of the
investigation -- the "facts" or "existence" or
"reality," which the investigator's conceptualization must fit. Hence, the existential details
of the individual case are extremely important.
However, the investigation would soon be hopelessly
mired down in detail were it not balanced by the
abstract conceptualization provided by the investigator. This conceptualization is an attempt to
capture the essence of the phenomenon -- to describe
how the experience is organized -- its structure.
Such a description attempts to provide a sort of
map or plan of the experience of anger, laughter,
distance, or whatever phenomena are under investigation. It describes how the person's experience
must be organized if he or she is to become angry,
to laugh, to be distant. It describes what changes
in experience occur with the anger or laughter,
what other organizations were possible, and how the

5

"choice" of the particular configuration that constitutes anger, laughter, or whatever, functions in
the overall context of the person's life.

Needless to say, a conceptualization that
accurately fits experience and that reveals a
hitherto unexpected order is almost an artistic
creation that can only occur after patient study of
numerous instances of the phenomenon.

In this task, the investigator is guided by
two quite different demands. First, the conceptualization must be true to experience -- it must fit
the various concrete experiences of the phenomenon.
It must be broad enough to include all instances of
the phenomenon yet narrow enough to exclude related
phenomena. Thus, a conceptualization of joy must
include all examples of joy but exclude cases of
elation or gladness. Second, the conceptualization
must be elegant. That is, it must be relatively
simple rather than cumbersome, it must describe
different aspects of the phenomenon and, ideally, it
should use concepts that are related to other investigations of interest to the psychologist. It is
the tension between these two poles -- the dialectic
encounter between concrete instances of the phenomenon and abstract, elegant conceptualization that
leads the investigator to create an interesting
nontrivial conceptualization. In one sense, in
order to formulate a good condeptualization the
investigator must move away from the concrete data.
That is, he or she can not simply select some concrete feature that seems important in many of the
experiences, or abstract concrete features which
different experiences have in common, or articulate
some "family resemblance" shared by the experiences.
Rather, the investigator must intuit an abstract
symbolic form that succeeds in capturing the essential relationships involved in all of the concrete
individual experiences. Like Michelangelo sculpting,
he or she must free the form that lies hidden in
the rock.

An adequate conceptualization usually takes a

long time to develop. At first the investigator may
not be aware of any particular pattern in the different experiences that are examined. Then, a pattern
may gradually emerge as he or she sifts through
examples of the phenomenon and reads through the
literature. Or there may be a sudden grasping of a
pattern, the report of one experience may be a revelation, an insight into the essential structure of
the phenomenon. On the other hand, the investigation may begin in a hit-or-miss style, the researcher
having a notion about the structure which is
thought in advance and only later checked with the
literature, the observations of others and self-
reflection. In such a case, repeated revisions will
occur. Regardless of personal style the formation
of a good conceptualization is a continual making
process as the researcher moves back and forth
between interviews, observations, literature and
reflection, gradually becoming more alert to the
nuances and patterns of the phenomenon.

The conceptualization develops through successive insights as it repeatedly encounters the
experience of different persons. In one sense it
can never be finished for there is always room for
development in science, mathematics, and art. But
there is a point where it is finished enough to
share with others, a point where a product has been
completed and publication is desirable. There are
at least three criteria for this point where a
conceptualization may be judged to be complete:

1. It is successful in explicating what has
previously only been implicit in the phenomenon.
Hence, it reveals the phenomenon in a new light so
that a person examining his experience has a better
understanding and appreciation of the experience.
This is particularly evident when the conceptualization provokes an "ah-ha" as a person suddenly
gains insight into his experience, realizes something that he or she was not aware of before.

2. It replicates in the sense that it fits

all the different experiences that different persons
relate or, at least, further encounters no longer
add anything new, no longer challenge the investigation.

3. The conceptualization is elegant and par-
simonious. It uses few but powerful concepts in a
precise way, concepts which may be related to the
work of other investigators so that the conceptualization becomes a part of a wider sphere of inquiry.
Rather than detracting from the precision of the fit
between conceptualization and concrete personal
experience, this systematic requirement seems to
enhance the power of the conceptualization so that
it is more apt to capture the essence of an experience. The requirement seems to function in much the
same way that requirements of rhyme or meter and a
sense of the history of literature seem to stimulate
a poet's creativity.

*   *   *   *   *

While the excellence of the investigator's work
necessarily depends on his or her attaining a thorough acquaintance with the relevant literature and
struggling to achieve creative insights, the
development and testing of the conceptualization is
ultimately dependent on the nature of the encounter
between investigator and research partners. In one
sense this is an intensely personal encounter. Its
fruitfulness depends on both persons feeling comfortable with each other and the situation so that
they can try to be completely open and honest with
each other. However, the encounter is clearly
structured with a research goal. Hence, it is not
personal in the sense of two friends sharing an
experience, nor personal in the sense of a therapeutic encounter. From the very beginning of the
investigation, when the investigator asks the other
if he or she would be willing to be a research
partner, there is an atmosphere of partnership
within the structure of objective inquiry. Open
communications about very personal experiences have
a meaning that is controlled (and often made pos-

8

sible) because of this research context.

    After the research partner has shared his or
her experience and the investigator has offered his
or her conceptualizaion, the two must work together
to determine whether or not the conceptualization
fits the experience. Of course, it may be immediately apparent that there is an excellent fit, or
that there has been a miscommunication and the two
have little to do with each other. Often, however,
and these are the most interesting encounters, some
parts of the conceptualization fit but others do not.
When these cases are pursued, either the conceptualization will help the research partner to attain
a new insight into the nature of the experience so
that he or she becomes more aware, realizing hitherto
ignored aspects of the experience, or the concrete
experience will convince the investigator that the
conceptualization is in error and must be modified.
Let us consider examples of these outcomes; first
the latter case, where experience forces a modification of conceptualization.

    When de Rivera initially began to investigate
the emotion of anger, part of his conceptualization
included the idea that when a person was angry,
there was a desire to hurt the object of anger.
This conceptualization seemed to fit his own experience and those of several other persons, so he began
to ask his research partners if they could think of
any exceptions to the statement. One responded with
an experience that was an exception: she once
became angry when her puppy wet the rug, yet did not
want to hurt the puppy. She said that she was simply
mad that the incident had happened and wished that
her rug were not wet. Now an exception to a conceptualization may only be an apparent exception.
The person in question may not have really been
angry or may have had the desire to hurt the puppy
but not let herself experience the desire because
she felt such a desire would be wrong. But these
alternative explanations did not seem to be valid --
the woman had acted angrily in other respects, and
she seemed to be capable of admitting her aggres-

9

sive impulses. Thus, the investigator concluded that his conceptualization needed modification and this particular encounter with a person's experience forced an important revision of the conceptualization.

On the other hand, a good conceptualization may change how a person conceives of his or her experience. Lindsay's conceptualization of gladness includes the idea that gladness occurs when a hope is fulfilled. One of her research partners reported feeling glad after spending an enjoyable evening with her fiancé and some of his old friends. She was not quite sure exactly what occasioned the feeling of gladness -- only that the evening was enjoyable; she did not spontaneously mention having had any particular hopes for the evening. However, when she was given the conceptualization and asked if she had been hoping for anything, she suddenly realized how important it had been for the evening to be successful -- that she had been deeply hoping that she would get along well with her fiancé's old friends and that they would like her.

Of course, there are times when it is simply unclear whether or not a conceptualization fits an experience. In such instances a delicate judgement is required. These ambiguities should be recorded as indications of possible problems with the conceptualization and carefully preserved as data for future investigation. Often, later encounters, or modifications in conceptualization, will resolve these uncertainties.

When we speak of encountering the partner's "concrete experience" we obviously refer to the details of a specific incidence of the phenomenon (as opposed to the investigator's abstract conceptualizations of the phenomenon in general). But this notion of encountering a concrete experience may be misleading if it is not qualified and elaborated. For one thing, we must note that the investigator is largely dealing with a narrative -- with the partner's account of the concrete experience -- and clearly it is essential to establish conditions of inquiry which will promote faithful rather than distorted accounts, conditions we shall discuss below. Usually, this account is a mixture of literal statements about actual events, more abstract reflections about what happened, and figurative evocative language. The partner attempts to get back into the experience and communicate it to the investigator, but can only narrate what he or she can articulate about the experience. Hence, the partner is limited by his or her personal introspective and linguistic skills and, to some extent, by the language of the culture. Obviously, the whole process of conceptual encounter is facilitated when it is possible to select research partners who are reasonably articulate and generally aware of their experience in the area under investigation.

Nevertheless, conceptual encounter is not completely dependent on the narrative skills of the research partners. In fact, we are not interested in the narrative per se but in the experience on which the narrative is based, and the investigator's encounter with this experience is not completely limited by the partner's narrative for the latter may be able to recognize much more than he or she can relate. Hence, the investigator can draw upon his or her own descriptive skill, and knowledge of other examples, and of English literature, to offer literal or figurative statements about the experience which the research partner can recognize as applicable or inapplicable. Further, in a successful encounter the partner's narrative develops as he or she gets more in touch with the experience. As the encounter continues, the partner develops a better comprehension of the experience -- becoming aware of previously neglected features and appreciative of the richness of its construction (something previously taken for granted) -- convincing signs that an experience and not simply a narrative is being investigated. Thus, when any individual conceptual encounter is conducted in a satisfactory manner we may be assured that we have a reasonably valid description of the concrete experience of a

11

phenomenon.

Nevertheless, this concrete experience is itself an "abstraction" in the sense that it is
created by a human being and may be a more or less
accurate representation of the lived event. Since
we wish to go beyond specific experience to the
general phenomenon we must question the validity of
the experience itself. Any concrete experience is
of something, and we are interested in the experience of psychological events, such as anger. An
experience ordinarily appears to be about a real
event, that is, the anger, love or whatever is
usually experienced as genuine. However, we know
that this experience may change. Thus, in the
course of either therapy or conceptual encounter, a
person may initially experience his or her behavior
as neutral but later experience the same behavior
as angry, or may initially experience anger but
later experience the anger as manufactured to avoid
an experience of hurt or anxiety. In such cases,
the initial experience is real enough but the events
referred to by the experience -- the neutral remark
or the anger -- prove somewhat unreal. If we are
interested in the general phenomenon of anger as it
is lived, then we must be alert to the possibility
of its manifestation in ways that are not immediately experienced by the angry person and to the possibility that its nature may be a bit different from
the description of an experience of anger that is
defensive rather than fully real. Fortunately,
while any particular experience may be partially
invalid, the investigator encounters many different
experiences in the course of studying a general
phenomenon. It would be unlikely to arrive at a
conceptualization which fits a number of different
experiences without the conceptualization having
some degree of validity.

This validity is, however, completely dependent on the honesty of the encounter between the
investigator's conceptualization and the partner's
experience. Hence, the investigator must be alert
to the possibility that the partner may distort the

experience, accepting the conceptualization out of suggestibility rather than because it really fits and gives insight. The likelihood of such a distortion depends a good deal on the configuration of the field of forces during the encounter. It is easy to imagine a situation where a partner who is not used to trusting his or her own experience and is not committed to the goals of the investigation wants to please the investigator and, hence, accepts a conceptualization that distorts the experience in order to avoid the uncomfortable tension involved in frustrating an enthusiastic investigator. On the other hand, to the extent that the partner discovers that the experience is valued in its own right, to the extent that he or she is committed to the goal of discovery, to the extent that it is clear that the way to please the investigator is to express one's own experience, and to the extent that it is clear that the investigator can tolerate the frustration of hearing discomforting evidence -- accepting it as a challenge rather than a defeat -- to that extent the partner will stick to the experience and reject an incorrect conceptualization.

There is significant evidence that persons give an investigator what he or she is looking for. If a person can see that the investigator is looking for the truth, genuinely wants a conceptualization that will fit the facts of the experience, then the person will make an honest inquiry. Hence, the best defense against the possibility of distortion is: (1) for the investigator to involve the other as a partner in the research enterprise, and (2) for the investigator to continually work on his or her ability to be personally accepting of the other's experience and to face disagreement as an opportunity rather than a defeat.

Conceptual encounter is a powerful and highly sensitive method that can probably be used in any area of inquiry. However, its power is completely dependent on the personal qualities of the researcher and somewhat dependent on the personal qualities of the research partner.

Different investigators naturally bring their personalities to the encounter. Some confidently assert their conceptualization and argue with their research partner, almost forcing their research partner to oppose the experience to the conceptualization. Others gently encourage the partner to speak and offer their conceptualization with diffidence. These differences do not matter; if it is clear that the investigator is honest in the pursuit of the truth, the research partner adjusts to the situation and will clearly assert the truth of his or her own experience. What is crucial is this: on the one hand, the investigator must be fully involved in and committed to the research so that the partner can experience a conviction that the results matter; on the other hand, the investigator must cultivate detachment in the sense that he or she is committed to the acceptance of whatever experiences are reported.

Even with the most articulate partner, the investigator must train to be a sensitive listener. He or she must be able to go into the other's position so that the partner's experience is fully comprehended, must be alert for any apparent incongruities in the narration of the experience. Such incongruities are usually a sign that either the investigator or the partner is fooling the self about the true nature of the experience. The data here are how the partner in fact experiences the situation, not how the partner or the investigator thinks he or she experiences it. A difficult problem is posed when the research partner may be out of touch with his or her feelings -- thinking he or she experiences something without really stopping to become aware of how it is actually experienced. When this seems to be happening the investigator may help by asking for concrete descriptions of the experience and what actually happened. For example, during an interview on the emotion of horror, the investigator noted a slight incongruity in his partner's report of his horror at reading an account of torture. The account related how some early pioneers heard a missing member of their party screaming for mercy as he was tortured by some Indians. The partner assumed (thought) that his horror was a horror of being the torturer. However, when he was encouraged to reflect carefully on the specific details of his experience, he realized that his horror was actually a horror of being in the position of victim -- specifically at being reduced to the point of having to plea for mercy.

Listening to the account of the partner's experience, the investigator compares it with his or her own experience. Is the experience recognized as an instance of the phenomenon that is being studied? If not, there may be some unreliability in the way the English term is used to refer to the experience. (In fact, we have found high reliability in word usage, but several instances where one word was used by different persons to refer to different "sub-species" of the experience). Does the investigator comprehend how the partner could have the experience in the context of the situation that is described, can he or she imagine acting in the way the partner acted? Any lack of recognition or understanding indicates a possible source of unreliability in the data. Perhaps the investigator lacks the necessary experience or imagination for recognition, or either the investigator or research partner is not in touch with some aspect of the experience that is difficult for him or her to acknowledge. Ultimately, of course, the final conceptualization must satisfy the investigator's own experiences. These personal concrete experiences of the phenomenon are extremely important instances because they may be studied from a privileged position, compared with one another, and examined for the essential similarities and differences which may provide the basis for abstract conceptualization.

The importance of the encounter between investigator and research partner and the fact that judgement as to the adequacy of a conceptual fit must come from this dialogue should not lead the reader to neglect the importance of the creative activity involved in formulating the conceptualiza-

15

tion. The investigator must take full responsibility for creating this conceptualization. She or he is the only person fully acquainted with the history of previous attempts, with the full range of experiences the conceptualization must fit, with the demands of logical consistency required by other conceptualizations and so on. The partner cannot be expected to do the investigator's work.

*   *   *   *   *

Psychological terms are a starting point, a way of gaining access to a range of experiences. If many experiences are referred to with the same terms, e.g., "anger," then perhaps it makes sense to look for what these experiences have in common. What ties them together? In its most simple sense, this is our starting point. The necessity of relying on the words and terms used to describe experiences arises out of the obvious fact that the experiences themselves are hidden until they are articulated, except possibly for one's own experiences, and even there exactly what process of knowing is involved is difficult to specify. Words help us clarify our own experience, and words are a major (though not the only) avenue to understanding the experience of others. Thus, while we are not interested in word usage but, rather, in a reality that lies beyond words, we have a basic trust in language as a gateway to experience.[2]

So we begin with words; we attempt to define an area of investigation by choosing a psychological word or concept (e.g., distance, joy, laughter), and then we attempt to gather examples of experiences which are related to our initial concept or term. What we would like is a collection of experiences; but of course what we necessarily get is a collection of descriptions of experiences, gathered from ourselves, from reading, and from interviews with other people. Each of these sources is important and though no one of them will give an accurate or full picture by itself, all of them taken together will give us a more complete picture of some partic-

16

ular experiential landscape than we would obtain from any one source. And we want as full a picture as possible.

If we simply wanted a series of pictures (or an average picture) of some experience, we might choose a random sample of subjects to provide us with such descriptions. But since what we want is a full picture of an experiential landscape, we instead seek out a particular kind of person to help us: someone who is sensitive, verbal, introspective, interested in nuances of experience, articulate in talking about those nuances. While the process of gathering examples cannot be unbiased in the conventional sense, we do endeavor to proceed with caution and are careful to be as circumspect in our methods of gathering information as we can. For example, although we choose certain kinds of people to talk with, we may tape-record our interviews and then have someone else listen to the interviews, to check our understanding of what is being said against someone else's. Or if we think a particular passage from a novel describes a particular kind of distance between two characters, we may ask another observer to read the passage and make a judgement about the kind of distance involved. We want to explore the meaning of psychological events; hence, we want to obtain descriptions of psychological events which are full and explicit and accurate.

The term "explicit" is a key word for us, since there is a sense in which our aim is to make explicit the kind of understanding of psychological events which many of us have only implicitly. There is an important distinction between explicit and implicit knowledge. The world most of us live in is crowded with occasions in which people do things with one another, which we observe and repeatedly attempt to make sense of. The sense we make of these events is for the most part implicit. If you ask a person to say what he sees in some interpersonal situation he is confronted with, he may fail miserably to specify explicitly and articulately its important features, and yet at the same time he

17

may demonstrate his understanding of the situation by his deft and tactful handling of it. This kind of understanding is at the basis of all skills such as that of getting along with people.[3] Language is perhaps our principal way of making explicit what we implicitly apprehend of what goes on around us. But language is helpful only insofar as it is synchronous with the structure which we assume exists in our experience. The structure of experience is what makes possible implicit knowledge (of the sort which enables us to act with tact for example) and explicit knowledge (of the sort embodied in psychological theory).

Much of our work consists of our attempt to elucidate the structure which we assume exists within the psychological events we are examining. There is some sense in which we cannot entirely justify this assumption of structure; that is, in a sense it is a given of our procedure, and so basic as to be beyond argument. However, we have certain arguments which we think persuasive. For example, we think that the fact that we can communicate with each other at all about our experience indicates there is some structure inherent in the experience, a structure which by being there enables us to talk about our experiences. That is, the experiences are not in constant chaotic flux; there is some element of order, some element of repetitive stability or organization in our experience, and it is order which is not totally idiosyncratic, else we could not talk to one another about our experiences. Further, we think that words are not applied entirely arbitrarily to experiences; at least once a culture has developed a language we think there is considerable agreement in language usage so that what one person calls anxiety will not ordinarily be entirely different from what another person calls anxiety. Of course, some persons may use some words bizarrely, differently than the rest of us, and there are often "sub-species" of meanings. But we could not do our kind of psychological investigation unless we believed that most persons use most words similarly, that words are applied to experiences in an orderly fashion, that experiences do have enough order to enable persons to apply words to their experiences in repetitively similar ways. Our results appear to support the validity of these assumptions.

We do not take a clear-cut position on whether the structures we are describing are inherent in universal processes (in the manner of the dynamics described by the Gestalt psycholgist), or an inherited pattern of organismic-environmental relationships (as some ethologists would assert), or are a consequence of the uniquely human child-mother relationship (as described by developmental psychoanalysis), or are cultural phenomena acquired early along with language (an ethnomethodologist might argue). In any case, it is clear that language is very tied up with the structures we are describing, and we want to leave open questions such as whether or not investigations carried out in other cultures would find structures which were not exactly identical with those we find. Indeed, the precision with which we can articulate the structure of experience by using conceptual encounter opens up an exciting new area of cross-cultural research. The results of an encounter within one language may be compared with the results from another language (using terms which are ordinarily presumed to be bilingual equivalents). Does a detailed comparison reveal equivalent structures or are there important differences in how the different cultures choose to structure emotional experience?[4]

So we assume that our experience is structured and that part of our job is to articulate the nature of these structures. Within social psychology, Heider (1958, p. 12) has clearly presented this position. As he states it, his own endeavor is to "make explicit the system of concepts that underlies interpersonal behavior, and the analysis of words and situations is considered only a means to this end." He uses the phrase "a system of concepts" where we have been using the word "structure," but the intent is the same.

Heider uses the phrase to "make explicit." Our procedure is best characterized as an attempt to make explicit the structure of psychological processes. This is a necessary beginning for our attempt to

19

develop psychology since so much of our experience in inarticulate. That is, often we are not clear about what we are experiencing or how to describe it, and certainly even when we are clear about what we are experiencing, we often do not see any connection between one experience and another; we do not comprehend the underlying structure. To return to our earlier emphasis on using words and psychological terms as a starting point: if we are interested in joy and we gather examples of what people call joy, we know that the same term is being used to describe many different experiences, but we do not explicitly understand what these experiences have in common that permits persons to identify them as recurrent events. The relation between the term and the various psychological events it is used to point toward is hazy and implicit until we begin to study those events to discern the inherent structure, and until we do this we can hardly begin to set the connections between joy and other aspects of our experience.

Such basic conceptualization, the explication of structure, is also quite useful for the therapeutic enterprise. Of course, therapy involves much more than a conceptualization of experience; it involves changing how one lives, influencing the very process of experiencing.[5] In fact, conceptualization can be misused, as when a person intellectualizes so that experiencing is avoided. But there is an important place for reflection and accurate conceptualization in therapy. A good conceptualization, like a good map, makes important discriminations and reveals important relationships; it is hardly the same as going somewhere, but it can be quite useful in helping a person get there.

*   *   *   *   *

We have said that when we explore a psychological event such as joy, we are attempting to articulate the structure of our <u>experience</u> of the event. But we do not conceive experience to be a private, subjective, mind-idea, that is "inside" a person. Rather, we are using the term to refer to an awareness of some way of being-in-the-world.[6]

Thus, when we refer to "joy" or "laughter" or a person being "distant," we do not mean merely a subjective feeling or a given set of behaviors. We mean a way of being-in-the-world, a unity, which is reflected in how a person perceives the world, the actions that are taken, the feelings we have and so forth. In our own work we make the assumption that any given way of being is a "choice," not in a conscious sense, but in the sense that there are always alternative ways of being and that a person can accept some responsibility for the way he or she lives. We find it useful to inquire into how any given way of being functions in a person's life. Thus, we may ask what function joy serves or what would go wrong if a person could not laugh. We want to clarify exactly how various ways of being are different from one another.

We examine accounts of experience in literature as well as the accounts of our research partners and it may be objected that since literary accounts are often acts of imagination, the investigation is dealing with imagined experience rather than actual experience. For that matter, it might be objected that since our research partners are usually recalling some experience in the past, we are dealing with remembered experience rather than actual experience. Such objections miss an important point about the nature of human experience. They assume that experience is a natural phenomenon that <u>happens</u> to us whereas, in actuality, experience is a <u>created</u> interpretation. The experience of the moment is just as much an interpretation as is the experience of a past event or the experience portrayed by a work of art.[7]

Of course, our experience may be more or less formed. Dewey (1934) has discussed this. Often, our experience may shift chaotically and be rather unclear, but when our experience is truly An Experience it has an internal unity of a successful work of art. By working with experiences which have been completed -- which are from the past or from works of literature -- and which are unambiguous instances of anger, joy, or whatever, we have deliberately selected experiences with good form and taken advantage of this good form to articulate clear structures. However, we have had to sacrifice a full investigation into the developmental dynamics of experience -- of how a person who is currently experiencing a situation attempts to structure his or her being-in-the-world. The description of this area, which is now largely the province of psychotherapy, will have to await future investigation.

It should be noted that regardless of whether we study past experience or current experiences we are not interested in studying experience as an objective event. One can study how different circumstances affect how a person perceives, or how the memory of an event changes as time passes and the person attempts to reconcile the memory with the rest of his or her life, or how different persons perceive the "same" event. Or one can study, as cognitive psychology does, what persons think about their experience -- how they conceive of anger, love, or any other phenomena. However, these are questions whose answers can be sought with traditional methods.

Conceptual encounter seeks to answer a radically different type of question. It asks how we can describe the meaning of an experience -- the organization of a person's experience at a given moment, the person's way of being-in-the-world -- the various choices that confront him as a creative participant in experience.

We could, of course, ask our research partner to participate in an experiment. We could contrive a situation in which our partner actually becomes angry, laughs, or whatever, and interview on the spot as to his or her experience. We could also interview other research partners who observe the situation. In fact, as we shall see, there is no reason why conceptual encounter could not be used in conjunction with an experimental approach. However, this would not necessarily allow us to grasp the "actual" experience any more accurately than via retrospective accounts. We would simply have additional accounts of experiences. On the one hand,

22

these more immediate accounts might give us a
different access into the meaning of the phenomenon -- and, hence, such investigation is worth
pursuing. On the other hand, the heat and focus of
the movement might blind the research partners to
important aspects of the experience, and such
accounts often suffer from the observers' not having
the time to reflect and contrast the experience with
others of the same or different type. While an
experience may be distorted by memory, it is also
true that the full meaning of an experience may only
become clear with the passage of time. It is
desirable to have as many accesses to experiences as
is possible, and if one wants to grasp the meaning
of experience, one may well look for it in a work
of literature or art where the essential features
of an experience are sometimes captured with a
minimum of confusing detail.

                *   *   *   *   *

     To comprehend the method of conceptual en-
counter fully, it may be useful to compare it
briefly to other methods, contrasting it with
traditional experimental and psycho-analytic methods,
and relating it to phenomenology and field theory.
Perhaps the sharpest points of contrast with the
usual experimental or correlational procedure are
conceptual encounter's regard for the "subject" as
a partner in the research enterprise rather than as
an organism whose behavior is being studied, and its
regard for the evidence obtained by detailed
analysis of single cases rather than the statistical
assessment of the differences between groups subjected to different treatment. In contrast to
classical psycho-analytic methodology, conceptual
encounter involves a dialogue aimed at the investigation of a particular type of human experience,
rather than a therapeutic encounter between an
analyst and a patient aimed at helping the patient
achieve an adequate historical comprehension of his
or her life. While the investigator offers a type
of interpretation of the other's experience, the
other retains the authority to argue whether or not

                        23

the interpretation fits his or her experience. (Of course, in principle this is also true in analysis but the dynamics of a treatment situation, as opposed to a research situation, seem to lead the patient's experience to change much more frequently than analytic theory.)

Since conceptual encounter seeks to articulate essential structures that are implicit in experience, it is closely related to the phenomenological psychology envisioned by Husserl and developed, in different ways, by Sartre and Merleau-Ponty (cf. Kockelmans, 1967). However, the investigator does not only reflect upon his or her own experience but also upon the experiences which partners report, thus almost immediately expressing a concern for inter-subjective validity. The group of phenomenological psychologists at Duquesne have been concerned with this problem of inter-subjective validity and Colaizzi (1973) has contrasted the method of reflecting only upon one's own experience with a method of empirical phenomenology in which the investigator attempts to articulate a structure that is common to the experiences of others, and to various combinations of these procedures.[8] While conceptual encounter is closely related to these procedures, it stresses the importance of dialogue between the investigator and the research partner and it emphasizes the inherent creative tension between concrete experiences and systematic conceptualization.[9] The latter has the ultimate goal of a network of systematic relationships that will, hopefully, relate different investigations to one another in an ever broadening map of human experience.

In this latter regard, conceptual encounter is closely related to Kurt Lewin's experimental methodology. Lewin emphasized the tension between the concrete details of the individual's experience and behavior and the investigator's abstract conceptualization of a dynamic genotypic field, the "life-space," which was conceived to underlie the phenotypic details of behavior and experience.[10] While the method differs from Lewin's in conceiving of the

24

person as a subject who creates the life-space as well as being an objective part of it, it shares his desire to construct a consistent body of abstract conceptualization that is responsive to the specifics of lived experience. It is important to note that this aspect of conceptual encounter permits the investigator to build on prior conceptualization and eventually to offer conceptualization to be built upon. A serious phenomenological investigation often attempts to see experience through fresh eyes with as few preconceptions as possible. Such radical beginnings have no place for prior conceptualizations. The benefits of such a procedure -- the freshness of viewpoint and the opportunity to build a new and more coherent structure -- are somewhat offset by the disadvantage -- the fact that one is bound to be operating with whatever cultural sets are most unconsciously taken for granted and the fact that one isolates the investigation from prior conceptualizations and may wind up rediscovering the wheel. If one places too high a value on radical beginnings and every investigation begins completely anew, there would be no way to build on each other's work and no cooperative community could form. Conceptual encounter attempts to work towards a balance between the desire for new insight and fresh beginning and the desire to share and build with others. Each new experience that is presented by a research partner forces a renewal as we encounter a new being-in-the-world. In fact, this aspect of the method resembles ethno-methodology in that the encounter may "breech" the reality of the investigator and certainly broaden his experience. However, the abstract conceptualization unites us with a community of others and permits us to build on their work and to contribute our own work to the building.

Conceptual encounter may be used whenever the object of inquiry is an aspect of human experience, whenever an investigator wishes to comprehend the structure or essential organization of some experience. Using the method permits the investigator to sample a far wider range of experiences than can be obtained from a given experimental situation. The investigator may even ask each research partner to

25

reflect over his or her entire life experience in an attempt to come up with exceptions to the proposed conceptualization. It should be noted that the requirements for articulate research partners do not necessarily restrict the domain of research. Many persons can be helped to become more articulate and aware of their experience, particularly if they are asked to compare their experience with the conceptualizations developed with more articulate partners. The latter may also be checked against observations of behavior in order to note whether the conceptualizations fit and can be consistently applied. One may even use conceptual encounter as a technique to work with the experiences of experts who have been working with small children or animals, inquiring as to whether or not the conceptualization fits their experience of the phenomenon as they observe it in their area of expertise. For example, we could ask an ethologist whether or not a conceptualization of anger relates to his or her experience of "anger" in dogs. Is there or is there not a close structural analogy?

In its present form, conceptual encounter uses words to gain access to experience and is, therefore, limited by the scope of language. For many purposes this limitation poses no problem. English is a very rich language and it is relatively easy to extend its own scope by going to other languages and working with the somewhat different structures of experience which another culture has chosen to name. However, if we wish complete access to the full range of experience, we must have some way of encountering the everyday behavior for which we have no words and the nuances of experience presented by the creative arts. That is, the method must be extended so that the investigator can use a piece of behavior or a work of art (rather than a word) to evoke the experience of research partners.

Actually the "experimental phenomenology" that flourished in Germany from 1900 until Hitler came into power made extensive use of the experience of behavior. The investigator would produce a piece of behavior in the laboratory and carefully tap into

26

his or her research partner's experience of the behavior as various experimental parameters were altered. Ach's study of will, Ovsiankina's study of the tendency to resume an interrupted task, Karsten's study of the satiation of behavior, Schwarz's study of relapsing into a prior habit, are all excellent examples. In these studies the "subject" is more of a research partner whose experience is carefully consulted and whose behavior must be individually explained without resource to random error terms. Elsewhere, I have described this method in detail and contrasted it with the "statistical experimentation" that is used today (de Rivera, 1976, pp. 10-20). It would be easy to modify such experimental phenomenology so that it became a conceptual encounter, having a type of behavior provide the concrete experience for the encounter. In a somewhat similar manner, conceptual encounter could be used in conjunction with the method of participant observation, modifying that technique so that the observed were taken into the investigator's confidence and asked to comment on the shared conceptualization. Likewise, it might be possible in some cases to use conceptual encounter as a way of investigating unconscious behavior and the experiential changes of persons undergoing psycho-therapy.

It might be more difficult to work with art, where the emphasis is on the uniqueness of the individual work. However, successful art seems somehow to capture universal experience in the unique instance. If one worked with a sample of persons who had learned to look at a painting -- were aware of the choices the artist must make in dealing with the canvas and open to what the artist was attempting to convey -- it might be possible to use an individual painting (rather than a word) to evoke experience. The investigator could then attempt to conceptualize the structure of the particular type of experience expressed by the artistic work. Such a study might be viewed as an aspect of art criticism and could conceivably both profit from and contribute to that difficult field.

While conceptual encounter can probably inves-

27

tigate any realm of human experience, it is not designed to be an all-purpose method useful for the entire range of psychological inquiry. A method inevitably reflects both goals and subject matter. In order to gain certain advantages, certain sacrifices must be made. The power of conceptual encounter lies in its ability to sample an extremely large variety of incidents and the fact that even a single incident may force a revision of the conceptualization. Hence, conceptual encounter leads to a rapid growth of sophisticated, logically consistent, conceptualization applicable to human experience. Further, it broadens the experience of the investigator. However, it is not designed to aid in the prediction and control of behavior. Moreover, to the extent that our experience is objectively determined, conceptual encounter alone cannot help us to reveal the facts of this determination and must rely on the experience of those who discover these facts by using other methods (observation, experimentation, etc.). Then, too, at least in the investigations up to now, the method has been used to uncover the structure rather than the dynamics of experience -- to articulate what is given, implied and what must be true, rather than how things come about. While we view every structure as functional it is still uncertain as to whether the method can be used to uncover how an experience develops and how it depends on the person's environment. As mentioned above, we hope that conceptual encounter can be wedded to experimental and observational methods to investigate these aspects of lived experience.

Regardless of how far conceptual encounter can be extended, of what its power and limitations eventually prove to be, we wish to establish its legitimacy as a valid method to investigate psychological processes. Earlier, we said that the final conceptualization of a properly conducted conceptual encounter had to have some degree of validity. We said some degree of validity because, of course, the establishment of full validity is always a research goal rather than an achievement. Any particular investigator may have a blind spot that limits the accuracy of his or her conceptualization; the full deepening of the idea may have to await the work of some future researcher. And there is always a question as to the limits of the breadth of a conceptualization: does it fit the experience of relatively inarticulate subjects, of children, of persons from different cultures? As further investigations proceed, the limits to a conceptualization emerge, new possibilities become apparent, and an altered conceptualization with more breadth may be created.

Finally, still another factor influences the eventual shape and ultimate validity of a conceptualization. A good conceptualization must not only fit the phenomenon with which it immediately deals, but must relate to other conceptualizations. As our understanding of other phenomena grows, these new conceptualizations may or may not be precisely related to the conceptualization in question and, hence, may either support or diminish its value, or possibly provoke some interesting revision.

* * * * *

An important aspect of conceptual encounter is its ability to accommodate itself to the different personalities and interests of different investigators. In the succeeding chapters the reader will see how each of us has used conceptual encounter in a somewhat different way. De Rivera's predilection is towards the precision of mathematics. Hence, he tends to favor the abstract pole of the encounter -- attempting to arrive at an almost geometric conceptualization of the experience of anger. At the other extreme, Goodman is a clinician and hence committed to working from the particularities of the individual case. Her investigation of anxiety is concrete and practical; it will be particularly appealing to those who like to begin with facts rather than abstractions. In spite of this difference, both Goodman and de Rivera tend towards "realism:" they sense that they are <u>discovering</u> structures of experience. On the other <u>hand, Lindsay</u> leans towards "idealism" insofar as she feels that the structures are not

29

really there before they are "discovered." Of
course, we can intellectually agree that experience
is interpretation but for some of us our experience
is an interpretation of reality while for others of
us reality is an interpretation!

In addition to these stylistic or temperamental
differences, our varying interests lead to different
choices of subject matter. Thus, Funk's interest in
the work of Reich and Lowen reveals itself in the
choice of topic that clearly depends on the body --
the behavior of laughter. He was concerned with the
odd behavioral pattern universally recognized as
laughter, the apparently pointless oscillations of
the belly, the turning up of the mouth, the helplessness ("the comic killed the audience") and so on.
In trying to find a function for this odd behavior,
Funk was forced to postulate that the world of the
laughter is quite separate from our normal reality.
On the other hand, Kreilkamp is interested in
literature. Hence, his investigations of psychological distance is basically anchored in material
from literature and many of his encounters are with
examples from literature rather than from an interview. Thus, his research partner is often an author,
who may have written his experience of an imagined
event long ago. Perhaps the fact that our human
differences are so easily manifested, that the use
of conceptual encounter provides us with a common
discipline yet does not require us to set aside
important aspects of our personality, is a feature
of the method which may particularly commend its use
in humanistic psychology or psychology conceived as
human-science.

Reference Notes
for Chapter I

1. The investigator need not necessarily begin with
   an idea. It may only gradually develop in the
   course of the investigation. In such a case,
   after listening to his partner's experience, the
   investigator simply presents his or her abstract
   understanding of the experience -- thus beginning an articulation of a structure that fits
   the experience.

2. It is interesting to note that Benjamin Lee
   Whorf (1956, p. 36), ordinarily an advocate of
   the view that different languages may structure
   experience in different ways, refers to a "...
   common stock of conceptions, possibly possessing
   a yet unstudied arrangement of its own...(which)
   ...seems to be a necessary concomitant of the
   communicability of ideas by language...and is in
   a sense the universal language to which the
   various specific languages give entrance."

3. See Polanyi (1958, Chapter 4). He discusses
   this in detail.

4. In this regard see Doi's (1973) description of
   the Japanese emotion of "amae," and de Rivera's
   (1977) discussion of the cross-cultural comparison of emotion terms.

5. See, for example, the description in Gendlin
   (1962).

6. This, of course, is the sense of the term as
   developed by Brentano, Husserl and Heidegger
   and closely related to what Lewin meant by
   "life-space."

7. This is not to say that there are no differences
   among perception, memory and imagination, that
   the first two are experienced as real, the
   second is experienced as referring to the past,
   etc., but all these modes of experience are,

necessarily, interpretations.

8. For a sampling of their thoughts and studies, see Giorgi, Fischer, and Von Eckartsberg (1971).

9. The emphasis on dialogue reflects the ideas of Martin Buber (1970). Such dialogue plays a key role in the "collaborative" assessment procedure developed by Constance Fischer (1978) and the research methodology suggested by Robert Sardello (1971).

10. For a complete discussion, see de Rivera (1976, pp. 15-20).

References
for Chapter I

Buber, M. I and thou. New York: Charles Scribner's Sons, 1970.

Colaizzi, P. Reflection and research in psychology: A phenomenological study of learning. Debuque, Iowa: Kendall-Hunt Publishing Company, 1973.

de Rivera, J. Field theory as Human-science: Contributions by Lewin's Berlin group. New York: Gardner Press, Inc., 1976.

de Rivera, J. A structural theory of the emotions. New York: International Universities Press, 1977.

Dewey, J. Art as experience. New York: Minton, Balch and Co., 1934.

Doi, T. The anatomy of dependence. Tokyo, New York, San Francisco: Kodansha, 1973.

Fischer, C. Historical relations of psychology as an object-science and a subject-science: Towards psychology as a human science. Journal of the History of the Behavioral Sciences, 1977, 13, 369-378.

Fischer, C. Collaborative psychological assessment. In C. Fischer & S.L. Brodsky (Eds.), Client participation in human services. New Brunswick, New Jersey: Transaction, 1978.

Gendlin, E. Experiencing and the creation of meaning. New York: The Free Press of Glencoe, 1962.

Giorgi, A. Psychology as human science. New York: Harper and Row, Inc., 1970.

Giorgi, A., Fischer, W.F., & Von Eckartsberg, R. Duquesne studies in phenomenological psychology:

Vol. 1. Pittsburgh: Duquesne University Press, 1971.

Heider, F. The psychology of interpersonal relations. New York: Wiley, 1958.

Kockelmans, J. Edmund Husserl's phenomenological psychology. Pittsburgh: Duquesne University Press, 1967.

Merleau-Ponty, M. The phenomenology of perception. New York: Humanities Press, 1962.

Polanyi, M. Personal knowledge. Chicago: University of Chicago Press, 1958.

Sardello, R. A reciprocal participation model of experimentation. In A. Giorgi, W.F. Fischer, & R. Von Eckartsberg (Eds.), Duquesne studies in phenomenological psychology: Vol. 1. Pittsburgh: Duquesne University Press, 1976.

Whorf, B.L. Language, thought, and reality. New York: Wiley, 1956.

THE STRUCTURE OF ANGER

Joseph de Rivera

I want to get at the essential nature of anger, at the meaning of the experience, in the way I imagine an early geometer wanted to get at the essence of a circle. The Greeks must have looked at a lot of "real" circles drawn on the ground before they intuitively grasped the essential properties of circleness by creating an "ideal" circle, where line had not breadth, whose points were all equidistant from one center. Once created, this ideal structure reveals certain necessary relationships. For example, if one draws a tangent to a circle, this line which touches the circle at only one point must necessarily form a 90° angle, with the radius that touches the circle at that point. It is my intuition that we can create a structure for anger (or any other emotion) that will help to reveal necessary relationships between that way of being and what happens in our life.[1]

As I began to examine instances of anger to see what they had in common, to see what made them instances of anger rather than instances of fear or some other emotion, it became apparent that there was no simple set of stimulus conditions, bodily states, or response sets that were present in all instances of anger.[2] For example, while frustration was often present and was conceivably a necessary condition, it was clearly not a sufficient condition for anger to occur. Often persons who were frustrated (in the sense of having their progress towards a goal blocked) simply found another way to their

goal or changed their goal. Other investigators reported that diastolic blood pressure increased in
the average subject, but sometimes it went down.
There was often a desire to hurt the object of anger,
but these were exceptions where persons who were
obviously angry and in touch with their feelings did
not have any impulse to hurt the other.

In order to grasp what the instances had in common, or (to put it more accurately), to create a
structure to which all instances could be related, it
was necessary to move to a higher level of abstraction, to see that the instances did not share common
elements but, rather, involved a similar relationship
between the person and the object of anger. On this
higher level of abstraction it was clear that in
every case the person wanted to change the object of
anger -- to make it other than it was -- to psychologically push away or remove the object of anger.
Such a wish stood in sharp contrast to the wish of
fear, where the person wanted to escape -- to remove
the self from the object of fear.

These wishes are usually reflected in the person's overt behavior. Sometimes this expression is
quite direct -- as when an angry person screams at
another to "stop it" or "get out," or a fearful person shrinks back from some danger. At other times
the expression is indirect -- as when an angry person sulkily withdraws or a fearful person strikes out
against the object of his fear. However, even in
these latter cases one's underlying way of being is
revealed in the quality of one's behavior -- in how
the person withdraws or attacks. Thus, the wish of
anger (to remove) and of fear (to escape) seem to
reflect the basic force or movement of the different
emotions. The emotions seem to transform the person's way of being so that these emotional ends
govern his or her behavior. It is as though the
emotion instructs the person "remove" or "escape" and
does not subside until the instruction is carried out.

Reflection showed that many other emotions, in
addition to anger and fear, could be described in
terms of abstract wishes that captured the inherent

"movement" of the emotion. For example, love could
be characterized by the instruction "give" while
desire reflected "get," and while the four emotions
discussed above (anger, fear, love, desire) all
involve instructions about how the person should
relate to an object, other emotions (such as depression, anxiety, serenity, joy) could be seen as
instructing the person how to relate to the self.
Elsewhere (A Structural Theory of the Emotions, Chapter 2), I have described how instructions may be
written for any emotion and how these instructions
appear to be related to one another in such a way
that they form an emotional system with a symmetrical
structure that relates each emotion to others within
the matrix of instructions. However, for our present
purpose of describing the development of a conceptual
encounter, we need only note that each emotion can
be characterized as having an "instructional transformation." That is, we can describe any emotion in
terms of how a person experiencing the emotion must
transform the world if the emotion is to disappear.
And in the case of anger the instructional transformation is to remove the source of the anger.

While the wish to remove the other seemed to
capture an important aspect of anger and to fit all
of the instances presented to the investigator, the
analysis seemed incomplete. When the experience of
anger was contrasted with that of fear, it was clear
that the difference did not lie only in the instructions or in a difference of the direction of movement
(remove vs. escape). Rather, these movements had
implications for the relationship between the person
and the object of the emotion. Anger, and the idea
of removal, implied that the person felt he or she
could somehow affect the other, that there was some
sort of possibility that the person's anger could
influence and transform the object at which he or
she was angry. On the other hand, fear implied a
gap, or breach of communality, a feeling that the
other did not identify in any way with the self.
Hence, the other could harm the person unless he or
she protected the self by escaping.

The Concept of Ought

When I examined the sense of power inherent in
anger, this feeling that one can influence the other,
it seemed based on ideas of what ought to be and an
assumption that the other should recognize these
oughts. That is, it is not just that the angry person is frustrated or would like things to be different; rather he or she seems to be acting as though
things should be different from what they are; the
object of anger (whether it be an other or the whole
world) ought to be different than it is. Persons
describing their anger make statements such as "I
was angry at the professor for not taking my study
seriously...and for underestimating my intelligence;"
"I demanded that she explain to me what gave her the
right to do what she did" (listened through a door
to a private conversation). On the other hand, the
person who is afraid has no sense that the other
ought to be different (at least at the moment of
fear). There is no unity, no moral order to which to
appeal; the other is wholly other and is not experienced as believing in the same oughts.

At this point in the conceptual encounter I again
turned away from contrasting immediate experiences of
anger and fear and turned towards abstract conceptualization about the nature and meaning of "ought."
I knew that the concept had been explicated by Heider
(1958) and turned to his analysis for ideas. Heider
points out that the concept of "ought" implies a
force that is supra-personal. That is, what ought
to exist is not just what some person desires, but
what is perceived as required by some objective order
of affairs. This corresponds to the experience of
the angry person who does not simply feel that his
or her wishes are being frustrated but that the
other ought to behave differently, that something is
wrong with the basic order to existence and needs
to be set right. For Heider, what a person desires
at a particular moment may be related to what the
person likes. What a person believes ought to be in
any particular instance is related to what the
person values. That is, if a person holds a given
value he or she believes that under certain condi-

tions persons ought to behave in certain ways. Note that this way of construing value (as the basis of what is required to be) is different from conceiving value as determined simply by what a person desires or fears (positive or negative valence) and oughts as simply stemming from the desires of some authority.[3]

Heider has explicated a number of important properties which oughts and values have. First, the concept is related to the concept of <u>can</u> (of ability), in that we cannot hold a person responsible, say that he or she ought to do something, if it is impossible for the person to do. If $\underline{P}$ ought to do $\underline{X}$, then it is implied that $\underline{P}$ can do $\underline{X}$. Second, since what ought to be is perceived as stemming from an objective order, oughts (and values) have the same status as beliefs about the nature of reality. Thus, while it is perfectly permissible for another person to have likes and desires that are quite different from our own, it is as upsetting as if the other saw red where we see green. If the person is close to us (and we are not protected by the distance of seeing them as foreign), the mere fact of a value disagreement creates tension in our relationship.

For that matter, the mere fact that something exists may suggest that it ought to exist, and we sometimes act as though what ought to exist actually does exist. If a person does what he or she ought to do, that person ought to be happy. If something bad happens to a person, it may be difficult to see him or her as simply unlucky. Innocent persons "ought" not to get hurt and, as Lerner (1974) has shown, we may tend to see them as somehow deserving their misfortune. Or we may feel that we ought somehow to have prevented their misfortune (as in survivor guilt).

We may extend this analysis of ought by noting that oughts imply some form of unity or unification. Thus, a given set of oughts do not apply to everybody, but only to members of one's community. No one feels that a dog ought to be charitable with its bones or that foreigners ought to be loyal Americans.

It is precisely the fact that they do not obey our own oughts that makes them a foreigner. To the extent that we do feel that others ought to do certain things, we are including them in the community to which we see ourselves as belonging. Of course, such "communities" may include various sub-sets of humanity. Thus, "property rights" with their related set of oughts and duties only apply within a national community, membership in a private club may require the acceptance of a specific set of oughts pertinent only to club members, and the rights of a husband or of a wife (or any couple who are committed to each other) include the right to expect a response to personal needs and, hence, involve values and oughts which only pertain to that particular couple. For this reason I shall call any group whose members recognize a common set of values a "unit." Thus, a unit may be as small as two persons or as large as the community of man.

When others belong in a unit with us, when they recognize the same oughts that we do -- share common values -- then we may appeal to these oughts if we are in conflict with them. If our analysis is correct, the person who is angry feels that he or she has some influence over the other because the person is experienced as in his or her unit, sharing some common values. Otherwise, the other could not be held responsible, could not be perceived as one who ought to act otherwise. One cannot be angry at a person who is not perceived to be responsible for his or her actions -- who either <u>cannot</u> behave differently (and hence is not subject to the force of ought) or who is in a different unit (is not subject to the same oughts).

It should be noted that we are speaking here of the subjective experience at the moment of anger rather than of what may be objectively true. Obviously there are occasions when one gets angry at a small child who, in retrospect, could not really help his or her behavior, or one explodes at a stuck door that is not really subject to the oughts of any of the units to which one belongs. However, <u>at the moment</u> of anger, the child <u>is</u> held responsible (no

40

matter how sorry one may feel later), and the door ought to open (though one knows intellectually that doors are not human). Adults are somewhat removed from the obvious magical thinking involved in such cases, but children may be quite aware that they are distorting reality. I once witnessed the angry explosion of a seven-year-old girl at a sled which kept falling down no matter how it was propped up against a wall. Talking with her afterwards I asked why she was angry and she patiently explained that the "darned old thing" wouldn't stay up. As she was talking a grin flitted across her face. I asked her why she had smiled and (after some "do tell me's") she stated, "Well, I told it to stay up -- I know it can't really do things but I haven't had a thing I wanted all day long, so I told it to and it should have" -- and here she smiled again. We can only wish that most adults were as much in touch with their infantile behavior!

It is important to note that each person has the choice of whether or not to join a unit -- of whether or not to belong. Fingarette (1967) has pointed out that one cannot force a person to be "responsible" (that is, to obey oughts) and that many persons living in our society (e.g., sociopaths) have never really decided to be responsible -- to join a community. While we may act as though the person belongs, in fact, only that person can decide whether or not he belongs.

When there is conflict and we do not experience the other as belonging to our unit, we may experience fear. We cannot influence the other through the medium of common values; the other will not be responsive to what ought to be. And just as fear is related to seeing the other as not belonging to our unit, we may postulate that anxiety is related to the possibility that someone we love does not see us as belonging to a unit with them.

The Concept of Challenge

While every instance of anger appeared to imply that the other ought to change his or her behavior,

41

it seemed clear that this condition was necessary but not sufficient. That is, it was possible for research partners to report instances where they believed the other ought to change his or her behavior and yet no anger occurred. In some of these instances the persons did not permit themselves to be involved; in others, the person had enough control over the situation to simply state a request, a reminder, or command that brought the other's behavior in conformity to what ought to be; or it became clear that the other was not intentionally violating the ought. On the other hand, when anger occurred it was clear that the person always felt challenged -- that is, the other was perceived as intentionally violating the ought and the angered person was involved yet lacked control. The person was involved in a situation where the other's behavior defined a reality that contradicted the reality of the angered person. There is a real contest over what ought to be, which one may win or lose; the contenders occupy the same "reality space" and one must leave.

For example, consider this instance of anger. Two class friends (Dorothy and Peter) were active in a youth organization and both decided to run for regional offices. They talked with each other and agreed that since Dorothy had been more active in the organization and cared about it a lot, she should run for vice-president (the more responsible and prestigious position) and Peter for treasurer. However, during the regional convention, "He suddenly... stated that people made him realize that he should run for vice-president and I for secretary...he was going to run for vice-president; if I wanted to run against him that was my decision, and abruptly walked away. For a month I was paralyzed...fighting tears...I was deeply hurt...Soon after Peter came over...I looked out at him. I told him I couldn't believe what he did, that our friendship must mean very little to him...Mostly Peter had allowed an outsider to penetrate the love and commitment between us...I very seldom became angry, mainly because anger frightens me. Usually I back down... this instance I was incapable of backing down when Peter challenged me. I wanted that office and Peter

42

knew how much it meant to me. I knew I was right...
he should never have challenged me...he went against
the unit we had formed."

The concept of challenge implies that the other
is a serious contender for the space and this suggests that an alternative to anger is to perceive the
other in such a way that he is not a real contender.
This may be done in a number of different ways.

The other may be perceived as "not responsible"
for his or her action, i.e., drunk, insane, only a
child, etc. Because the other can't really control
his or her behavior, the behavior does not challenge
the ought.

The other may be regarded as unqualified to be
a challenger because of the person's status, i.e.,
a foreigner, a woman, a member of a different caste.
The other does not challenge the ought because his
or her position as an outsider does not permit a
challenge.

The other may be seen as having a character
structure that works against his being an adequate
member of the group, i.e., as "phoney," "disagreeable," "basically weak," etc. In this case the other
is usually disliked and this sentiment takes the
place of anger.

Notice that all of these ways of perceiving the
other involve increasing a distance between oneself
and the other. Rather than getting angry the other
is seen as different from oneself so that he or she
cannot present a real challenge. Instead of the
emotional force of anger, we have a structural
change -- in effect a change in psychological space
so that a person who may have been close is now
distant.

The Concept of Assertion

First, our analysis simply suggested that anger
instructed a person to remove the object of anger.
Then it became clear what this object was -- a
challenge to what the person believed ought to exist.

43

But implicit in this idea of removing a challenge is the notion that the person _can_ remove the challenge -- that the person not only has a belief about what ought to exist but also that he or she has the power to _assert_ that belief, to maintain his or her position about what ought to exist. This is not always easy to do. While both the angry person and the other belong to an identical unit, and hence, recognize the same values, the two persons do not necessarily agree on what ought to exist. Just as liking only becomes desiring when a person also has a need, values become oughts only when a person recognizes that objective conditions require the value to be expressed. In most contests there is a disagreement over what is recognized as the situation; to one person the salient features of the situation indicate that X ought to be done; to the other person the situation calls for Y. The contest itself is over what the situation actually requires (and this depends on the meaning of the situation). It is a contest over what reality is like and, hence, what ought to be done. The presence of anger implies that, in this contest, the person continues to assert his or her own position to will what he or she recognizes as existent and, hence, to determine what oughts apply in the face of the other's will to define reality differently. Thus, anger supports a person's position and if it is not present the person may "fold" and give in to the other's position.

We may inquire what happens when a person who is challenged fails to become angry and assert his or her will. We postulate that when a person abandons his or her position, the person becomes depressed. This will occur when there are forces which prevent the challenge from being removed and when there are reasons not to exercise the alternative of distancing the challenger. The depression may be seen as analogous to the surrender mechanism that some species use to signal the acceptance of defeat and, hence, to end the fight.

For example, a college student is going to eat with a group of friends. They decide to eat early, so that they can be seated right away, but one of

44

the group delays them with an unnecessarily long
phone conversation. The student has a lot of work
to do and a slight headache, she experiences some
anger but does not say anything. When they finally
get to the dining hall, it is crowded and there is
a wait for seats. At this point the student suggests
that they go to a nearby dining hall that is quieter
and less crowded. Most of the group is amenable,
but the woman who delayed the group says that she
likes this room better. On hearing this, the group
appears to accept the wait (they turn their bodies
back to the door). At this point the student
abandons her position. Rather than stating that she
really needs to eat right away, she sees the situation
as one in which there is nothing she can do. She says
she has a headache and goes back to her room experiencing anger at her protagonist and depression over
the group not seeming to care about her. She feels
she ought to have said something, but she couldn't.
The group as a whole cared more for her protagonist
than for herself.

From our perspective depression is not simply
a passive reaction to a situation of loss. On the
contrary, a conceptual encounter by Kane (1976) has
shown that depression may be regarded, like anger,
as transforming the person's situation. In fact,
we may understand depression as an emotion whose
structure is the reverse of the emotion of anger.
That is, whereas anger instructs the person to remove
the challenge, the instructional transformation of
depression is "remove the self." Just as anger works
to strengthen the person's will so that he or she can
remove the challenge, depression works against the
person's will so he or she can't fight against the
challenge. Thus, part of the experience of depression
is that one cannot do anything about the situation
one is in.

The instruction, "remove the self," is not
necessarily dysfunctional. It prevents distancing
from the other and although the person's position is
abandoned, the person's values are preserved.
Ordinarily, if a person failed to assert his or her
position, the person would be abandoning his or her

45

values. But in depression one can't act; therefore, oughts cannot apply and the failure to act does not mean that the person no longer subscribes to the group's values. Kane has shown that in many cases of situational depression, the person is caught in a situation where his or her values require an action that would have unfortunate consequences. When the depression occurs, the person can't perform the required action, thus preventing the consequences while still preserving the person's commitment to values and, hence, to group membership. For example, in one instance a teenager became pregnant and was caught in a situation where her value for human life required her to have the child in spite of the fact that her young boyfriend could not marry her and that she believed she could not confide in her mother because of her mother's opposition to premarital sex. While there were moments of anger at the mother -- when she was perceived as one who ought to accept sex -- the predominant emotion was a mild depression which lasted for about a month as the young woman decided that she had to have an abortion. (Note how the depression structures the situation so that she does not really act against her values -- she experiences having to get the abortion rather than wanting it). Thus, her values are maintained in spite of the fact that she does not act upon them.

Returning to the emotion of anger, we now see that in both anger and depression there is a challenge to the person's belief in what ought to exist but that in the former the person continues to assert his or her position while in depression the person no longer can assert what ought to exist.

The Situation of Anger

It is now possible for us to state a conceptualization which may be the necessary and sufficient conditions for anger. We postulate: if an other (O) challenges what a person (P) asserts ought to exist, then P will be angry at O. And conversely: if P is angry at O, then O is challenging what P asserts ought to exist.

46

This conceptualization is really a statement about what we might term the situation of anger. Note that it rejects the idea that under some objectively determined stimulus conditions a person will necessarily react with anger. There is no situation that is independent of the person. It asserts that anger is one structure, one way, that a person may be-in-the-world. It asserts that when a person is in the world in an angry way, the person is necessarily experiencing a challenge to what he or she is asserting ought to exist. There are other ways in which the person could structure the situation. Thus, as we have seen, the person could experience the other as alien and feel fear, or could create a distance between the self and the other rather than experience a challenge, or could become depressed and fail to assert what ought to exist. But in such other cases the person would not be angry. The person has a number of degrees of freedom; the situation can be structured in a number of different ways. However, there are definite consequences to whatever alternative is selected (or comes into being). If one perceives the other as belonging to one's unit but does not get angry then one must increase distance (or become depressed), etc. Our freedom involves the recognition of these psychological necessities.

Implicit in this way of experiencing one's situation is the "response" of anger, the instruction to remove the challenge.

The Structure of Anger

At this point in our conceptualization we had statements for the situation of anger and the "instruction" or response of anger (remove the challenge to what ought to exist). These statements were shared with colleagues and students and critical responses were solicited. While the statements themselves were accepted as valid, two sorts of questions were raised. The first of these asked about what might be termed the "embodiment" of anger. Granted that there was a challenging situation and a force to remove his challenge, but was it not also true that anger affects one's body and could even be

47

said to be based upon bodily changes? Should not the conceptualization speak to this aspect of anger? The second type of question raised a different issue -- granted the structure of anger, what place did this way of being have in a person's life? Why should a person get angry, what role did it serve, when was and when wasn't it functional? While the interview data did not permit complete answers to these questions it seemed clear that they did furnish at least partial answers and that a full conceptualization of anger should respond to these sorts of issues. Accordingly, I proposed that anger, or any other emotion, could be described as a structure with four interrelated parts: the situation, the instructional-transformation (the goal which would terminate the emotion when it was reached), the transformation of the person's body and its relationship to the perceived environment (which served as a means towards realizing the emotion's instruction), and the function of the emotion (that is, the role of the emotion in the person's life, the reasons that the particular emotion occurred rather than some other structuralization).

When a person was angry it seemed clear that his or her body was transformed in a particular way. It tightened and seemed about to explode, an embodiment which appeared to strengthen the person's will so that he or she could assert the self to remove the challenge. When the person avoided anger by creating distance, the person failed to exercise his or her will to remove the challenge. This was shown in numerous incidents such as the following examples.

A woman in public relations work was given a contract to change the image of a firm that was expanding its business. After doing some work on the contract she had lunch with a member of the firm and happened to express her political views. She noted that the conversation grew strained and realized that she had made a mistake in speaking so openly about her beliefs. The job called for further contacts with the firm, but the other did not call and "could not be reached." This placed the woman in conflict. Clearly a contract had been signed,

48

some work had been done, and she should attempt to collect her fee. On the other hand her client was in a position where he could injure her reputation with other clients if he promulgated his judgements of her and, consequently she hesitated to press him for payment. However, she was angry about the client's condemning her professional ability because of her politics and failing to cancel the contract in a responsible way and because of her anger she had her lawyer write a letter threatening court action and, thereby collected half the fee called for by the contract.

By contrast, a student wrote a paper for a course and felt that she had done a good job. It was returned with a mark of D+. She later reported that rather than becoming angry she had two thoughts in quick succession: "She (the grader) obviously doesn't know what I am talking about" and, "The course has a pass/no record option anyway, so nuts with grades." In the first thought, distance was created by considering the reader unintelligent, whereas in the second thought the student saw her-self as uncommitted to doing well in the course, as no longer involved. If she had become angry she might have confronted her professor with the assertion that she ought to get the grade her paper deserved. Without the anger she did not risk an actual con-frontation about the grade. Of course, we do not know whether the student was maturely reacting to an obtuse reader with false grading standards or whether she was avoiding a confrontation out of an insecurity about what the paper was really worth. In either case, in the absence of anger and an actual confrontation the student is able to maintain her belief that the paper is good but the grader's judgement determines social reality, and the paper's actual grade is uncontested by an assertion from the student's position.

It is such examples that lead us to postulate that the embodiment of anger seems to strengthen the person's will so that he or she risks the attempt to remove the challenge to what they assert ought to exist.[4]

A full description of the role which anger plays in the lives of persons is beyond the scope of the present study. However, we can note that anger functions to preserve the person's position as to what ought to exist, the values that these oughts reflect, and the closeness inherent in perceiving the other as a member of one's unit.

We are now in a position to propose a structure for the experience of anger. We suggest that anger is a way of being-in-the-world in which the angry person's will is strengthened so that he can remove a challenge to what he asserts ought to exist, thereby preserving the unit between the angry person and the object of anger and the shared values of this unity.

Of course, these ways in which anger functions may or may not be functional in the sense that they help a person lead a strong and creative life. The person's position may be valid or egocentric, the closeness may be a loving union that would ideally be maintained or a defensive hostile integration (cf. Pearce & Newton, 1969) that would ideally be relinquished. Anger may function to help a person maintain his or her integrity and to change the world creatively, or be used as a defensive mask that hinders growth and leads to injustice.

In any case, however, anger will always function to preserve the person's sense of what ought to exist. If this is acknowledged, anger may be appreciated in its own right and worked with so that the person may use his or her anger in construc-tive ways.

Note that the above structure is a whole with four interrelated parts. Thus, when we are angry, we cannot really separate the response (remove the challenge) from our perception of the situation (there is a challenge -- which is something to be removed). And one cannot make this response (the emotion's instruction) without the particular trans-formations of the body that characterize the expres-sion of anger (one cannot remove a challenge without a strengthend will). Finally, the emotion would not exist if it were not motivated by the way in which it functions in the broader scheme of the person's projects and personal relationships (the perception of a challenge that can be removed, functions to maintain a unit with common values and, hence, avoids having to create distance). We propose as a working hypothesis that any emotion is a way of being-in-the-world that functions to advance the projects to which the person is committed. Each particular emotion may be described by specifying its own unique structure. And every structure may be conceived as composed of four interrelated parts: (1) a way of perceiving one's situation, (2) "instructions" how to transform the situation, (3) a set of transformations that alter the person's body and its relation with the environment, and (4) its particular function within the person's life.

Continuing the Conceptual Encounter

In order to continue refining the above conceptualization of anger, I asked students in my classes to write short (3-5 page) papers based on an encounter between the conceptualization and their own personal experiences of anger. I pointed out the difference between a sort of mild meeting where one sticks to generalities and is satisfied with an easy fit between idea and experience, and an exciting encounter where the power of the conceptualization reveals aspects of the experience that were previously unnoticed or the details of the experience forces a modification of the conceptualization. I made it clear that I valued exciting encounters more than mild meetings and that the former occurred when one went into the concrete details of some specific experience and pitted them against the specific terms of the conceptualization.

In the following pages I want to present lengthy excerpts from four papers which illustrate the results one obtains from this type of conceptual encounter. (Names within these excerpts have been altered in order to preserve anonymity). After each of these papers I will consider implications for the conceptualization and mention whatever related problems or suggestions stem from other papers which I have not included in detail in order to conserve space.

Example 1 (from a paper by Jay Dudley)

This year I lived in an apartment with two other males. One of them, Alan, and I have been friends for a long time without ever having quarreled. We thought we knew each other pretty well. Monday night, January 20 of this year, Alan and I and some friends were at a bar and had a good time together. Everything was fine. On Tuesday morning I woke up freezing as the heat had been turned way down. I was furious that some skinflint would freeze rather than pay the price for comfortable heat, and would disregard the needs of the others in the apartment. Also, I had a cold at the time and felt extremely poor. After I turned up the heat I went to water my plants. I had one plant in the living room (which is the warmest room) as it was recuperating from a disease. I found that a new shoot had been twisted off, as to make room for another plant, which I knew to be Alan's. I looked in the waste-basket and found the broken shoot. I cannot describe the intensity of the anger that I felt. I was totally blind to any other thought other than to kill Alan. My plants are like people to me, so I viewed his action as an assault against a child of mine. When Alan returned from work that day I asked him if he broke the shoot on the plant. He answered yes and I told him if he ever did it again I would smash his_____ face. My anger was forceful and direct with a verbal hardness. I used no violence, and never could. After I said this I left the house and didn't talk to him for two weeks. As far as I was concerned he didn't exist.

Coincidentally, the emotion of anger was the subject of our class that very week. It was said that an "ought" is an assertion of one's values. This "ought" protects our values as there is a want for something to exist that doesn't. This "ought" holds another person responsible. I thought this was all trash. All I knew was that my anger only made me view him with hatred. Then my other roommate, who is not friendly with Alan at all, told me that he didn't know shy I was so angry. He said that Alan was a jerk and nothing that Alan does matters to him. It was then that I realized that he didn't hold Alan responsible for anything and that I really did. This "ought" also signifies a unit between people. This unit was broken and created anger in me for him because he had gone against the values that I had been asserting all along, on my plants, and on his caring for them also.

I later found out that Alan accidentally broke off the shoot. I then realized the rashness of my having expressed anger on him, and was sorry for it. However I was glad that he did know how I valued my plants and the need of his responsiblity toward them. Also I must admit that I did feel as if I had got rid of a burden when we did make up. I had no realization of these things when I was in the midst of anger, but I certainly do now. Alan and I seem to be closer now than ever, as we have accepted each other's "assertions of values."

       *   *   *   *   *

This example shows how the conceptualization helped a relatively non-introspective person begin to understand his experience. While the person himself is content with the analysis of his example, we may note some interesting problems which the example poses for the conceptualization. First, the person appears to have been in a bad mood when he woke up and this may have influenced his subsequent anger. This fact reminds us that the conceptualization does not really deal with the precursors of the experience of anger, nor offer us an analysis of how anger develops. Later, we shall see that an early experiment by Tamara Dembo may help us to understand the development.

Second, the intensity of the anger responses -- the thought of killing and the harshness of the verbal assault -- reminds us that the current conceptualization does not help us understand the difference between constructive and destructive expressions of anger. Here we may be helped by an interesting paper by Barbara Deming (1974). Working from her own experience with anger, Deming distinguishes between anger as a murderous affliction that stems from viewing the other's existence as a threat to one's own, and a healthy anger which reflects a determination to bring about change, and an assertion "you can and must change" that is based on hope.

The above distinction is related to yet a third problem posed by the example. The person states that for two weeks, "As far as I was concerned he didn't exist." This seems an extreme reaction that goes beyond the simple removal of a challenge. In some current studies by Lee Walker, we are finding this sort of response as a part of the structure of hate. In the experience of hate the other is seen as unchangeable; the person does not have the power to assert what ought to be in the face of the other and hence can only wish the other out of existence. It is interesting to note that in the very next paragraph the person states, "All I knew was that my anger only made me view him with hatred." Hence this example requires us to distinguish precisely between anger and hatred. Our own interviews suggest that hatred is related to a person feeling threatened rather than challenged; it may be equivalent of Deming's "murderous" anger. However, we do not yet understand when the person structures his experience in this way. Certainly it is unclear from this particular example; we would need more information why the person felt threatened by his antagonist and why such a threat is invariably associated with the absence of power and of any hope that the antagonist can change. In hate there is a sort of paradox: the hated person is perceived as not having the values which he ought to have! The insistence that the person ought to have certain values implies that the other is part of one's unit-- human and responsible -- while the fact that the person does not hold those values defines him as out of one's unit -- as inhuman, evil, and incapable of change.

54

In the above example, the encounter between experience and conceptualization primarily resulted in an illumination of the experience and only secondarily served to expand the conceptualization. In other papers, the reverse was true. The student used the encounter primarily to force a change in the conceptualization and only secondarily to understand the experience.

For example, one student felt that a close friend ought to have phoned at a time which had been mutually agreed upon. The conditions for anger appeared to have been met -- the other was held responsible for not having called, thereby offering a challenge to the value of responsive friendship -- yet the person did not experience anger and did not create distance. Instead the person "chose" another alternative that the conceptualization had not forseen -- the student reported feeling very <u>hurt</u>.

The report of such an experience forces us to expand the conceptualization of anger so that we may discriminate the conditions underlying hurt from those underlying anger, and show the relationship between these conditions. Clearly there is some sort of close relationship between anger and hurt, often when a person is subjected to a sudden physical hurt the person reacts with an outburst of anger. Further, the etymology of the term suggests a connection. Anger stems from the Icelandic <u>angr</u> (grief) and is related to the Latin <u>angro</u> (<u>anguish</u>). If we were simply to speculate about the relationship we might conclude that anger was simply an expression of hurt or that hurt was simply a form of inner-directed anger. However, it is clear that anger and hurt <u>feel</u> differently, the experiences are quite distinct, <u>and</u> our existential perspective leads us to consider them to be alternative ways of structuring our experience to meet a violation of what ought to be. Rather than speculate we must carefully describe the experience of hurt and attempt to articulate a conceptualization for the experience which will allow us to systematically relate it to the conceptualization of anger.

55

How then can we describe the structure of hurt? From the examples I have examined, it appears that the person retains a sense of what ought to have happened and a sense that the other is responsible, but the person does not really assert his or her will in an attempt to remove a challenge. Rather, the will collapses and the person suffers the hurt. This seems to occur along with a loss of confidence or trust in the other's regard for the self, and a realization that one cannot will the other to love the self. The reaction to the suffering is often to close off, pull in, tighten up, in order to deaden the hurt or prevent its future occurrence. The alternative is either to share the hurt or to "choose" to experience anger, the emotions often shifting back and forth.

During the experience of hurt, the other's response seems to have challenged the very existence of the personal unit and the closeness which would sustain anger. Rather than the person distancing the other, the other seems to have distanced the self -- so there is no longer a common ground for anger to occur.

While we can begin to relate hurt to anger on the basis of this crude sketch, a more accurate analysis of hurt would require a complete conceptual encounter, testing the sketch against the details of a number of concrete experiences. Such an analysis would have to take into account the fact that the experience of hurt must be related to the somewhat different experience of psychological pain. The latter appears to occur when self boundaries are broken -- as when a person has to separate from a union, or has to recognize some new aspects of the self, or even, at times, when a person must break open the self to experience love. In fact the intimate connection between pain and the realization of love is shown clearly in the works of writers such as William Blake and D. H. Lawrence. (See, for example, Blake's poem, "The Little Black Boy," or Lawrence's short story, "Daughters of the Vicar.") Such pain appears to have a somewhat different structure from the "hurt" of rejection which we have been considering.

In any case, for our present purpose of illustrating the method of conceptual encounter, we note how a personal experience provoked by the conceptualization forces a modification in the conceptualization. Examples show that a violation of what ought to exist may result in hurt rather than anger; remind us that there is an intimate connection between the two; and challenge us to define hurt and specify when it will exist rather than anger. Tentatively, we propose that as an alternative to either structuring a situation so that there is a challenge to what ought to exist, or to distancing the other, the person may suffer being distanced. The next example not only illustrates how hurt is an alternative to anger but shows how both of these emotions are related to distancing.

Example 2 (from a paper by Jane Raley)

This paper revolves around an incident that took place about a month ago. It concerns a close friend of mine named Bill. Because of our closeness and trust in one another, we share many confidences. He came to talk to me on a Wednesday night abut his relationship with his girlfriend. He was upset because her boyfriend from home was coming up here for the weekend. Naturally enough he just didn't know where he stood with her. We talked the whole thing through for about three hours. For the next three days I devoted a lot of my time to him, mainly just listening. Throughout all these discussions I had just kept saying, "Well, let's wait and see what happens this weekend and then take it from there." On Sunday evening I knew that his girlfriend had been to talk to him after her other boyfriend had left. As I was leaving the library I saw Bill and we talked for a few minutes, but he did not mention the fact that he had talked to his girlfriend. As I left the library I was a little stunned but then it definitely turned into anger. I hadn't necessarily wanted to know the whole story but just for him to say something like, "Sue, I talked to Sally and everything is all right." I thought that he ought to have mentioned it because of all the time we had spent talking. I didn't see him for a day but when I did I was with a group of people doing a crossword puzzle. When Bill came in and said hello, I didn't look up from the puzzle and even when he addressed me directly I didn't answer him verbally. I just sort of looked up and nodded my head. I reacted to him in this manner for about two days. I really wasn't consciously deciding to react this way. In fact, I was very amazed when I realized how I was acting, since I don't usually react in this manner. I was even more amazed, however, when I realized that this was clearly an instance of distancing, in order to avoid anger.

...All three of the criteria (for anger) were present in my incident with Bill. There was a challenge to what I thought ought to be. I thought Bill ought to have said something to me about the outcome of the weekend. I had been through too much of it with him just to be left hanging. Also we had a well established unit. We had a close, trusting relationship for quite a long time and during the time that we had been doing all this talking it had been implied that we would talk over the outcome of the weekend. Lastly, I really cared that he had challenged my values and I felt very strongly that he should change his behavior and support my values because he was a responsible member of the unit and also, in my eyes, at fault. However, I did not react with anger. Instead I chose one of the alternatives to anger that de Rivera suggests: increasing the distance between oneself and the other. There are many ways of doing this. I seem to have broken up the unit that Bill and I belong to, physically by not speaking to him at all. By doing this I was getting rid of one of the criteria of anger and thus avoiding a confrontation.

When I noticed that this incident was closely following the pattern of anger presented by de Rivera I realized that the thing to do would be to go and talk to Bill about my anger. A unit cannot maintain a close bond without the anger being expressed. I very much wanted Bill and me to be close again but I was afraid of expressing my anger because I thought that he might react the wrong way. I was

58

afraid that he would say to himself, "If I have to be this careful about what I do or don't say to Sue, if she's so sensitive, then it's not worth all this hassle to confide in her." Consequently our whole relationship would be destroyed. I was losing my power of assertion. De Rivera suggests that this loss of assertion is connected with depression. However, I was not depressed because this would involve turning the circumstances around until I was holding myself responsible, saying that I had acted in the wrong fashion. This was not in the least bit true. I always felt very strongly that it was Bill who had behaved in an unacceptable manner.

In thinking about the emotion that I felt during this incident, it didn't seem entirely correct to call the emotion anger. I believe that an alternative to anger that I used was hurt. When I saw Bill I realized that anger could stem from the situation, so consequently I distanced myself from him to avoid it. When I was alone, however, and thinking about what had happened, I felt hurt. As I see it the difference is that when I saw Bill, I felt like shaking him and saying, "Can't you see that you didn't do what you were supposed to do?" and wanting to change him, which constitutes anger. On the other hand, when I was alone and thinking, the pain was much deeper and felt as if there was nothing I could do to change him, that that is just the way he is. In feeling hurt I am aware of the loss of our relationship as it had previously been. In anger, however, there is still a bond, so I am not aware of a loss.

I was having tremendous difficulties trying to organize this paper because I was still having such inner turmoil over the incident. I finally came to the conclusion that I wouldn't be able to write the paper unless I talked to Bill and told him what was on my mind. At this point I didn't even care about what the outcome would be, I just wanted to know one way or the other so that I wouldn't be as confused. I finally did get the opportunity to talk to him and I told him exactly what I was feeling. He did not react in the manner which I had feared

59

he would. Instead he was upset that I hadn't told
him earlier but also glad that it had bothered me
because it showed that he was important to me. Since
our discussion it appears as if he had been much
more aware that there is a relationship between the
two of us and has been behaving as if he is fully
aware of the values and responsibilities that go
along with it.

*   *   *   *   *

This example clearly reveals a relationship
between anger, distancing and hurt. The person is
afraid to express the anger to her friend because he
might not continue the relationship. (After all,
the anger is about an apparent lack of caring for
her). Rather than risk the relationship, she distances from her friend and, thus, avoids the anger.
Such a maneuver occurs rather frequently in the
examples I have collected and appears to reflect
both a general unease with anger and an uncertainty
about one's worth.

Of course, eventually the maneuver undermines
the very relationship it is designed to preserve.
Ultimately, one must either continue to cling to a
relationship which does not really meet one's needs
and which undermines one's sense of worth or must
risk expressing one's anger. If one does not take
this risk, the relationship slowly dies out or may
be put at risk or even ended when the person uses
his anger to end the relationship assertively. In
the example at hand, Sue resists the temptation to
continue to forget the lack of the attention she
wants but only reluctantly shares her anger and
risks rejection.

It is quite clear from this example how feeling
hurt is yet another alternative to anger. In the
friend's absence she feels he does not really care
about her or thinks of him as the kind of person who
quickly forgets the past as soon as its problems are
solved. It is evident that she is not going to get
what she really wants from the relationship, that
she must accept the fact that she is really not the

kind of personal unit which she desires, a relationship where friends are eager to communicate. Her
friend simply does not care that much about her and
this hurts; therefore, she must dissolve the unit
and stop caring about him. Note that the type of
distance that is called for here is qualitatively
different from the distancing that is used to avoid
experiencing the anger which she feels in his presence. In the latter case she is personally close
but does not want to experience or express the
emotions that are called for, whereas in the former
she is personally distant. The realization that
there are different types of psychological distance
led to the investigation of distance that is reported in chapter six. At the close of this chapter
we will use some of the results of that investigation
to make a more precise conceptualization of anger.

Example 3

     At the beginning of this last module I decided
to do well in my organic chemistry lab. This was
prompted by the fact that I didn't do so well in the
previous three modules. It's not that how I did in
lab wasn't of concern to me before, just that it
wasn't important enough to me to make me devote my
fullest effort to it. I accepted it as a challenge,
as a task. I did not foresee failure, I was confident I could do it. Implied in this task was the
assertion: I do not fail at what I really try to do.
The first lab of the module was a support to this
assertion in that it was efficiently done and rather
successful. There was one hitch though: I spilled
some sulfuric acid on my hand at one point and
suffered a minor burn. It was painless, but it made
me angry. I felt a tension and a desire to smash
one of the glass beakers. This was associated with
the thought, "This should not be happening!"

     The next week I started a series of nine tests
in identifying unknown compounds by indicating
characteristic chemical properties. That day I
completed four tests moderately successully and again
strengthened my confidence in the decision to do well.
The following week I did the next four tests with

61

little trouble. The last test, however, was marred by a minor disaster. This test consisted of slowly adding nitrous acid to a test tube containing an organic compound which was cooled in an ice bath. There were three different compounds in separate test tubes. Two of them behaved nicely. The third (quite comically in retrospect) started foaming madly and started to come out of the top of the test tube. Obviously I had either added the acid too fast or had not cooled it down enough. I tried to cool the test tube down some more by moving it around in the ice bath, but only managed to knock one of the other test tubes over, loosing its contents to the icebath. Then I impulsively removed the troublesome test tube from the ice bath, propping it up against my lab towel. But it managed to fall over and spill its contents on the lab table. At that moment I was feeling my anger. I felt an incredible tension which seemed directed at holding back from shouting innumerable obscenities. I felt that what was happening shouldn't have been happening. I felt a strong desire to smash all of my glassware. I decided not to finish the experiment and started to clean up. While cleaning up I managed to break, unintentionally, two beakers. This didn't relieve my anger, though, because they merely broke, they didn't shatter. It didn't add to my anger either because I didn't care that I broke them.

Upon leaving the lab I released my anger by turning in my mind everyone that I passed into pillars of salt and by blowing up my dorm while I approached it. When I got back to my room and to the presence of my roommate and some friends, my anger dissipated, as if I left my anger behind when my "life space" changed into that of my social world.

It is important to note that my anger was not directed at anyone or anything specific. While in the lab it wasn't at myself, nor the lab assistants, nor the professor, nor the students around me, and certainly not at N,N-dimethylaniline (the nasty organic compound that started the whole mess). My desire to smash the glassware wasn't because I was

62

angry with the glassware, but because I desired to destroy something. And against whom or what would have shouting obscenities been directed? Again, when I did at least in my mind release my anger I didn't turn my professor, lab assistants, or fellow students to dust, but anonymous people I passed. And I didn't blow up Jeppson Laboratory nor Jonas Clark Hall, but my dormitory. Admittedly, there was a social pressure to refrain from expressing my anger while in lab, but that social pressure was not the object of the anger.

I propose that the statement that anger is felt, "when there is a challenge to what we assert ought to exist," is a specific case of a more general statement, "when there is a violation of what we assert should (or does) exist." With this new statement there didn't have to be social norms, social units nor an antagonistic character involved in the anger. Should refers to what one sees as the structure of the world and the violation is the interpretation of an act. This act could be caused by an intentional being (who may have a different view of the world) or by the encountering of the view of the world and the real world.

* * * * *

This example poses a different sort of problem for the conceptualization -- what happens when the challenge to what the person asserts ought to exist is not issued by an opposing will? In the above example, it is an impersonal reality that challenges the person's will. In other examples, persons may unintentionally challenge the presumed order of the world (e.g., accidentally knock one's head during a game, or not hear what one says, or have to cancel an anticipated meeting for legitimate reasons). In all these cases, no other is really challenging what the person asserts ought to exist. There is only a violation of the reality that should be. Nevertheless, it is important to note that the angered person responds as if he or she were challenged. He or she responds with the same disbelief that occurs in examples of personal anger. And although the person realizes the irrationality of the anger, that he or she "should" not really feel anger, and though he or she controls its expression in various ways, there is still the impulse to deal with a sort of challenge -- to see some other as responsible, to smash something, to somehow restore his or her power to act in the world, to regain confidence in the world as it should be. However, since there is no challenge in the sense of an opposing personal will, there is no obvious target for the anger (unless the person begins to attribute intentionality to the object that has violated his sense of how the world ought to be).

This distinction seems to be related to the different types of anger reported by investigators who have conducted naturalistics studies. In at least two such studies (McKeller, 1952; Richardson, 1918) persons reported instances of anger to the investigator as they occurred in the course of everyday life. Both studies report two different sorts of anger: an impersonal sort of anger that is occasioned by frustration, and a personal type of anger occasioned by insult, humiliation, or oppression. The first type is easily relieved by any sort of explosive discharge while the second type is only relieved by some sort of redress in the balance of the relationship.

Cases of the first type -- simple frustration -- pose a different sort of problem for the control and management of anger than cases which must deal with the will of an other. Rather than attempting to create an appropriate assertion that is timed correctly and based on a hope that the other can change, the person may attempt to release the anger with destructive imagery (as in the above example) or run it off in physical exercise. In either case, interesting questions about displacement are raised. In classic frustration-aggression theory the person displaces an aggressive impulse when there is some fear of punishment. The displacement is to a stimulus which: (1) bears a resemblance to the original

64

frustrating stimulus, yet (2) provokes little fear of punishment. However, in the above example, the person could have smashed the test tube or imagined blowing up the laboratory. Instead he chooses innocent bystanders and a non-academic building to be the targets of his fantasy aggression. Is he perhaps seeking to avoid the irrational implication of his anger, or is he displacing anger at himself?

Rather than displacing anger, one may cope with frustrating situations by avoiding anger and accepting the situation by altering one's goals. Thus, the person may give up the goal of a perfect experiment and patiently seek to discover how to correct the frustrating condition. Some persons seem much more able to use this strategy. Rather than insisting on the way things ought to be, they accept the fact that things have gone wrong. Rather than exploding with anger, they step back and then fit themselves into the new situation. Earlier we noted that certain moods, particularly states of tension, seem to predispose a person to anger. We learn a good deal about the conditions which predispose a person towards anger from an early investigation by Dembo (1976) which used experimental phenomenology to study the dynamics of frustration.

Dembo gave her subjects a problem that was impossible to solve. She carefully observed each subject's behavior and interviewed each person immediately after the experiment. The subjects were highly motivated -- they had solved previous problems -- and attempted numerous solutions. As long as a subject had hope that he or she could solve the problem, the subject persisted. With the loss of hope the frustrated subject did not become angry or aggressive, rather he or she simply attempted to leave the experiment. That is, frustrating a person by placing a barrier between a person and his or her goal does not lead to anger or aggression, but to withdrawal. However, when the subjects discovered that they were not free to leave (the experimenter simply told

65

each one that she was sure that they could solve
the problem and should try again), tension began
to build. That is, tension only builds when there
is also an outer barrier that holds the person
in the situation. In the experiment, the outer
barrier was maintained by the will of the experimenter. In everyday life, this outer barrier may
be a time pressure, fear of what another person
will think, self-ambition or self-doubt, anything
which prevents a person from having the freedom
to step out of the frustrating situation and see
a way of restructuring the problem.

It is important to note that the tension
which builds is not conceived to be "in" the
person but is, rather, a quality of the field
which surrounds and includes the person. As the
person returns to the task and suffers another
defeat, tries again to leave and is reminded that
this too is impossible, the tension within the
field begins to rise. The field has been rather
differentiated, that is there are boundaries
which enable the person to distinguish between
himself and the problem, to separate reality
from unreality, to see different aspects of the
problem; but as the tensions mount, these
boundaries begin to disappear and distinctions
are obliterated. The field becomes increasingly
primitive and the person loses the freedom to
restructure the situation in any way. In fact,
until the pressure is relieved by an outburst
of anger, or some other irrational action, the
person is trapped in an impossible situation.

The fact that a person is always kept in a
frustrating situation by some outer barrier
suggests that some expressions of anger may be
directed at this outer barrier rather than at
the direct cause of frustration. This may be
particularly true when the outer barrier is
supported by another person's will. In fact,
certain displacement effects may be understood
in terms of anger that is related to an outer
barrier. Thus, in the previous example, the
fact that anger was directed at fellow students

and a dormitory may reflect the fact that what
held the person in the situation -- his determination to perform the lab experiment successfully --
may have been grounded in his relations with his
peers and his determination to be a successful
member of the peer group.

Clearly we need to have a precise statement
that relates Dembo's conceptualization of the
tension to our own conceptualization of anger.
Such a statement cannot be simplistic. It is
true that tension appears to predispose a person
to anger and may be released in anger, but it
is also true that anger which is unexpressed may
lead to tension and that this may be released in
irritability or tears.

Example 4

This semester, both my roommates, whom I am
very dear friends with, are student teaching.
Their interships involve an intense commitment
in terms of time and energy. As a result of
their burdensome work load, I was indirectly
and implicitly allotted a greater proportion of
responsibility for keeping the house clean and
preparing meals. I began to feel I was exerting
more effort than I should have, or wanted to,
in maintaining the household. One night I came
home from the library and found the dishes from
dinner spread on the table and the dirty pots
left on the stove. Lynn and Janice were each in
their rooms with their doors shut, studying. I
threw my books on the floor, went into the bathroom and slammed the door. When I came out, Lynn
and Janice were standing outside their doors.
Lynn asked me what was wrong. I angrily told
her that it was the second time that day I was
doing the dishes. She exclaimed that I did not
have to get up the next morning and chase thirty
kids around a classroom. At her remark, my anger
erupted. I yelled at them both, saying that
even though I do not chase thirty children every
day, I work hard, lead a life that can be
physically exhausting at times, and should not

be made to do all the work in the house. I
told them I was sick of hearing what went on
in their classrooms and how much they had to
do when neither of them cared or knew about
what happened in my life. Janice told me to
look at her and asked, amazed, "Do you think we
don't care about you?" With an intensity of
emotion, I said, "It doesn't seem you care if I
live or die. Nobody wants to do anything for me
or listen to me anymore. After you graduate you
won't even think about me or care if I'm your
friend or not."

   It was immediately after I made these last
remarks that I became aware of the true source
of my anger. Although the disorder in the house
was a partial contributor, I knew my angry behavior was triggered by other, deep-seated
reasons, that I had not been fully conscious of
before becoming angry. First, I was angered
by the change in the established pattern of
behavior in the apartment. In many ways, I had
been the "child" in the household. The triad
of roles each of us had taken on was disrupted
when my roommates became student teachers. The
second reason for my anger was the diminished
amount of emotional support I was able to draw
from my roommates for my life activities. It
seemed they were too busy to take an active
interest in my daily life or listen to minor
personal problems. Third, I was angry that my
roommates were leaving me and graduating at the
end of the semester. Because they knew we would
not be together much longer, I felt they should
spend more time with me. After realizing I had
indirectly stated the primary causes of my emotional
outburst, I told my roommates the dishes were
only part of the reason I was angry. My anger
remained on the same level, but I was able to
coherently and straightforwardly discuss with
them why I had exploded and what I thought had
to be changed to allow for all three of us to
be content with our home lives.

   The concepts of ought, challenge, and

68

assertion, which are manifest in the situational conditions to anger according to de Rivera, can be evidenced in my personal experience. My roommates challenged my ought systems concerning intimate friendship and household management. The oughts I felt applied to intimate friendship were exhibiting caring behavior, consideration of the friend's needs, and a high level of interest in the friend's daily life. With regard to household management, I valued a cooperative orientation and a communal set-up. The challenge my roommates posed took the form of their neglect of the house and my own self. The expression of my anger was an assertive declaration of my oughts and a persuasive imperative that our household environment conform to my view of what reality should be like. Expressive transformations were apparent in my personal experience, such as my slamming the bathroom door. Instructional transformations also occurred. Because I chose to preserve our friendship unit, I necessarily took steps to make compatible our lifestyles and my values by demanding a removal of the challenge my roommates posed and a change in their behavior.

Although my experience contains the essential constituent features of de Rivera's structural analysis of anger, I feel it necessitates a modification of his theory in that it exposes events occuring in the process of expressing anger which he does not discuss and contradicts the functional effects he ascribes to anger concerning the preservation of the values of the angry person.

According to de Rivera, the emotion of anger persists until instructional objectives are adhered to or the situation takes on a new meaning. I feel that, in the process of expressing anger, the situation inevitably accrues new meanings. In my experience, expressing my anger led me to see that my oughts were not based in an objective, accepted order, but rather on my subjective needs. The egocentric nature of the reality I was asserting should exist became apparent to me. I remained

69

angry, as I felt the behavior of my roommates still needed to be changed, but my situation was restructured by the inner dimensions of my psychological make-up brought to the fore of my consciousness during the course of expressing my anger. Revealing my anger resulted in a self-revelation. I believe expressing anger possesses the potentiality for functioning as a self-revealing process. If this is true, situational transformations may be intrinsic to the series of actions which occur during the course of expressing anger, as are expressive and instructional transformations, and need to be emphasized in a structural analysis.

My anger also served to reveal to me the necessity for personal change. Rather than functioning to affirmatively maintain my view of reality and endorse my oughts, my anger led to a necessary re-evaluation and reordering of my value priorities. I began to view my ought system concerning intimate friendship as overly demanding and my need to be a "child" as a preventive barrier to achieving personal autonomy. I realized I value maturity and self-reliance more than dependency and that I must work to live according to these priorities. The process of expressing my anger served to be as functional to me as the specific ends it achieved.

*   *   *   *   *

Encountering this example challenges the conceptualization of the function of anger. While the anger initially functioned to remove the challenge to the person's position as to what ought to exist, and while it was certainly in the service of the person's values and the preservation of the unit, the expression of the anger freed the person to see the egocentricity of what she was asserting. This changed her perception of what ought to exist and she realized that certain needs (to be a child, to receive emotional support, to not suffer separation) motivated the anger in addition to her values (of cooperation and friendship). In other examples, it is also clear that

70

anger can enable one to separate oneself from a unit that has not been meeting one's needs. In such cases, as well as in the above example, the anger is certainly in the service of the person's ultimate values, but clearly may lead to a change in the person's own position as to what ought to be or may destroy rather than preserve the unit.

Of course, at the moment of anger the conceptualization still holds. That is, even in the above examples, while anger is occurring the person is removing a challenge to what he or she asserts ought to exist within the unit with the other person. And this assertion is in accord with held values and the expression of the anger maintains closeness and the connection between the person and the other. However, regarded developmentally, the expression of the anger may allow one to change one's position about what ought to exist or to separate oneself from the unit with the other.

Needless to say, the expression of anger does not necessarily lead to such beneficial growth (compare for instance the first example we examined). In some examples, going through the expression of anger enabled the person to separate and grow, while in others it merely preserved the status quo, or triggered feelings of guilt. Such facts call for an extended conceptualization that can deal with the role of anger in personal development. Ideally, such a conceptualization should help us understand the best ways for anger to be expressed and received.

Further Development of the Conceptualization

As our conceptualization encounters new experiences, it has to be modified and expanded. Sometimes such accommodations are relatively easy. We can enlarge the concept of challenge to include impersonal violations or we can add the alternative of being hurt to being angry or depressed. However, there are times when it is not clear how to change the structure, or the structure becomes increasingly cumbersome and inelegant, top-heavy

71

with the weight of too many accomodations. In such cases, a restructuring is needed; the investigator must have a new insight into the relations between different aspects of the structure so that he or she can reorganize the conceptualization. Often such restructuring is made possible by examining connections between the structure and the conceptualizations of other investigations.

In the case of the anger conceptualization, it soon became clear that the concept of distancing had to be clarified. The conceptualization pointed out that distancing was an alternative to anger because the distanced other could not really challenge the person's values (e.g., he's a jerk, why care about what he does). But there seemed to be different ways to increase distance. Hence, Thomas Kreilkamp began to study psychological distance as a concept in its own right (rather than as simply a part of the conceptualization of anger), an investigation that is presented in Chapter six. Meanwhile, the anger conceptualization encountered examples of other types of distancing (such as number two above) where a person "distanced" from the self as well as the other in order to avoid an anger that might disrupt the unit, and examples (such as number two and others cited) where hurt occurred instead of anger and the person seemed to "withdraw" from the other and consider relinquishing the unit. If a person used "distancing" in the sense of "he's a jerk, so why care what he does," the person experienced a change in psychological space rather than the emotion of anger. On the other hand, if the person distanced from the self, or "withdrew," some affect was still present and the person's behavior appeared to be an expression of emotion rather than an alternative to it. In spite of these differences, in all cases of distancing the person still retained a sense of what the other ought to do, or of what friends or lovers in general ought to do, even though the particular other could not be trusted to meet expectations and the particular relationship might have to be relinquished. Thus, all cases of anger or distancing could be contrasted with experiences of fear or danger, where considerations of what ought to be was never inherent in the experience.

How can we formulate a new conceptualization that will capture what we have learned from our encounters with experience? Previously we stated that anger was a way of being-in-the-world in which the will was strengthened so that the person was enabled to remove a challenge to what he or she asserted ought to exist. And we suggested that the anger functioned to preserve a unit that existed between the person and the other, and to maintain the values that were shared by members of this unity. We now see that almost every aspect of this structure needs to be qualified. For example we find that while a challenge often reflects an opposing will, it is sometimes merely an impersonal violation of how the world ought to be and sometimes constitutes a threat to the person's identity and values. In the one variant there is no opposing will to be changed and the anger is usually discharged in some harmless fantasy, outburst, or activity. In the latter varient the opposing will is not seen as change-able, its very existence constitutes a threat which must be removed from existence rather than a challenge which must be met, the person experiences hate rather than anger and wishes the other did not exist.

In all of these cases the person is held in the situation where he or she is confronted with what ought not to exist, by some outer barrier that prevents the person from reducing tension by leaving the situation, restructuring, or distancing. If the person is able to accept what exists the anger vanishes but anger itself works against this acceptance by strengthening the person's sense of what ought to exist. Paradoxically, experiencing and expressing the anger may reduce the tension so that the person can see the situation differently.

73

While anger always seems to strengthen the person's perception of what ought to be and removes any challenge about what ought to exist in the person's own perception, it does not automatically strengthen the person's will so that he or she attempts to remove the challenge in social reality. The person's body is necessarily affected, but if the person is unable to create a safe and appropriate expression for the anger, the person may avoid the other, become sullen or passively aggressive, or become tense or upset. In such cases, the anger still seems to function to preserve the person's sense of what ought to be and still affects the person's body and behavior, but does not directly operate to enable the person to remove the challenge. When the "energy" of the anger is not used to directly remove the challenge in social reality, it seems to persist until it can be expressed or the person's situation is changed by external events. It still appears that when the anger is not expressed in some way, the sense of what ought to exist is lost, and the person begins to become depressed, feeling that behaving in the way he or she ought is impossible.

In discussing the concept of "ought," we noted that it reflected the person's values, his or her sense of what some impersonal order wanted to exist rather than simply what the person wished to exist. And it is true that in every instance of anger the person seems to have been asserting what ought to be, making some requirement on the world or the other, rather than simply expressing some personal wish. However, in assessing any instance of anger there are two important ways in which the assertion of ought needs to be qualified. First, what a person asserts ought to be may in fact be based on personal needs as well as a person's values. Hence the assertion may be egocentric or may reflect insecurities as well as true values. Nevertheless it may be necessary for the person to express and acknowledge his or her anger in order to separate and distinguish the true assertion of value from the egocentric expression of need. Second, for a

74

person to fully "own" his or her anger, to take full responsibility for the anger, the person must not hide behind some impersonal ought, but must create a direct personal assertion which expresses his or her position. (For example, compare an indirect statement such as "people ought not to make prejudicial remarks" with the direct, "I don't like you making a prejudicial remark").

Finally, we have seen how distancing, in the sense of a transformation of psychological space, is not the only alternative to anger. Another possibility is to feel hurt. Possibly, the experience of hurt occurs when the person perceives the self to be distanced by the other. That is, the other seems not to be treating the self as a worthy member of the unit. Yet another alternative to a complete anger experience involves the person "distancing" from feelings of either hurt or anger by withdrawing from the relationship with the other. However, such cases constitute an expression of the emotion rather than an alternative to it.

We may summarize our findings by sketching the rather complicated diagram shown in Figure 1. Such a diagram attempts to show how different emotional relationships are dependent on how the person structures his or her situation. It tries to reveal the alternatives that exist and is a sort of crude map of how different ways of being-in-the-world are related to each other. It is crude for two different reasons. First, to be more accurate one would have to construct similar maps for each of the alternatives shown (e.g., fear, hurt, etc.) rather than simply focusing on anger. This would begin to reveal the entire complex web of interdependent relationships. As it is, the map does not necessarily show the correct relationship between the different parts. While it is probably correct in portraying the close relationship between anger and hurt, it may be incorrect in failing to show a relationship between fear and hate (perhaps both involve the experience of being threatened) or in suggesting a relatively close relationship between being hurt and being depressed (when depression charges the self rather than the other with responsibility). Second, the ways of being-in-the-world that are located on the map are only a part of a larger whole that includes possibilities such as acceptance, anxiety, and laughter. Yet there is no indication of how these other alternatives are connected to the ones that are portrayed.

Constructing a map is an interesting technique that may be used as part of a conceptual encounter. It forces us to make choices about how concepts are related to each other. It makes us realize specific deficiencies in our knowledge, sends us back to concrete experience with specific questions that we previously failed to ask. For example, in drawing the map I had to decide where to place depression. I decided to show depression as related to hate the way hurt is related to anger. However, this questions my earlier statement that depression maintains closeness. If the map is correct, it must involve the suffering of a loss of unity with the other. I'm not sure whether this is so. The next time I do an interview on the experience of depression, I'll check it out. So we need further study, a more precise inquiry.

Still, we understand more now than when we began our exploration. The first charts of America were equally crude, a stretch of mainland later turned out to be an island and a possible passage became a large bay. May this current chart like those before it aid further exploration and lead to the revelation of an entire new world!

ANGER AND ITS ALTERNATIVES

O – choice point
p – person
o – other

"Distancing" of o

Removal of o's challenge

p asserts

ANGER

p fails to assert

tension in p

Obliteration of o

HATE

o challenges p

o is not worthwhile

What ought to exist

hope

no hope

o threatens p

p suffers distancing by o

HURT → Withdrawal

DEPRESSION

p is responsible, not worthwhile

a violation

of what ought exist

A NEGATIVE EVENT

danger

no ought involved

FEAR

77

Reference Notes
for Chapter II

1. Such an endeavor is not dissimilar to the
   project elaborated in Spinoza's Ethics. However,
   I am more concerned with the revelation of
   necessary relationships than with deduction
   from axioms. Of course, I am aware that "many
   persons view modern mathematics as nothing but
   a consistent set of conclusions deduced from
   rather arbitrary definitions and postulates
   that may be created at will by the mathematician." However, as Courant and Robbins
   (1941) point out, this is a "deceptive half-
   truth." In fact, the mathematician must reveal
   structures and relationships and can only be
   "guided by intrinsic necessity" and constructive invention.

2. Of course, it is conceivable that there is
   nothing in common to all different instances
   of anger, that they simply bear what
   Wittgenstein (1953) would call a "family
   resemblance" to each other, the way different
   New England towns might share somewhat
   different sets of features. To the extent
   this were true one might want to use the
   tactic that Rosch (1973) has described --
   creating an ideal type that persons agree is
   a "typical" example of a New England town
   (or instance of anger). However, I feel that
   there is an essence common to all instances of
   anger. This commonality does not exist
   because instances of anger have some common
   element. Rather, as Cassirer (1953) argues,
   the various concrete instances of anger are
   unified by the concept of "anger." There are
   intimate connections between each specific
   instance and a general form which we structure
   to include all instances and exclude non-
   instances. For an event to be experienced as
   anger it must already be seen as an example
   of the concept "anger." The substance of any
   specific instance of anger, of any particular

78

experience, any member of the series or set
that we conceptualize as "anger" is cate-
gorically different from the form of the
series, the functional whole that is the
concept "anger." The latter is the result
of a "synthetic act of definition" that
differentiates the form from other concepts
in the same domain.

References
for Chapter II

Blake, William. The little black boy. In Songs
of innocence and of experience. New York:
Orion Press, 1967.

Cassirer, Ernst. Substance and function and
Einstein's theory of relativity. New York:
Dover Publications, 1953.

Courant, Richard and Robbins, Herbert. What is
mathematics? London: Oxford University Press,
1941.

Dembo, Tamara. The dynamics of anger. In Field
theory as human science, Joseph de Rivera (Ed.).
New York: Gardner Press, pp. 324-422, 1976.

Deming, Barbara. On anger. In We cannot live
without our lives. New York: Viking Press,
pp. 36-51, 1974.

de Rivera, Joseph. A structural theory of the
emotions. Psychological Issues Monograph 40.
New York: International Universities Press, 1977.

Fingarette, H. On responsibility. New York: Basic
Books, 1967.

Heider, Fritz. The psychology of interpersonal
relations. New York: Wiley, 1958.

Kane, Richard. Two studies on the experience of
depression. Unpublished Masters Thesis, Clark
University, Worcester, Massachusetts, 1976.

Lawrence, D. H. Daughters of the Vicar. In The
complete short stories, Vol. I. New York:
Viking Press, 1961.

Lerner, M. T. Social psychology of justice and interpersonal attraction. In Foundations of interpersonal attraction, T. Huston (Ed.). New York:

Academic Press, pp. 331-351, 1974.

McKellar, P. Provocation to anger and the development of attitudes of hostility. British Journal of Psychology, 1950, 40, 104-114.

Pearce, Jane and Newton, Saul. The conditions of human growth. Seacaucus, New Jersey: Citadel Press, 1969.

Richardson, R. F. The psychology and pedagogy of anger. Baltimore: Warwick and York, 1918.

Rosch, Eleanor. On the internal structure of perceptual and semantic categories. In T. M. Moore (Ed.) Cognitive development and the acquisition of language. New York: Academic Press, 1973.

Wittgenstein, Ludwig. Philosophical investigations. New York: Macmillan, 1953.

III

THE EXPERIENCE OF ANXIETY
AS DIFFERENTIATED FROM PANIC

Susan Goodman

In this chapter I identify the tangible,
particular elements of an experience that make it an
experience of anxiety, as distinguished from an
experience of panic. I also specify the life
circumstances that accompany the emotions of anxiety
and panic. The two emotions are discrete states
and should not be thought of as being on one
continuum.

The Method of Investigation

I used a clinically-oriented form of conceptual
encounter, described in detail elsewhere.[1] The
intention behind the method of proceeding was to
stay as close to the data of experiencing as possible.

The sources of data for the study included
informal observation of my family, friends, acquaint-
ances, students, patients, and strangers met in the
street, introspection, and works by masters of
English prose. I held extended and repeated tape-
recorded interviews with 48 people who agreed to act
as research partners. The people interviewed spoke
about specific instances during which they were
certain that they had had emotional experiences which
they would call by the names "anxiety" or "panic."
All of the research partners were introspective,
skilled at making fine discriminations about their
experience in words, and spoke English fluently.

Now names are tricky things. Words like "anxiety" and "panic" are very formal words that are not used by all sections of the population. The emotional experience labeled "anxiety" by the research partners may well be what some other people mean when they say they are "nervous," "tense," "feeling bad," "out of it," "going through changes," etc. The experience labeled by the research partners "panic," may be what other people mean when they say they are "crazy with fear," "flipping out," "falling apart," "dying," "losing my head," and the like. Also, some people do not even use such terms for the formal words "anxiety" or "panic" but, instead, communicate via hypochondriacal symptoms, bodily movements, significant silences, recollections of dreams, or vivid situational descriptions from which the appropriate emotion is to be inferred by an empathic listener.

The use of qualifying adjectives such as "mild" or "severe" may point to phenomenologically quite different psychological experiences. A person who says he is "severely" anxious, for example, may be having an emotional experience with the characteristics described in the section on "panic" below. Or, he may mean that he is "anxious" in the sense described in the section on "anxiety" below, but be having a repetitive bout of anxiety extending over several days.

Also, some people may use the word "anxiety" incorrectly, in the sense that they would apply it in circumstances for which people with a feel for the English language would suggest another word. An instance of this would be the sentence, "I am anxious to meet you," when the intended meaning, in fact, is, "I am eager to meet you." Of course, the sentence "I am anxious to meet you" is correct when that is what is meant.

Language, in short, is a guide, but it is only a rough guide to reality.[2] In conducting my ongoing dialogue with the research partners, I therefore tried to get them to be as explicit as possible about the experience they were referring to when they said

84

they were "anxious" or "panicked." Our interviews together were lengthy and repeated because it was important to be sure that we both were talking about the same experience and not getting misled by words.

It took a while to figure out a way of interviewing that would enable me to find out both what probably happened when someone was "anxious" and what the meaning of what happened was for the person.[3] I originally just jotted down notes of my conversations with the research partners. Later I tape-recorded the interviews and found that this made a marked difference. The existence of a mechanical memory for what transpired in the interview served as an important protection against selectively screening out statements by the person interviewed that I did not, for whatever reason, want to hear. Also, I found I could attend fully to the subtleties of wording and phrasing when reading the transcriptions over in the absence of the person being interviewed. Finally, the tape recorder brought home the fact that there were two people in the interview situation, the research partner and I.

I noticed the role that I played in how the interviews went. It seemed to me that the other person and I did a verbal dance with each other, setting up the right positions, rhythms, distances between us so that we would both be comfortable with what was spoken about. It was clear from the tapes, for example, that at first I did not want to get into particular aspects of panic experiences and would close off with an arch remark, or a topic switch, any intimations of a willingness by the other person to open up about an area of experience troublesome to me. It took me a while to be able to listen with comfort to the apparently crazy things connected with panic experiences. Once I began to respond to them in a matter-of-fact everyday way, I began to hear many more accounts than before about crazy experiences which accompanied panic.

I also picked up my tendency to interrupt on the tapes. I would let people speak for about fifteen minutes and then start firing questions at them. Needless to say, what followed either just confirmed my question or else was a denial given in an increasingly irritated fashion. I finally taught myself to shut up and listen.

Because of my unsystematic style of asking questions, I also noticed that one tape had lots of material on one aspect of an emotion while another would be filled with information about another aspect. There were marked similarities in the information found on all the tapes but I could not tell if the discrepancies were due to idiosyncratic differences or to the fact that I had not directly inquired into the informant's experience of a particular aspect.

I finally evolved a method of interviewing which took account of the difficulties discussed above. The interviews usually took four hours, divided into two two-hour sessions, the first comparatively unstructured and the second, quite structured. Sometimes a third session was required.

In the first session I asked the person to think of an episode to which they would definitely apply the name "anxiety" or "panic." Then I gave this instruction:

> Please recall, moment by moment, what happened during the course of the episode. Start from just before you felt the emotion, go through the beginning of the emotion to the sequence of events that occurred while you were experiencing the emotion to what happened just before the end of the emotion. Then describe the end and what happened immediately afterwards. Try to describe it as if you were re-living it, as if it were happening right now. Try not to leave anything out and try to tell me everything that you think is important to understand what happened. I do not want to bias you by my questions, so I won't ask you anything until you have completely finished. I trust your own mind to know what is relevant anyway, more than I trust mine.

This instruction usually led to a monologue of at least an hour. When the person finished I asked, "Is there anything else that comes to mind?" This question often provoked either further detail about the episode or additional associations about the meaning of the event for the person's life. I then said, "Well, can you think of anything else? What you have been telling me is marvelously helpful and I trust your mind more than mine to know what is relevant. Does anything else occur to you?" Some people then spoke at length; others didn't.

During the first, comparatively unstructured, interview, I listened in an empathic mode, experiencing in myself what the other was saying and deliberately inhibiting any critical thoughts I might have had. I found that this facilitated the fullest communication. After the person had clearly finished all that he had to say, I used the remaining time to ask questions that flowed directly from the material. My questions surprised me by coming from seemingly nowhere, yet they had a "right" feeling to them.

The questions which came from the creative encounter I had been having with what the research partner was recounting about the episode of anxiety or panic illuminated the episode in a way that was surprising to both of us. If I had been fully and relaxedly listening, if I had genuinely wanted to hear the other's experience, I observed that I frequently learned something I had not known before. Both of us shared a revelation.

People told me afterwards that they felt unusually "understood" from my manner, questions, and statements. I have had similar experiences of being understood and of deep clarification when other people have had the time, skill, and interest to reach out of themselves to attend to me fully. A different sort of knowing occurs here than that which takes place when you "check conceptualizations" (or "test clinical inferences") against another person's reality. It is a knowing of the previously unknown that happens almost by a giving up of the attempt to "know," by a relaxation of the attempt to master the world by imposing your own vision on it.[4]

At the end of the first interview, I sounded the research partners out about their reactions to it, thanked them and made another appointment. In the interim, I listened critically to the tape and noted down unanswered questions I had about it. I also noted how much of the material fell into conceptual categories I had already formulated from previous interviews on anxiety and panic, as well as some I was doing, for contrast, on apprehension, fear and terror. I eventually devised a check list (with some 200-odd items!) to ensure that I had covered all the categories -- such as the physical experience, the experience of the self, the experience of others, the experience of time, the experience of danger, ad infinitum. The interim time was more than a mulling time. It was a time in which I let myself tear into the body of the "data" (not the person) and get angry at it for not being the way it ought to be.[5] It was a point at which I confronted my conceptions and some of my preconceptions with the real world.

In the final structured interview, I tried to relate with the research partner in an analytic, rather than an empathic, manner. That is, I asked a series of questions drawn from the check list plus others drawn directly from our first interview together. The questions were intended to analyze or discriminate what had already been said. I checked to see if what had been said did or did not fit certain conceptualizations and, if not, why not. My subjective experience was one of serious and thoughtful questioning, of explicitly testing research inference, but it was not an experience of the mutual sharing of a reconsideration of a deeply felt emotional experience.

I stress the different modes of listening -- empathic, critical and analytic -- because I think they determine to some extent the sort of material obtained. They each seem valid in their proper place.

All of the 48 people I interviewed were people

I liked and wanted to know better. I avoided both
people I did not like or those who I thought, for
whatever valid or invalid reason, might be overly
disturbed by what transpired. The people who eventually became research partners volunteered to take
part after hearing a brief summary of what I was
working on in the course of casual conversation.
Since I was aware throughout that the outcome of the
interview depended on the person's willingness to
participate genuinely, I took many and varied steps
to ensure they were comfortable with the situation,
felt their confidentiality would be respected, and
the like.

        Almost everyone interviewed was white. Of the
48 people, 29 were female and 19 male. Half of the
sample was Jewish and there were definitely more
Protestants than Catholics among the remainder. They
ranged in age from ten to seventy, but most were in
their twenties and thirties. A few had not graduated
from high school but the majority had at least some
graduate education. Most were already in one of the
professions; well over half were in psychology. There
were a few artists and writers. A couple were rich;
a couple were poor; the rest were within the middle
class and likely to remain there.

Previous Literature

        There is an extensive psychological literature
on the subject of Angst.[6] I found this literature
bewildering until I became quite familiar, through
interviewing, observation, and introspection, with
experiences of anxiety and panic in the real world.
Then, I realized that the theory of Angst advanced
by Kierkegaard and others within the existential
tradition -- a theory which will be called here the
"transitional paradigm" of Angst -- made sense if I
regarded it as being about the experience of "anxiety"
I had observed. The theory of Angst advanced by
Freud and others within the psychodynamic tradition --
a theory which will be called here the "repression
paradigm of Angst" -- made sense if I regarded it as
being about the experience of "panic" I had observed.

89

The transitional paradigm of Angst is that
Angst occurs as a person makes the choices involved
in going from one way of being in the present to
another in the future. Kierkegaard, the originator
of the paradigm, spoke of Angst as inherent in the
"qualitative leap" (1944/1957, p. 39) that takes
place as a man moves from a state of innocent
ignorance, in which "spirit is dreaming" (p. 37), to
a state of knowledge. He held that Angst is ontological in that it is a constitutive element for the
self; a person never actualizes a potentiality without going through what Kierkegaard calls the
"intermediate determinant of (Angst) (May & Basescu,
1963, p. 78). For Kierkegaard, the "greater the
Angst, the greater the man" (1944/1957, p. 135).

Goldstein (1940) follows Kierkegaard in his
discussion of the appearance of Angst in the normal,
self-actualizing adult as he comes to terms with a
new milieu.[7] Schachtel's presentation of Angst as
the emotion which occurs when "there arises the
necessity or desirability to emerge from a particular
form or aspect of life in which one has been embedded
and to make the transition to a new and different
way of life" (1959, p. 43) is also similar. Sabert
Basescu (1962), William Fischer (1970), and Abraham
Maslow (1962) are further representatives of this
tradition.

Unlike the "transitional paradigm" of Angst,
the repression paradigm is that Angst occurs when
experiences previously barred from awareness in the
past attempt to force their way into consciousness
in the present. The term "repression paradigm" is
taken from Eugene Gendlin, who describes it as
follows:

Most personality theories (in different words
and with somewhat different meanings) share...
the "repression paradigm." They agree that in
an individual's early family relations he
introjected certain values, according to which
he was loved only if he felt and behaved in
certain ways. Experiences which contradicted
these demands on him came to be "repressed"

90

(Freud), or "denied to awareness" (Rogers) or
"not me" (Sullivan). Later, when the individual
encounters experiences of this contradicting
sort, he must either distort them or remain
totally unaware of them. For, were he to notice
the contradictory experiences, he would become
intolerably anxious. The ego (Freud), or self-
concept (Rogers), or self-dynamism (Sullivan),
thus basically influences awareness and perception. This influence is termed "resistance"
(Freud), or "defensiveness" (Rogers) or "security
operations" (Sullivan), and a great deal of
behavior is thereby explainable. A personality
is as it is, and remains as it is, because it
cannot take account of these experiences. Or
if, somehow, repression is forcefully lifted
and the individual is made to become aware of
these experiences, the ego will "lose control,"
the self will "disintegrate," and intolerable
"uncanny emotions" will occur. In psychosis,
it is said, the individual is aware of such
experiences and the ego or self-organization
has indeed broken down.
If the individual needed merely to be reminded,
or to have the "repressed" factors called to his
notice, he would soon be straightened out.
There are always helpful or angry people who
attempt this, and many situations grossly demand
attention to these factors. The individual,
however, represses not only the given factors
within him but also anything outside of him
which would relate to these factors and remind
him of them. He misunderstands or reinterprets
so as to prevent himself from noticing the
aspects of events and persons which would bring
these factors to his awareness.
Thus, the specific personality structure maintains itself and change is theoretically
impossible. Whatever would change the individual
in the necessary respects is distorted or goes
unnoticed just to that extent and in those
respects in which it could lift the repression
and change him (1964, pp. 104-105, my italics).

I believe the "repression paradigm" of Angst

91

applies to the experiences of panic I studied.
Freud's second theory of traumatic anxiety as
occurring when the ego is overwhelmed by an influx
of stimuli too great for it to master (1933/1965,
Chapter 3 and Brenner, 1957, pp. 76-107), Sullivan's
(1953, 1954, 1956, and 1964) theory of panic as
occurring when the "self-dynamism" is threatened by
the emergence of the "not me," Roger's theory that
anxiety is a "state in which the incongruence between
the concept of the self and the total experience of
the individual is approaching symbolization in awareness" (1969, p. 204), and Horney's (1937) theory that
anxiety results from the surfacing of repressed
hostility, all make sense if read as being about the
structure of experience characteristic of panic
discussed below. They are not intelligible, it seems
to me, if read as being about the experience of
anxiety as identified in this paper.

The discussion below of the structure of
experiencing of anxiety, as distinguished from panic,
builds upon the work of the theorists of the "transitional" and the "repression" paradigms of Angst.
The relation of this discussion to the work of other
authors will be indicated in text and in footnote.

Categories of Explication

Emotions are a holistic experience. Anxiety,
panic, etc., permeate the immediacy of one's entire
being. You are anxious or you are panicked or you
are confident in the world. You think, dream,
remember the past, envisage the future, talk, see,
hear, act, move, touch, etc., differently with each
emotion. Anxious breathing cannot really be separated
out from anxious bodily posture nor that from anxious
seeing, nor that from the anxious self that anxiously
thinks and sees. The anxious self you try to describe
in the present cannot really be described apart from
who it has been in the past, who it is becoming, who
it is with others, or from the physical, historical,
cultural environment which constitutes its anxious
world. In like fashion, panicky breathing cannot
really be separated out from panicky bodily posture
nor that from panicky seeing, etc., etc. Neither

can confident breathing be separated out from confident bodily posture, nor that from confident seeing, etc., etc.[8]

For purposes of explication, however, the consideration of the holistic experiences of anxiety and panic have been divided into the following categories: the physical experience, the experience of intellectual, perceptual and muscular functioning, the experience of the self, the experience of self-criticism and the conscious experience of what the emotion is "about." The remarkably consistent way in which the pattern of experiencing appears in the various categories will be demonstrated, first for the case of anxiety and then for the contrasting case of panic. The sections on anxiety and panic conclude with a discussion of the life circumstances accompanying the pattern of experiencing characteristic of the respective emotions.

ANXIETY

Physical Experience

When anxious, people are uncomfortable with their bodies and clearly experience them as not being right. The impaired sense of physical well-being is noted to different degrees and extents. It is an unpleasant but tolerable sensation.

Manifestations of bodily discomfort include: constricted breathing, dry mouth, a choking feeling in the throat, a sensation of having a hollow chest, "butterflies" in the stomach, vomiting, diarrhea, an inordinate need to urinate, heart beating, shaking, weak knees, wooden legs, cold hands, sweating, and eyes out of focus.

Tension, ranging from an experience of being "as tight as a steel drum" to a slight edginess, is reported. Some speak of a generalized body tension while others remark upon headache, frozen brows, tight shoulders, rigid back or a crick in the neck. A sense of being out of touch with the feeling in one's muscles and of one's muscles moving is also

93

occasionally noted.

Some people remarked upon a sensation of having
energy and holding back from using the energy at the
same time, as if they were about to get very excited
but felt that they were rushing too much for appro-
riate action in the situation. A few said they felt
as if they could do nothing that they wanted to and
said that they felt either tired or as if they were
"almost but not quite paralyzed." Others noted that
they used the word "anxiety" to apply both to times
when they were holding back from eager action and to
times when they felt nearly immobilized but were still
considering acting.[9]

The following four quotations illustrate the
experience of impaired physical well-being felt by
people who were anxious:

> I get a stuffed head, cotton in the whole body,
> sand running through the arteries and veins
> instead of blood, like as if the throat was a
> faucet and the spigot had been turned off tight;
> everything is constricted.

> I used to feel anxiety on the way to the class-
> room. It was hard to walk, difficult to carry
> books, climb stairs. I had sinking feelings,
> butterflies in my stomach and I felt very
> uncoordinated, very tense. I was always afraid
> of being late to class because I had trouble
> walking.

> (I felt) kind of very irritable, tight skinned,
> tight cheeked, like your skin could be pricked
> or scratched, like I should be darting all
> around looking at things with my eyes. My neck
> wasn't comfortable, not resting easily on my
> shoulders.

> I got a hard knot of pain in the small of my
> back. But, in the rest of me, there wasn't
> really feeling but a kind of numbness. I was
> walking but I didn't really feel the ground I
> was stepping on, nor my feet nor my ankles, my

legs, my back, my body, shoulders, head or any body parts. When I was walking I wasn't breathing or flowing; I was just a jerky body with a hurting back getting there somehow.[10]

The Experience of Intellectual, Perceptual and Motoric Functioning

People report that, when anxious, there occurs a definite, but tolerable, impairment in their ability to think and perceive. There is also a diminution of the ability to remember, to speak, to see, to hear, to touch, to kinesthetically sense one's body and to move. There is a shrinking of the bounds -- inner and outer, and also temporal -- of focal awareness and of free physical or psychological locomotion. These impairments are tolerable in the sense that one can often function adequately enough in the world with such limitations but not as well as one can when not anxious.

The impairment in thinking is evidenced in different ways by different people. The following is a suggestive, but not inclusive, list of areas of possible difficulty: in abstracting categories from particulars, in imagining alternatives, in envisaging times other than the immediate present, in planning flexibly, in reasoning appropriately from probable cause to likely effect, in picking out essential from inessential details of a situation, in assessing the relationship of wholes and parts, in shifting figure and ground relationships, in appreciating nuance and complexity.

Anxious speech is different from the person's normal speech, but, depending on the characteristics of the latter, it can be glibly rapid, hesitant, repetitive, rigidly insistent, shrilly nagging, bland, dogmatic, pompous, boring, floundering, circumlocutionary, etc.

Some people forget what they were going to say and others seem to have selective memories in which only certain aspects of experience are recoverable.

95

Blurred perception in which the obvious is missed, the trivial highlighted and the just proportions of things generally distorted is another way in which anxiety is evident. Some people mis-hear when they are anxious or so lose the context of what is being said that certain phrases seem to echo loudly to the exclusion of others. Literally being "out of touch" with physical sensation or tensing one's muscles seems to be related to such things as sexual unresponsiveness, ungraceful dancing, clumsily dropping things, poor tennis playing, still posture, fatigue while shopping and the like.[11]

The following four examples from the interview transcripts were selected to provide a sense of the nature and variety of the experience of impaired intellectual, perceptual, and motoric functioning while anxious:

From a ballet dancer about the morning before a performance: I'm just very distracted. I'm not putting together a series of movement in a direction. I do something and then I begin something else and then I forget that and I start something else. A lot of interrupted activity and picking up where I left off, so I'm not very well organized toward getting out of the house quickly.

A person describing himself about to talk in a group: I felt as if my head was filled with cotton, literally as if my brain had stopped working except for the top one-fourth of an inch...things got cloudy at the edges. I couldn't take in too much action at the same time. I could see what's going on in front of me but I didn't pick up what's going on at the edges...I wouldn't quite understand what was happening or see the depths of things. I'd only understand the most literal simple meaning of what's going on; I wouldn't see the innuendoes, the subtleties. I'd barely understand the literal meanings. I'd miss such things as the tone of voice. For example if someone said "I'm fine" in a sarcastic voice, I'd miss the

sarcasm. All the richness is gone...I feel it's
hard to think straight. I have to struggle to
get my thoughts together but then I can get them
together and say things which I later find out
are comprehensible to other people, coherent,
not necessarily very deep or anything but, at
least, not really foolish or incoherent.

A housewife about planning political action:
My thoughts go around and around like a broken
record that never finishes the song. I seize
upon something in the situation that's not that
important and I blow it up way out of proportion
in my mind until it gets to be a BIG thing. I
don't let go of it. I can keep it up all night
so I'm exhausted the next morning from insomnia
...When I'm anxious like that, I can shop, make
dinner, feed everybody but I don't really pay
attention to what I'm doing. I don't taste the
food, really see the colors on the dinner table,
notice what's going on with my husband and kids
or hear what they're saying. I couldn't repeat
to you what my husband said about what happened
at his job or tell you what my son was wearing
or describe how the milk got spilt. I'm not
even sure who washed the dishes; maybe I did.
Everything's hazy except those half-thoughts
that kept going through my mind.

A student about dropping out of college: Sometimes I didn't hear. I'd try so hard to hear
that I could see someone's face just moving and
it goes completely past me like so many dots on
a page. I was embarrassed to ask someone to
repeat themselves; you're a damn fool if you
ask someone to repeat themselves...As soon as I
tried to remember, I'd forget. I couldn't see
the words in my mind or book in front of me. I
remember spending hours at a time trying to
study...Stuff that would be easy to talk about
I couldn't write down on paper. I couln't make
the transfer between what I have in my head and
the typewriter. There's anxiety there. There's
some kind of cutoff that takes place where I
cannot move. Obviously, in other circumstances

97

I can move. I can do complicated things...I
couldn't take notes. I looked over a notebook
recently and there were fourteen different kinds
of handwriting. I couldn't think. Even thoughts
that had been clarified at one time, I couldn't
put them together...I feel as though there are
tremendous gaps in mind, like lots of these
little concrete or brick walls erected. I can
almost see and feel them. I feel like there are
whole sections, like even in the middle of
sentences and paragraphs in my mind, that are
solidified or atrophied, like calcium deposits,
like there are actual blockades of something,
like whole cities of blocks. So if I were asked
to go through a whole paragraph that I had spoken
when I was seventeen, I'd probably get three
words out and then nothing. You could beat me
and I wouldn't be able to tell you what it was.
This is what really scares me sometimes that I
can forget so completely.

The impairment of functioning suffered by the
anxious person is sometimes noticed by other people.
However, it is often not recognized as a phenomenon
of anxiety[12] and instead the person is believed to
be such things as: boring, rigid, ideological,
unintelligent, inarticulate, clumsy, insensitive,
indifferent, unperceptive, rude, unable to see the
nose on his face, unable to take account of the
other person's reality, lying, repressing, etc.[13]

Definition of the "Self" and the Experience of "Being Myself" Contrasted with the Experience of the Self While Anxious

Chein (1972) defines the self as:

That which is at the origin of perceived space-
time (origin, of course being understood in the
mathematical and not in the historical or
genetic sense); or, if you will, the self is
the hereness in the thereness. All of one's
own experience as it occurs -- and, more generally, all of one's own behavior -- has an
implicit reference to this origin; I am here in

98

space-time and the objects with respect to which
I act are there...(p. 197).
I have no fixed position in the body. That is,
I seem to be able to move about more or less
freely within it. Also, there are circumstances
under which I can contemplate the body from
outside, as it were, that is: the space-time
center from which the body is contemplated is
external to the body. As an inevitable consequence of these experiences, the body appears
as a nonimprisoning abode of the self...(p. 202).
Subjectively, the responsible agent for all of
one's apprehended behavior is the self, regardless of the source of motivation. To be sure,
many...behaviors have an alien quality about
them, as if one were possessed and compelled to
carry out these behaviors as if they occurred
of themselves. But it is the self that is
possessed and becomes, as it were, the compulsory
agent of these actions and the very need for the
alibi of compulsion or the very repression of
the awareness of the action testifies to a con-
tinuing sense of responsibility (p. 280).

The experience of the self, as just defined,
appears to vary with different emotions. A description of the confident state of "being myself" follows,
with accompanying quotations from the interview
transcripts. It is intended to serve as a background
upon which to view the contrasting state of the self
while anxious. A description of the experience of
the self while panicked is incorporated into the
chapter on that emotion.

The "hereness in the thereness" of the confident
state of being myself is like a firm ground in a
crisp, brilliant day. Expressions such as "centered,"
"whole," "together," "present," "there," "grounded,"
"with it," "in touch," "responsive," "clear," "alive,"
"free," and "arrived" are commonly used to describe
this state. In it, people feel integrated with their
bodies. They also feel themselves subjectively
responsible and able to carry out the commitments
they choose to fulfill, which involves feeling that
they have a living context within which to act freely

and with unselfconscious grace.[14]

The following three quotations from the interview
transcripts contrast the experience of "being myself"
with that of anxiety and panic:

From a musician: There's a whole feeling, that's
a feeling of being filled up by the music, of
being whole inside, of being just one person.
I didn't have that while anxious and panicked.
It's interesting -- that wholeness to me is a
very moving experience. It's what music does
to me all the time. That's a really important
thing. It's being in touch. I feel like I can
take in what's around me and I'm whole.

A dancer about being on stage: I feel very
composed and confident and there's no hesitation
and no sense of inadequacy. I think that I am
a very good judge of what I can do and what is
dangerous to do...There's a vitality there that
is very pure. I feel very alive and strong and
capable and colorful...If I'm feeling very together in a room full of people, it's like that.
I can sense them and I can sense them sensing
me and I can sense me sensing them sensing me.
I can see what's going on; but, if I'm feeling
anxious, I only react blindly. When I feel
together, not only do I see myself as a whole
but I see myself in a situation as a whole and
I can perceive patterns and what's happening in
the situation. I can see it and I'm aware of
being seen...(I remember the first time I felt
the "together" person). It was when I was
crossing the street. It was a sensation of
clouds lifting. It was very tangible, very
concrete and I related it to clouds lifting and
I could see. The world was colorful and I was
in it. I was crossing the street. It became
an act of will -- something I could choose to
do or not do. I stopped scurrying and started
stepping. There was a real, tangible difference.
I stopped feeling like a rat running across the
street and looking like one too. (When I'm
dancing) I'm present in the way I was when the

100

clouds lifted.

A young woman: There are certain days that I do things like take a walk or I'll have a meal by myself which I used to do as a kid. I'll feel the breeze. I'll enjoy the meal, feel very much in life. It's very sensual. I feel very free. What I'm describing is the opposite of what I feel when I'm anxious...It's all one. There's a kind of unity in which my body is very much felt within my skin. I feel very alive. I think that's partly why I feel the breeze in the way I described to you. If I describe it, I lose it, which is a problem with describing anything that feels like a whole. I'm very grounded. I have a core. I feel I have a core. It's not even all that conscious. If it were conscious, I wouldn't enjoy it that much. But I'm all integrated in a way.

In contrast to the confident state of "being myself," the "hereness in the thereness" of the anxious self is like a marsh in a heavy fog. The self is experienced as present but as insubstantial and diffuse, rather than as solid and coherent. The "I" with respect to which all experience is in relation was described by the people interviewed with such terms as: "vague," "wispy," "uncentered," "spaced out," "not together," "there but not quite there," "flimsy," "like quicksand," "like all the starch was gone out of me." Neither the location of one's self in space-time nor the world with respect to which the self acts are clear.

A number of the people interviewed spoke of feeling spatially located in their bodies but also of being "out of touch" with them at the same time. The sense was of not being fully present in an alive, integrated fashion within one's physical being. There were, however, no accounts, among those inter-viewed about anxiety, of being located in any par-ticular place in the body or of contemplating the body from a space-time origin external to it.

While anxious, people view themselves as

101

responsible for their behavior but somehow not adequate to exercise that responsibility.[15] There are persistent accounts of feeling a loss of a sense of being at home in the world, of no longer having a definite living context within which to act or a clear set of meanings with which to inform and give direction to freely willed actions. Statements such as "I don't know who I am or where I am going" often accompanied indications that the person felt unprepared to carry out a responsible commitment that was nonetheless felt called for in the situation. A potential for responsible action was dimly sensed as being in the future rather than vividly present as an actual, immediate reality.

The insubstantial anxious self, however irresolute, is felt as responsible. It is a case of the "I" being present and irresolute. It is not a case of the "I" being either absent and acting against its will or of the "I" being present but about to be taken over by an alien behavior that threatens to possess the self.

The Experience of Self-Criticism

An increase in the salience of self-criticism accompanies the experience of the insubstantial self and the experience of impaired physical and intellectual functioning. The self-criticism is possibly an attempt to anchor such experiences in a stable reality by explaining their occurrences, possibly a component of such feelings and possibly even the origin of such feelings.

The reports of self-critical feelings while anxious were consistent among the people interviewed. People repeatedly said such things as: "I am... false," "dumb," "incompetent," "lazy," "fat," "ugly," "cowardly," "clumsy," "phoney," etc.

The people interviewed varied with respect to the severity with which they felt criticized, the source--internal or external--from which the criticism was perceived as coming, the allocation of blame for the criticism, and the effect the criticism

102

had on their desire to withdraw from the company of others. Some felt everyone criticized them; some felt only a few did; some felt that there were people who liked them despite the criticism; others felt little or no support from other people. These aspects differed from person to person and from episode of anxiety described by the same person.[16]

The following four examples were selected from the interview transcripts to illustrate the experience of the insubstantial self and the experience of self-criticism:

A student therapist describing a discussion of a patient with his therapy supervisor: I felt like I didn't matter, as if I had no social weight. I'm not the equal of my supervisor. It's like he was a solid, real person who knows all there is to know in a genuine, sophisticated way and I'm a faker. He's got the power in him. He's a heavyweight and I maybe shouldn't even be in the ring. When we were talking, I couldn't remember what had happened with the patient. I had a few semi-thoughts in my head but they all led to things I had done wrong and why. I wasn't together. I felt like I was using first-grade sentences and he was talking super-Freud. He seemed to be very critical of everything I said and I couldn't marshal my forces against him. I expected him to say I shouldn't see any patients. It's funny. I can't see his face. It's like he was in a grey fog and I'm in a grey fog, too. But he's the sun and I'm just a wispy haze that could get burnt away...I'm much surer of myself now. I think I'd feel more equal in power if I saw him again. He probably isn't as nasty, or as much of a rigid Freudian, as I remember him as being. Or, if he is, I would know how to deal with it.

A law student about preparing for the Bar examination: When you're anxious, your self is not there. It's like being a zombie looking through your own eyes. Physical things are all wrong. Your body is just an uncomfortable

garment. Like all of a sudden, you're strobing
in and out. Aren't I here? There I am, aren't
I? Every once in a while, you come to, but
don't know anything about anything. I doubt
everything, absolutely everything. I don't feel
I can do anything positive...Sometimes I feel
foolish. There's nothing wrong with feeling
foolish. Fuck them. I don't care. I'll wind
up a bum drinking alcohol, sink into the exact
opposite of perfection. One wrong thing would
follow upon another and all the insecure bases
of social snobbery would disappear. My friends
would lose respect for me. Last but not least,
I would need money and would be fed intravenously
by my parents...I have a lot of friends who are
more clever than me. If the situation were
reversed, I would lose respect for me. I don't
understand why they like me.

A girl recalling her adolescence in boarding
school: I was afraid to ask questions, to show
myself up as stupid. The "brilliant" science
students always understood but I was stumbling
along in the dark...If the teacher asked me to
recite, even if I knew the answer, I could tell
that everyone thought I didn't know it...I was
something hollow living in something hollow...
I felt awkward and ugly. Everyone else looked
sharp. I didn't have the clothes suited to
their cliquish dressing style. I thought the
other girls thought I was dumb, not important,
that I didn't have anything to offer them. I
felt as though they looked down on me.

A ballet dancer about the evening before a
performance: I have this image of myself being
a total rag doll on this big stage and not having
any control over the stituation whatsoever. I
feel completely inadequate to it and frantically
nervous about doing it even though I want to do
it very badly...When I think of myself walking
to the theatre...I see myself through a filter
that's very grey and colorless and bloodless
with no feeling but with a kind of intense
yearning for something I know I'll never get,

as if I'll be rejected. It's as if there were a grey filter over the picture and I were very strained and wanted something I would never have. There is a lack of vitality or purity... I tend to think that whatever is said to me when I'm in this state is an imposition and I resent it. My thinking tends to be a little paranoid, I guess. For example, my husband might want me to do something like walk up to 8th Street to get the paper. Why I can't do that! You KNOW I'm DANCING tomorrow kind of thinking. I'm always distressed about my thinking when I'm anxious. I don't like the way I think. It's very narrow, shortsighted, kind of unconscious thinking. There's a lack of perspective. When I'm anxious, I can't ever imagine life is not like that. Life is wrong... I'm sure I'm inaccessible. If you're very tense and react resentfully to an intrusion, then you're inaccessible. Also feeling very alone. That's part of the paranoid thinking I was describing -- everyone's trying to keep me from doing this well. You know. I have to sleep eight hours a night and if people come over, they are keeping me from sleeping the eight hours. You know, which means I'm all on my own! Nobody else will help me -- no one is going to make the bed, help me get the eight hours, make sure that nothing upsetting happens so that I can fall asleep.

The Experience of Confusion About Who One Might Be Becoming

The impaired physical well-being, the interference in intellectual, perceptual and muscular functioning, the insubstantial sense of self and the self-critical assessments of oneself are facets of anxious experiencing immediately present in the center of conscious awareness. At the fringe of consciousness, however, is a vast inarticulated but articulatable, confusion about more or less obscure core issues related to who or what[17] one might be becoming in the future.

Thoughts on this subject go in and out of awareness in a fragmented fashion. They are not fully
formed thoughts. They are not resolved in an integrated, coherent structure of commitments. They are
not about clear, felt beliefs. They do not provide
a groundwork of considered principles upon which to
base pragmatic action suited to the actual conditions
in the world. They revolve, instead, in an incon-
clusive, inarticulate, unfocused manner.

The fragmented thoughts turn in a confused way
around issues raised by the potentiality that one
might be on the verge of becoming someone -- or
something -- one presently is not. The event is in
the future. It is experienced as obscure and hard
to define and yet it is there, pulling at one like
a magnet.

For example, a woman anxious about her agreement
to get married would not experience herself as having
an integrated, coherent vision of how one went about
getting married, let alone of the life commitments
involved in the social contract of marriage. Getting
married and marriage are relatively abstract ideas
for her, not immediately real, fleshed-out, alive
conceptions reflecting the living through of her own
life. "Who" she is at present is a not-married
woman not able to fully grasp what she might be
becoming, that is, a married woman.

The anxious woman might have a succession of
images and thoughts hovering around the edges of her
consciousness in an apparently unconnected way. The
images might range from episodes in her own family
life to such scenes as elderly ladies alone on park
benches, mothers struggling with whiny children, a
couple walking along talking companionably, a friend
whose husband had left her, a house full of people
celebrating Thanksgiving, a planned trip cancelled
at the last moment, a birthday party. These might
be mixed with self-critical thoughts that she's without energy, stalling about going to see a doctor
about the pains she's started to have in the back,
a fretting that she can't think straight, has been
blurring out on the events of the past few days and

106

in general has not been "together" as a person. Her relations with other people may get quite tangled because she might do such things as blow up small remarks way out of proportion, not follow through on a relative's offer to help with the wedding, or start blaming a woman friend for being insufficiently liberated.

In her muddle, she well might not recognize that the object of her anxiety is the difficult-to-imagine change in her way of life that marriage would involve. However, were she able to tell someone else at some length about the seemingly disconnected images or fragmented thoughts she had been having, as well as her associations to them, the relationship between the thoughts or images and the implications for her life of the forthcoming wedding would most likely become clear. She would then become aware that her laziness, back pains, withdrawal and outbursts of temper were part of anxiety about getting married and assuming the recognized position of a married woman held by other members of her family.

There appears to be a wide latitude in the degree to which people recognize that they are anxious about what the present implies for what they might become in the future. Some people immediately connect up the experiential aspects of anxiety discussed earlier in this chapter -- the impaired sense of physical well-being, etc. -- with the awareness that these experiences are part and parcel of being con- cerned with who or what one might be becoming in the future. Others do not make the connection.

The people who do not make the connection between the present impaired sense of physical well- being, etc., and a concern about who or what they might become in the future, appear to live in a world sensed as more ominously dangerous than those who do make the connection. They live in a world populated by scare images -- possible cancerous growths, portents of brain damage connected to memory loss, thoughts that someone is going to jump on them with big, hob-nailed boots, etc. -- which loom vague and large.[18]

At its worst, the experience of living in an ominous world does not begin to approach the experience of facing an imminent, inexplicable danger which characterizes panic. In panic, the danger is in the immediate present and so urgent that the person must instantly flee from it. In anxiety, the danger is vaguely in the future and the person does not feel any urgent necessity to do something about it in the present.

Also, when a person is anxious he can usually recognize the connection between the vague scare images he experiences in association with the impaired sense of physical well-being etc., and a concern about who or what he might be becoming in the future. A discussion with someone else might be required for the connection to be recognized -- but it usually can be made with some ease. This is not the case with panic.

The Life Circumstances of Anxiety

When anxious, people experience impaired physical well-being, interference in intellectual, perceptual and motoric functioning, a sense of themselves as being insubstantial, and an increase in the salience of their self-critical assessments, as well as a sense of confusion around core issues related to what they might be becoming in the future. The following section describes the essential structure of the life circumstances which accompany the appearance of such experiences in awareness.

Anxiety occurs as part of a transitional stage of identity formation in which the person believes there is a real possibility that he can become what he envisages he must become. In becoming what he envisages he must become, the person lives up to the expectations shared by himself and by the members of the social unit to which he belongs. An anticipated risk situation is in the future when it will be mutually determined by the person and by others in his social unit whether or not he has met the criteria for becoming what he must become.

The anxiety starts after the person recognizes that the risk is approaching and ends at the point at which the person decides whether or not to confront the actual moment of risk. During the interim period, a working through process takes place in which the person inconclusively evaluates more or less obscurely envisaged alternatives with respect to an uncertainly and often incorrectly apprehended future. While the working through process is going on, the person experiences himself as especially vulnerable to the opinions of others. At the end of the working through process, the person makes a decision either to confront the risk or not to confront the risk or to postpone the decision for the time being. At the point of making the decision, the anxiety ends.

If the person chooses to confront the risk and successfully confronts it, his identity changes. He then feels he has become what he had to become and believes he is entitled to the rights as well as the responsibilities of the new identity. If the person chooses not to confront the risk, or to postpone the decision, his identity remains the same. If the person does not choose to confront the risk, not to confront the risk, or to postpone the decision, he remains anxious.

Some terms used in the above description of the essential structure of the life circumstances in which anxiety occurs are discussed below.

Identity

Erik Erikson (1968a) defines his concept of epigenetic, psycho-social identity in one passage as:

A sense of sameness and continuity as an individual -- but with a special quality probably best described by William James. A man's character, he wrote in a letter, is discernible in the "mental or moral attitude in which, when it came upon him, he felt himself most deeply and intensely active and alive. At such moments there is a voice inside

109

which speaks and says: 'This is the real me!'"
Such experience always includes an "element of
active tension, of holding my own as it were,
and trusting outward things to perform their
part so as to make it a full harmony, but
without any guaranty that they will." Thus
may a mature person come to the astonished or
exuberant awareness of his identity.
What underlies such a subjective sense, however,
can be recognized by others, even when it is not
especially conscious or, indeed, self-conscious:
thus, one can observe a youngster "become
himself" at the very moment when he can be said
to be "losing himself" in work, play or company.
He suddenly seems to be "at home in his body,"
to "know where he is going," and so on.
The social aspects of identity formation were
touched upon by Freud when in an address he
spoke of an "inner identity" that he shared
with the tradition of Jewry and which still
was at the core of his personality, namely,
the capacity to live and think in isolation
from the "compact majority." The gradual
development of a mature psychosocial identity,
then, presupposes a community of people whose
traditional values become significant to the
growing person even as his growth assumes
relevance for them. Mere "roles" that can be
"played" interchangeably are obviously not
sufficient for the social aspect of the
equation. Only a hierarchical integration of
roles that foster the vitality of individual
growth as they represent a vital trend in the
existing or developing social order can support
identities. Psychosocial identity thus depends
on a complementarity of an inner (ego) synthesis
in the individual and of role integration in
his group (p. 61).[19]

Certain aspects of Erikson's concept of identity
are particularly useful for understanding the
experience of anxiety. They are: the view of the
person as an active, responsible agent who picks and
chooses among ways of life presented to him by society
seeking to find the path best suited for himself;

the emphasis upon the self-sameness and continuity of the individual as he grows up within a community of people who exemplify traditional values of genuine significance to him; the stress on the mutuality of the fitting process between the person and others in his community; the awareness that people enter upon new developmental tasks as they grow older; the observation that people have goals to strive for but never quite attain which they try to live up to and live out within the social reality, arriving - perhaps! - at a point of "ego identity" when these goals are attained (but forever to be revised).

Another aspect of Erikson's concept of identity useful for understanding the experience of anxiety is his description of the subjective sense of identity. The passages quoted -- about the feeling experienced by William James that "This is the real me!" or about the absorbed child who seems "at home in his body" and "to know where he is going" -- coincide to a considerable extent with the accounts of "being myself" given earlier in this chapter. These were volunteered by the people interviewed as instances of an experienced state, to which they sometimes gave the name "confidence," which was felt as different from anxiety yet intimately related to it.

People become anxious when their already accomplished identity, subjectively sensed as "This is the real me!," is in the process of undergoing a potential transition. The transition may be to a not yet formed new identity which, if accomplished, will be felt as a continuation of the old identity and will be experienced, in turn, as "This is the real me!" Schematically, the process is:

Identity A	Transitional Stage of Identity in Formation	Identity A
"The real me!"		"The real me!"
confidence ("being myself")	—— anxiety —— ("insubstantial sense of self")	confidence ("being myself")

111

The extent of the potential change in a person's identity varies widely. The potential from the old identity to the not yet formed new identity can involve broad areas of a person's life, such as the basic choice of sexual identity, profession, marriage, religious belief, country of residence, allegiance to family, etc. It can involve more circumscribed areas of a person's life, such as the choice (for an intern already committed to a particular medical speciality) of which hospital's offer of a residency to accept, or the decision of just how to teach a course in one's area of expertise, or just what to say in a social situation that one knows well, or just whom to invite to a party.

No matter how broad or circumscribed the scope of the potential change in the person's identity is, the change being considered is related to the vital core of who one is, to one's me-ness. It is not a matter of what social role one will perform, leaving one's identity intact and unaffected, but what genuine commitment one will make by which one can, and will, in fact, live. At times of anxiety, one's life is on the line. The choices made, to change or to remain the same, determine who one will be.

Must Become

The potential identity change about which one is anxious is experienced as something that one must become. The experience that one must become an X refers to those expectations (or aspirations or ego ideals or, in Erikson's language, to-be-striven-for-but-forever-not-quite-attainable goals) that a person has for himself which are congruent with his already established line of identity development. That is, it is consciously acceptable to the person while anxious that he must become a doctor, a lawyer, a ball player, a guy who "makes it" with girls, a girl who is asked out, a person who stands up for the disenfranchised, a person able to think in isolation from the "compact majority," a Christian, a Communist, a person trusted by others for advice, a person who hates outsiders, a person who laughs, a person who cooks delicious dinners, someone who makes money, etc.

112

Whatever it is that one must become is a natural continuation of the already established line of identity development that one has.

That one must become an X feels, when one is anxious, like a pull from the future in relation to which all of one's behavior is of necessity oriented. It feels as if the pull comes from outside of oneself, not as if it is a want of one's own.[20] It feels as if there is no alternative to being oriented toward the pull, as if it is a matter not of choice but of necessity that one becomes what one must become.

This experience varies some in intensity. In many episodes of anxiety, it is a matter of importance but of more or less importance, that one becomes what one must become. In others, it is experienced as a matter of life and death that one either will become what one must become or else one cannot continue to be who one is.

The experience of must become is similar to Heider's account of the experience of an "ought" in the following three respects. First, both experiences have a quality of requiredness, that is, of filling a gap in an uncompleted situation. Second, they both have the character of a force field, that is, of something that exerts an actual prompting influence on the person. Third, they both have the status of reality in that they are givens of the universe that belong to a suprapersonal, objective order which applies invariantly to everyone in one's situation independently of personal whim.[21]

The experience of must become differs from Heider's account of the experience of an ought in the following respect, however. The experience of ought refers to social norms to which the person feels presently obligated. The experience of must become refers to social norms to which the person does not presently feel obligated but which he nonetheless dimly apprehends he will be required to fulfill in the future if he lives up to what is expected of him. An ought, that is, implies an actual responsibility within the social order whereas "must become" implies

113

only a potential responsibility which one will assume in due course within the social order.[22]

Heider says that the concept of "ought" implies the concept of can in that one would not say a person ought to do something if it is clearly impossible for him to do so.[23] In like fashion, the concept that a person must become an X tacitly implies a belief that the person can become an X. That such a belief is sometimes an illusion does not enter into the experience of the person when anxious. He thinks that his fate rests in his hands, not in the hands of others nor with fortune.[24]

De Rivera (1977, p. 79, 80) extends Heider's discussion of "ought" to include the concept of social unit.

> ...oughts do not apply to everything or every-
> body but only to members of one's community.
> Most persons do not feel a dog ought to be
> charitable with his bones and many persons do
> not feel a foreigner ought to be patriotic or
> respect the dead, etc. To the extent that we
> do feel strangers ought to do certain things,
> we are including them in a broad community of
> humans to which we see ourselves as belonging...
> ...call any group whose members recognize a
> common set of values (oughts), a unit. A unit
> may be as small as two persons or as large as
> the community of humans but in every case persons
> decide whether or not to belong to it, and if
> they accept the responsibility of belonging
> they become subject to and may take advantage
> of the values (oughts) held by members of the
> unit.

De Rivera's definition of a unit can be extended to the experience of anxiety.[25] For when a person becomes what he must become, he fulfills the expectations of the unit to which he belongs and whose expectations he shares. The unit can be the unit of his childhood -- e.g., he must become what his parents expected he must become -- or it can be a unit which he decided to join later in life --

114

e.g., he must become what his employers think he must become. Whatever the case, the person shares the expectations of the other members of the unit to which he belongs, just as he shares their oughts and their value-system in general.

Risk Situations

In every anxiety situation there is an antici-pated risk approaching: person believes it will be evident both to himself and to others in his social unit whether he has, in fact, lived up to the expectation to become what he must become.[26] That is, the person either will or will not find a job, reach orgasm, drive a car, ask a favor from a friend, talk in class, hit the ball, get married, etc. The anticipated risk is real, for one can lose out. It is also public, for others will know and will fre-quently be required to take an active part -- e.g., accept an offer of marriage or agree to publish a book. In short, it is a situation in which the person will either have to put up or shut up and faces the possibility of losing either way.

The risk situation poses a new task for the person.[27] The newness of the risk is always evident to the person, even if to an outsider it looks as if the risk has been surmounted many times before. Thus a practiced performer will experience anxiety before going on stage for the umpteenth time because each new show represents a new goal for him in his line of identity development as a performer.

Not all risk situations provoke anxiety. The only ones that do are the ones that matter to a person's developing sense of his own identity. Thus for one person this could mean becoming anxious before taking a mathematics test and for another it could mean becoming anxious before asking a relative to pass the salt. Also, in addition to feeling that one is being judged in an area that matters, there are implicit in an anxiety-provoking risk situation re-spect for the judges, a sense of the inherent worth of the task, and some indicator of whether one will have passed the risk.[28]

Some people work out their lives so that they encounter very few situations which pose risks that provoke anxiety. Others continually place themselves in risk situations in which they feel that they are on the line. Also, some people allow only a short interim to pass between the recognition that a risk is approaching and the decision to confront or not to confront the risk, whereas others allow the interim to stretch on for years.[29]

Criteria for Meeting the Risk

Definite criteria for meeting the approaching risk are envisaged by the person who is anxious. To him the criteria seem obvious and objective. To an outside observer the contrary is often the case. At best, from the perspective of an outside observer, the anxious person's envisaged criteria bear only an approximate relation to what will, in fact, be needed in the future risk situation; at worst, the envisaged criteria are completely unrelated to what will be needed.

Inherent difficulty attends the task of foreseeing, with even approximate accuracy, what the criteria for meeting the approaching risk will be. The gap between expectation and reality is, of necessity, often unbridgeable. One's present imaginings are likely in the course of things as they are to be thin and abstract, not grounded in a sensible understanding of the conditions that will arise in the future.

The odds of envisaging criteria appropriate for adequate performance in the forthcoming risk are, of course, greater for some sorts of risks than others. For example, a student preparing for the New York State High School Regents Examination in Intermediate Algebra has copies of previous tests available to him from which he can acquire a probably correct estimate of the sorts of questions he will encounter on the examination. Or a seasoned trouper will have enough accumulated stage experience to judge the range of responses he is likely to meet. However, a person imagining criteria for being liked by someone he has never met, delivering a new lecture before a strange audience, getting an A on an English paper, etc., is less likely to assess correctly the criteria by which his performance in the forthcoming risk situation will be judged.

Criteria for such things as the pursuit of truth, being loved, being a scholar and a gentleman, promoting peace on Earth, acting honestly, being a good Christian, etc., often appear impossible to assess either in advance or afterwards. To an outsider it can often look as if a person committed to such ideals is engaged in a phantasmagoric search for perfection. Thus, it can look as if the anxious researcher not only wants to write a paper but also to win the Nobel prize, as if the anxious housewife not only wants to clean the house but to do a job worthy of a photograph in Good Housekeeping, or as if the young piano student not only wants to play the piece but perform it as well as her teacher of many years experience. By judging themselves failures against such ideals, it looks, to an outsider, as if the anxious "perfectionistic" researcher, housewife and piano student have lost all sense of proportion and humor.

It should be noted, however, that the apparently overblown criteria often point in the direction of a potential future for the person in which the criteria will be used as models for actual attainments.[30] Thus, the researcher may write a paper and get it published in a reputable journal, even if he does not win the Nobel prize; the housekeeper may eventually straighten up enough to receive her guests in a fashion acceptable to her family if not to Good Housekeeping; the piano student may eventually play the piece with enough musical spirit to set her audience of proud relatives beaming, even if she does not equal her teacher in skill.

An artist, interviewed in the course of the research for this study, said that he felt he was continually "living under false pretenses." He added in describing his persistent anxiety:

I can do my work as well as the next guy. But

117

I always think there will be someone who will
see through the work and say, "It's okay as a
piece of craftsmanship but who needs that?"
Sometimes, in fantasy, when I receive this new
commission, I've had a fantasy of doing this
magnificent thing. Great stuff. Matisse,
Picasso. The moment after if I try to put it
down, I see that the whole thing is disappearing into what I am in fact capable of and that's
not enough.

His work hangs in museums across the country. I
decline to judge whether his is the statement of a
neurotic or of a creative man.[31]

Working Through Process

A working through process occurs as the person
potentially readies himself to meet the envisaged
criteria of the forthcoming future risk. Fragments
of the thoughts pertaining to the working through
process appear and disappear on the fringes of
consciousness. My impression, however, is that much
of the real work of the working through process must
go on outside of conscious awareness. I think of
the analogy to the experience of insight. This
experience itself gives ample evidence of the reorganization that has taken place, but except in the
case of gradually dawning insight, one cannot observe
the reorganizing; one observes the product, not the
process.

Delicate assessment of a large number of complex,
subtle motivational and situational factors seem to
be involved in the working through process. The
assessments seem to be responsive to, and entail,
more or less obscurely envisaged alternative possibilities, rife with illusion and error, with regard
to an uncertainly apprehended and risky future.

The following list is a suggestive and, by no
means exhaustive, listing of the issues that are
probably being confronted, at least tacitly, during
the working process:

Can I meet the requirements of reality? Is there

any place in the world for what I want to become?
Do I have the capacity required? Will I ever have
that capacity? Will others recognize and acknowledge
that I have that capacity? What sort of person am I
right now? Do I want to continue to be that person?
Will making a new commitment destroy previous commitments of value to me? What will be the actual and
imagined reactions of significant others to me? If
I lose their esteem, can I survive? Do I care enough
for their esteem to change myself in order to obtain
it? Whose values are right? What is the standard
of judgment? Is my reality greater than their consensual reality? Have I assessed my own motives and
those of others correctly? What are the consequences
and am I able to bear them? Does it really matter
to change? Will I have sold myself out if I don't?
Am I giving up something for a possible nothing?
Have I set my sights too high? Too low? Am I engaging in magical thinking when I try to anticipate and
predict the consequences of my choice? Do I have the
control that I fantasize that I have? Perhaps it is
better to drop this enterprise and go back to an
existence in which I am adequate to the requirements
of the situations in which I am liable to find myself?
And so forth.

A part of the working through process deserves
special mention: the feeling that one is deficient in
meeting up to the criteria imagined for the forthcoming risk and the recognition that this deficiency
points up the necessity of doing further preparation
before encountering the risk. Thus, for a student
who feels he "must become" a scholar and yet who also
feels himself inadequate to the envisaged criteria
of having read the books on his professor's shelf, a
part of the working through process involved in
meeting the risk of a forthcoming examination would
be to read and understand the books. To a certain
extent, the self-critical assessment that he is a
"phoney" with regard to scholarship is an accurate
one, remediable only by doing work.

Vulnerability to Others

What Erikson says in an already quoted passage

with regard to the process of identity-formation
also applies to what is here called the working
through process:

> ...identity formation employs a process of
> simultaneous reflection and observation, a
> process taking part on all levels of mental
> functioning, by which the individual judges
> himself in the light of what he perceives to
> be the way in which others judge him in com-
> parison to themselves and to a typology
> significant to them; while he judges their
> way of judging him in the light of how he
> perceives himself in comparison to them and to
> types that have become relevant to him (1968b,
> p. 22).

During the interim of the working through
process, the person experiences a marked increase in
his vulnerability to the opinions of others.[32] An
astonishing variety of people -- his wife, a stranger
in the street, an infant, an esteemed teacher, a
deceased grandfather, the janitor, St. Augustine,
an unknown guest of some friends, etc.--are endowed
with the power to pass judgment on him. It is as if,
while anxious, the person views himself with another's
eyes, using almost any available other for this
purpose, and finds himself wanting. It is basically
unimportant to assess whether the fantasized or real
other person, in fact, holds the negative opinions
he is perceived to hold by the person who is anxious;
the important point is that the person who is anxious
believes he is being criticized and feels vulnerable
to that criticism.[33]

The perceived negative judgments often discourage the person from plunging into new activities
when anxious. The feeling of being more or less
clumsy, stupid, ugly, false, etc., often acts as
something of a brake on precipitate action. If the
negative judgments seem particularly strong, the
person can approach a point where he barely acts
and feels nearly paralyzed by anxiety. Depending
on a variety of circumstances, such a state can be
either essential or detrimental for survival in

society.

The Decision

The interim in which the working through process occurs can last for a few seconds or for years. Why this is the case is probably a function of many variables including such things as: the developmental stage which the person has attained (e.g., adolescence or maturity), the presence or absence of facilitating conditions (e.g., economic depression·or prosperity), the importance of the issue for the person's identity (e.g., vocational choice vs. asking someone to dinner), the interrelationship of the potential change with other areas of the person's life (e.g., moving to another country to study history vs. staying home and studying history at a local college), the reactions of other people concerned with the person to extended periods of anxiety and so forth.

While the person is engaged in the working through process, it is as if he is "out of life" being anxious. The person re-enters life after a decision has been worked through with regard to the potential change. The decision can be a decision to go ahead and meet the risk involved in becoming who one "must become," a decision not to become who one "must become,"[34] a decision to postpone dealing with the matter until some specified time, some indefinite time or possibly never.

If the person decides either to postpone meeting the risk involved in becoming who he "must become" or even declines to become who he had hitherto envisaged he "must become," a variety of consequences ensue which are beyond my scope here. It should be noted, however, that extreme caution ought to be observed before labeling such decisions as indications of "inhibitions in ego development," of "constructed personality," of a "rigid personality structure," of "failure," of "cowardice," of "copping out," of "abandoning pretensions," or any one of the other terms in our vast vocabulary of ordinary and sophisticated abuse. Such negative evaluations tend to ignore the problematic nature of the notion of progress so dominant in our culture.[35]

If the person decides to meet the risk, then he becomes, in his eyes, who he had envisaged he must become. He regards being who he had envisaged he must become as now being himself and reacts, in James' language,[36] with a feeling of "This is the Real Me!" The identity change appears to occur at the point at which the decision is made to meet the risk, rather than at the point of the risk itself.[37]

Once the person decides to meet the risk, he feels entitled to the rights of the new identity into which he has entered. He acts in such a way that -- perhaps because of his very demeanor, perhaps because of his behavior in meeting the risk -- he is treated by other members of the culture as if he is entitled to those rights. At the point of assuming the rights of the new identity, he concurrently assumes the obligations of the identity into which he has entered, the oughts that apply to a person of that position in society. He is treated, in turn, as if he is responsible for those obligations by the members of his culture. He is free to act meaningfully, as if he is being his real self, within the new social context.

His identity has changed and yet he has remained the same, for the new identity is but an affirmation of the ideals of the former identity.

PANIC

The experience called "panic" in this section can be distinguished from the experience called "anxiety" in the previous section. The reader is reminded that panic experiences are labeled by different people in a variety of ways including "unreasoning fear," "severe anxiety," "flipping out," "going crazy," "horrible dreams," "dying," and the like.

What is meant by panic in this chapter can best be conveyed by two examples. The first is an account by William James of an experience that happened to him and the second is a description of remarkably similar experience that his father, Henry

122

James Sr., reported as having happened to him.

William James (1947, orig. 1902) describes what he called an episode of "panic fear" in the following passage:

Whilst in a state of philosophic pessimism and general depression of spirits about my prospects, I went one evening into a dressing-roon in the twilight to procure some article that was there; when suddenly there fell upon me without any warning, just as if it had come out of the darkness, a horrible fear of my own existence. Simultaneously, there arose in my mind the image of an epileptic patient whom I had seen in the asylum, a black-haired youth with greenish skin, entirely idiotic, who used to sit all day on one of the benches or rather shelves against the wall, with his knees drawn up against his chin, and the coarse grey undershirt which was his only garment drawn over them enclosing his entire figure. He sat there like a sort of sculptored Egyptian or Peruvian mummy, moving nothing but his black eyes and looking absolutely nonhuman. This image and my fear entered into a species of combination with each other. That shape am I, I felt, potentially. Nothing that I possess can defend me against that fate, if the hour for it should strike for me as it struck for him. There was such a horror of him, and such a perception of my own merely momentary discrepancy from him, that it was as if something hitherto solid within my breast gave way entirely, and I became a mass of quivering fear. After this the universe was changed for me altogether. I awoke morning after morning with a horrible dread at the pit of my stomach, and with a sense of the insecurity of life that I never knew before, and that I have never felt since. It was like a revelation; and although the immediate feelings passed away, the experience has made me sympathetic with the morbid feelings of others ever since. It gradually faded, but for months I was unable to go out into the dark alone.

In general, I dreaded to be left alone. I
remember wondering how other people could live,
how I myself had lived, so unconscious of that
pit of insecurity beneath the surface of life.
My mother in particular, a very cheerful person,
seemed to me a perfect paradox, in her uncon-
sciousness of danger, which you may well believe
I was very careful not to disturb by revelations
of my own state of mind. I have always thought
that this experience of melancholia of mine had
a religious bearing.
...
I mean the fear was so invasive and powerful
that if I had not clung to scripture-texts like
"The eternal God is my refuge," etc. "Come unto
me, all ye that labor and are heavy-laden," etc.
"I am the resurrection and the life," etc., I
think I should have grown really insane (pp.
157-158).[38]

William James' father, Henry Sr., underwent an
experience of almost the same sort which he eventually
decided was a "vastation" of the kind reported by the
Swedish mystic, Emanuel Swedenborg. Henry James Sr.
described (Allen, 1967) his experience as follows:

One day...towards the close of May, having
eaten a comfortable dinner, I remained sitting
at the table after the family had dispersed,
idly gazing at the embers in the grate, thinking
of nothing, and feeling only the exhilaration
incident to a good digestion, when suddenly --
in a lightning-flash as it were -- "fear came
upon me, and trembling, which made all my bones
to shake." To all appearance it was a perfectly
insane and abject terror, without ostensible
cause, and only to be accounted for, to my
perplexed imagination, by some damned shape
squatting invisible to me within the precincts
of the room and raying out from his fetid
personality influences fatal to life. The thing
had not lasted 10 seconds before I felt myself
a wreck; that is, reduced from a state of firm,
vigorous, joyful manhood to one of almost
helpless infancy. The only self-control I was

124

capable of exerting was to keep my seat. I felt the greatest desire to run incontinently to the foot of the stairs and shout for help to my wife -- to run to the roadside even, and appeal to the public to protect me; but by an immense effort I controlled these frenzied impulses, and determined not to budge from my chair til I had recovered my lost self-possession. This purpose I held to for a good long hour, as I reckoned time, beat upon mean-while by an ever-growing tempest of doubt, anxiety and despair, with absolutely no relief from any truth I had ever encountered save a most pale and distant glimmer of the divine existence, when I resolved to abandon the vain struggle, and communicate without more ado what seemed my sudden burden of inmost, implacable unrest to my wife (p. 17).

With variation in detail, the accounts of the "vastation" of Henry James Sr. and the "panic fear" of his son, William James, are essentially similar to the sorts of phenomena I was told about by the research partners under the labels panic and/or severe anxiety.

In this chapter, the holistic experience of panic will be considered under the following four categories: (1) the physical experience; (2) the experience of intellectual, perceptual, and motoric functioning; (3) the experience of the self on the verge of disintegration; and (4) the experience of fleeing from an inexplicable, intolerable, imminent danger. The chapter will conclude with an account of my understanding of the essential elements of the life circumstances which are present when the phenomena characteristic of panicking according to each of these categories are also present.

The ways in which the phenomena characteristic of panicking can be demarcated from the phenomena characteristic of anxious experience will be indicated as the chapter progresses.

Panic

Physical Experience

Almost everybody interviewed reported a striking
sensation of energy or flooding. Some spoke of
"running," "having to move fast," "needing to walk
quickly," "waves going from my head to my feet,"
while others used images like "this dybbuk injected
me with adrenalin." To quote from a number of
different transcripts, the sensation was: "frozen and
chaotic, like someone being electrocuted through whom
a tremendous amount of unchanneled energy flows,"
"a flooding, a breaking, inside me," "a being revved
up to some exploding point," "like I could shatter in
a million pieces," "like a dam had broken and I was
being swept up by wild, incredible rushing forces,"
"like a cancerous invasion that was rapidly filling
me up."

A number indicated that the sensation of energy
approached being intolerable. For many, the sensation
of energy was accompanied by a distortion of body
boundaries. To cite three examples from the interview transcripts:

I felt I was floating, that I had no belly or
upper thighs, that I had a reality but no
reality. Certainly I was not upright.

I started to get hot all over my body, all over
me. The heat didn't feel like my body, it felt
like me. There wasn't an outline to my body in
the usual sense of the word. There was some
awareness of heat. It wasn't even localized
geographically or spatially. It didn't even
have boundaries; it was unlimited. It was like
all-over-the-place...But HEAT, unbearable heat,
in my head, all over the place. HEAT! Really
HEAT, positively all over my body...Now that I
look back at it, I could have been two feet
above the ground and at an angle. It's funny,
I never thought about it like that. When I
look back at it, I see a mass. I don't see a
person. When I look at me, I see myself

126

literally two feet above the ground and arched
backwards like that. It feels like a real
image. Something in me was so powerful that it
distorted my "body image" if you want to put it
that way. Though I wasn't aware of it then,
like I say. At that point, I was aware of some
heat, some nondistinct mass that was me, that
mass was the heat; it wasn't as if there was
heat in a mass, although I think it was heat
filling out to the boundaries of a mass. I
think I also felt I would blow up or something.
Not quite blow up but blow out of my boundaries
or something.

The real thing was the whole solar plexus attack.
It's hard to describe because the feelings themselves seemed to come from within but they also
seemed to come from without. It's like this
whole area was cut open and it was a flood. The
main area of sensation was the chest. It's
almost as if this (chest area) was pulled beyond
my body. I was scared of losing it or whatever.
It would start from the chest. It wouldn't
start from my legs or anywhere else; it would
start from right in here and go geeep! It
would start with a thud like my heart was
beating too much and then it would just go out
of hand, incredibly out of hand...(The panic
attacks) were a regular thing (for months).
Oh NO! It was TOO MUCH! Too much life! Too
much energy. Unbelievable! It was like being
zapped continuously with a psychoelectric
current that always threatened to become more
and more. It always threatened more energy.
The question was will it be at the top or will
it go down? That was the overriding question
of every day -- will the energy go over or will
I have a day where it will subside?

One person, who lost the distinction between the
inside and the outside of his body, stabbed himself
with a pair of scissors to re-establish the boundary.
He did this, he said, because:

There was some relief in letting the blood run

127

out. There was a feeling of too much pressure
inside, of being on the verge of an explosion
and somehow opening up the skin and letting
blood out was like letting out steam from a
pressure cooker and that had something of a
soothing effect.

Aside from the report of floods of nearly
intolerable energy and the distortion of body
boundaries, there was little consistent agreement
about the physical symptoms of panicking among those
interviewed. A number, however, did mention noticing
that their heart was pounding, that they wanted to
vomit or that they were gasping for air. Some spoke
of feeling "closed in," a feeling that may possibly
be one of not being able to breathe or of becoming
encased in one's final lodgement of casket or grave.

Unlike the physical experience in anxiety, it
is not physically tolerable to panic. Panicking is
felt as an emergency state that cannot continue in-
definitely, whereas anxiety, while unpleasant, feels
physically tolerable and as if it could continue for
weeks without being life threatening. Panic <u>must</u>
stop.

Experiences of Intellectual, Perceptual and Motoric Functioning

Extreme disorganization of thinking, remember-
ing, speaking, hearing, seeing, touching and moving
is characteristic of panic. People literally cannot
cope with the world while in this state. There is a
real question as to whether they are capable of
exercising full moral and/or legal responsibility
for their actions.

The following quotations from transcripts are
cited to give a sense of the variation and extent
of the disorganization which characterized panicking:

The word blind in connection with panic is very
important...I wasn't assessing the situation,
making a plan to get away. It felt like an
instinctive reaction, getting cornered, being

128

trapped...I was active, as I say, my muscles
were mobilized but there was a kind of wildness
to it. There was no deliberation at all. I
didn't know where I was going. It's like I was
flailing around. My motions were alert but very
incoherent...My eyes were flying all over the
place, just casting around, trying to see where
I could no...It was a matter of getting away but
very random...The reason why is that even though
I was trying to get out, I couldn't go anywhere,
so it was senseless motion...I wasn't making
these motions that were directing me. I got
taken over by this impulse to move, get out, to
go -- no assessment -- just a need to go --
that's what was in my body and mind combined.
Almost a kind of visceral thing, so I didn't
feel willful. Neither deliberative, nor willful.

It's not like a loss of consciousness because
there's intense pain but until I noticed the
people stiffening around me nothing in the world
existed except this horrible feeling -- unable
to speak, my heart pounding at maybe heart attack
level, loss of contact with what I wanted to say
or whatever the issue was. It's like a total
preoccupation with the pain...The circuits were
blown. If it stayed that way, they would have
carried me out. I mean how long could I have
stayed there with my face flushing and my hands
trembling without somebody doing something?

The pattern of the sidewalk strangely distorted
from a rectangle to an ovoid shape...Fighting
against this untruth, I felt stronger panic as
the day seemed suddenly darker and things seemed
to float in a mendacious manner. Things don't
lie. Solid bodies don't float...There was
blankness of color, absence of gravity, "pure
fear." The total eye distortion thing was the
most frightening side effect. I remember we
all went to see A Day at the Races. I remember
not being able to see the movie, sitting there
and not being able to see it. Everybody around
me was reacting, laughing at what was on the
screen. I remember trying to use the entire

part of my mind just to be able to see what was
going on in the screen, just to be able to say:
"Oh, there are horses going along." Just breaking everything down to its simplest components,
horses going along the track. There was nothing
funny going on. The complete context was gone.
Just horses going around and then losing it and
this terrible feeling of panic. I've lost it.
I can't see any more what's on the screen.
Everybody's laughing and I'm completely out of
the picture. I'm spun off the human context.
Everybody's laughing, having a good time; there
I am off, just trying to hold onto the bare
essentials just to keep from completely going.

Everything was electric, affectively not per-
ceptively. Like everything was charged. I was
charged. Not good energy. Like when you're
going to run but undifferentiated, freaking out
all over the place. Like if you are anxious --
it's a tension -- but this was going out of my
body in a way, not quite out. So much was going
out or around that I didn't have much connection
with my physical form any more. I didn't say:
That muscle is tense. I couldn't say anything
like that. My head was all mixed up. I couldn't
think straight. If someone had asked me to
"pass the ashtray," I would have said "GASHTRXKZ!"
I couldn't have said, "This is an ashtray." I
would have just looked at them. If my husband
had come along and said, "This is an ashtray,"
I couldn't have coped with it at all. That's
light years away from this. That's someplace
else. It couldn't have been, "Can't you see
what state I'm in?" I would have been NO communication. I couldn't have added numbers,
even two and two. The outside lost the perceptual organization -- you know, these blobs of
light that make up Tom and those blobs of light
make up Harry -- that we all do. Tom and Harry
just weren't there at that point. There were
sounds that I couldn't attribute to anything in
particular and light. It was like sparkly, too
vivid. The whole perception was random. The
light also. It was the light and dark created

130

by someone's shirt and somebody's lighter face but I was not experiencing it as such. This must be what an infant experiences, total diffusion of stimuli...They were making word sounds but I couldn't make it into words. It's not "Not Hearing." It's not recognizing it or putting it into a framework that one is used to....And it was exactly what the bodily sensations were....I felt funny when I told you the physiological reactions of panic because none of those served to make me any more aware of my body as distinct from what is not my body. Usually, when you have a headache, you are very conscious of having a head. But they didn't do that. Even the internal sensations of the electric knot in my stomach and the pounding heart didn't make anything internal feel any more real. They were sensations existing on a totally different sensory level than before what the brain does to interpret sensations, like before all that learning that has taught you inside from outside and me from you....Yet, I can't make it fit with the feeling that "I" am in danger and "I" have to get out. Maybe the best way I can describe it is to say that the confusion was not total.

The degree of disorganization described in the above quotation was experienced by most of the people interviewed for a brief time and then they began to think in a more usual fashion. Two of those quoted, however, were hospitalized because they began to panic fairly continuously and were not with people who could take care of them in the outside world.

The impairment of functioning while anxious ranges from mild to severe; it never reaches the point where the person cannot function in the ordinary world, as is the case with panic.

The Experience of the Self
on the Verge of Disintegration

In anxiety, the self is sensed as present but diffuse and insubstantial. In panic, the self is sensed as present but on the verge of disintegration. The experience is that it is possible, but not definite, that the "I" may vanish any moment. Since the space-time frame-of-reference itself becomes disrupted, the danger looms that what Chein calls the "origin in space-time" or the "hereness in the thereness"[39] may simply no longer continue to be present, leaving an unstable void in a sea of chaotic nothingness. To the person, who is panicking, this is an unacceptable contingency.[40]

As in anxiety, the "I" in panic is located within the body. There were no reports among those interviewed of the experience of the origin of space-time being located outside of the body. However, in contrast to the descriptions of the anxious self, there were a number of accounts of panicking in which the self was described as being located in particular parts of the body. For example, some people reported that they experienced their "I" as being "in my stomach" or "withdrawn into my head" or "hiding near my heart."

While anxious, people regard themselves as responsible for their behavior but somehow irresolute and not able to exercise that responsibility in a fully meaningful way. While panicking, people feel that they are responsible for their behavior but only barely. It is as if they are about to be taken over by an alien force that threatens to possess the self. This alien force is experienced as being so strong that a real question whether responsibility in a moral or legal sense can be exercised by the panicking person.

The "I" that is responsible -- that wills, knows, thinks, chooses, prays, acts, commands, etc. -- is under siege in panic. The person still feels responsible but does not know if he can continue to exercise that responsibility. The "I" is sensed as teetering on the brink of losing control.

The phenomenological experience is of an "I" that is still present but about to be wiped out. The transcripts are filled with statements of the

following sort: "I thought I was...dying, going
crazy, being engulfed, blacking out, about to faint,
having my soul torn from my body, going to disappear,
being flooded, losing my self," and the like.

What is experienced as threatening the "I" is
variously described. One group of people described
the source of the danger to their "I" as something
which came from within their bodies but which nonetheless belonged to an "it" or a "not me." A second
group of people described the source of the danger
to their "I" as something which came from without
their bodies and belonged to something that was
"not me."

The following examples are from the first group
of people who described the source of the danger to
their "I" as coming from within their bodies but as
nonetheless belonging to an "it" or "not me:"

It seemed to have nothing to do with me. It
seemed like a dybbuk entered me. There's a
flashing wave of light and darkness that sweeps
in on me. It's not me. Something pounded
wildly on that door but it didn't feel like:
"I am pounding on the door." It was more like
I watched while my body and arms, not connected
to me for that particular moment, hit the door.
I was there telling myself, "Don't panic!" --
but it, the wave that wasn't me which seemed to
activate the body that wasn't me -- was acting.
I was in my body, almost like I was in my head
someplace, and these arms that should have felt
like "mine" but didn't were flailing at the
door. It's a remarkable sensation.
The things that were coming out of my mouth no
longer felt like I had directed them. My voice
began feeling like something I had been listening
to from somebody else and I started getting very
panicky that I was losing control of how I was
reacting and how I would appear....I felt I had
no control over my body movements at all, that
I was making gestures that weren't me. I was
watching myself and listening to myself do these
things...I was trapped in a body with a mind

133

that was trying to destroy me. My mind was
playing tricks on me, was causing me to hear
things that were not real and it was doing this
to torment me. I felt very split at this time.
I mean the body wasn't mine. I'm not sure what
I was referring to when I said it was trying to
torment me but the feeling was that there was
no way out, no way out of my body, no way to
escape from this thing that was making me crazy.

A second group of people also experienced the
danger as coming from within their bodies. These
felt the danger as if it belonged somehow in a
category of "almost me" or "potentially me." To
quote from William James' description of "panic
fear," and then from a transcript of the person who
was interviewed:

There arose in my mind the image of an epileptic
patient....He sat there like a sort of sculptored Egyptian or Peruvian mummy, moving nothing
but his big black eyes and looking absolutely
non-human. This image and my fear entered into
a species of combination with each other. That
shape am I, I felt, potentially. Nothing that
I possess can defend me against that fate, if
the hour for it should strike for me as it
struck for him. There was such a horror of him,
and such a perception of my own merely momentary
descrepancy from him, that it was as if something hitherto solid within my breast gave way
entirely, and I became a mass of quivering fear
(James, 1947 orig. 1902, pp. 157).

It was like something that was not me, although
it was me, was taking over at the same time. It
was threatening in that sense because what it
was that was coming out was a hostile, to me was
a hostile, at the same time it was me; it was
very much against me at the same time it was me
and what I needed to be at that point.

A third group of people experienced the danger as
coming from without their bodies and belonging to a
source that was "not me." In most cases, outside

134

observers would probably classify such experiences
as phobic (e.g., unreasoning fear of being in an
enclosed space) or as hallucinatory (e.g., unreasoning fear of a "shark" just "known" to be in the
water or a "devil with evil vibrations" which is
"sensed" within the room, or "dangerous" people
"seen" on a peaceful street).

Panic persists as long as the person is teetering on the brink of losing control of himself. Some
descriptions of the attempts of the "I" to maintain
control against the onrushing "it," "not me," or
"almost me," "potentially me" or "outside of me"
sensations follow:

> (The panic pain) escalated to total disorgan-
> ization for a second and then enough organization
> came for me to put the coffee cup down clumsily
> and light a cigarette...There was a feeling of
> pushing the panic down enough so that my head
> could coordinate to say the words, the minimal
> number of words, to get me out of the situation.
> The strength of will came from the fear of it
> getting worse.

> (I deliberately took control). For a moment it
> felt like I was almost out of control. Like,
> "I am going to faint. I am going to faint. I
> must not faint. I must not faint. I must turn
> around and get out of here. I can't. I must.
> I can't. I must"...and I'm guiding myself out.

> Then there was this split. There was part of
> me that knew I was panicking and was saying to
> myself: "Now, look. You've had this before.
> If you do this and this and remember it takes
> a while for the tranquilizer to have an effect."
> It was kind of an observing operation, a holding
> operation, that was going on at the same time
> but sometimes the waves of panic would over-
> whelm the other for a second but I could pull
> myself back. So the balance sort of tipped
> different ways and this continued for a while
> until I was all right.

135

A method of retaining control quite consistently spoken of by those interviewed was calling upon reserves of will power, e.g., "TAKE HOLD OF YOURSELF!" "DON'T PANIC!" or "YOU MUST NOT LOSE YOUR HEAD!" or "GET OUT!" A number of people said they felt like they heard a voice giving them such commands and monitoring their execution of those commands. Other methods of retaining control included rapidly leaving the physical location in which the panic occurred, touching oneself or deliberately moving to re-establish body boundaries, even to the extreme, in one case already mentioned, of stabbing oneself, taking tranquilizers which were then perceived as "being in control." Creating external tasks in order to consciously structure the internal chaos, e.g., "go eat a doughnut," "go to Z place," was said to be helpful. In addition, mentally labeling the episode as one of "panic" -- rather than as a "heart attack" or "going crazy" -- was useful in retaining control for some.

A few sought someone else to hold onto for a while, such as a friend, a doctor, a "mommy" substitute. Some turned to God. To cite James' description of his experience of "panic fear" again:

I mean the fear was so invasive and powerful that if I had not clung to scripture-texts like "The eternal God is my refuge," etc. "Come unto me all ye that labor and are heavy-laden," etc. "I am the resurrection and the life," etc., I think I should have grown really insane.

The experience of the self being about to lose control, but not actually losing it, seems central to panicking. When persons are panicking, their concern is with the survival of the self; other issues are irrelevant. The problem is to keep their "I" afloat in the midst of something that potentially threatens to overwhelm it.

The unfavorable assessments of the self so characteristic of anxiety does not occur in panic. People are concerned with sheer survival of the self when panicking, not with relative goodness or badness of the self.

The Experience of Fleeing an Inexplicable, Intolerable, Imminent Danger

While anxious, people report that fragmented thoughts related to confusion regarding who or what they might be becoming flicker in and out of conscious awareness. This concern with what might possibly occur in the future is what the anxiety is said to be "about." Panicking, in contrast, is usually described as being "about nothing," as "inexplicable," as "an irrational fear without an object," as "a crazy fear of something that can't be the real object."[41]

What people report as being in awareness while they panic is that there _is_ an intolerable, imminent danger from which they mu__st__ flee instantly. Thoughts related to the experience of a present emergency flood consciousness, such as: "Get out!" "Run!" "Move!" "Get a tranquilizer!" "Find Mommy!" "Crash through the window!" "Out the door!" or "Closing in!" "Too much!" "Heart attack!" "Balance going!" "Crazy light!" "I am dying!" or "Keep calm!" "Don't panic!" or "Hold on!"

Nothing exists in consciousness but fleeing the emergency or, at most, how best to flee the emergency. Panicking is felt as intolerable. It has to stop. Tremendous urgency is created by the sensation that the panicking is getting worse and worse very second. Something must be done before things get out of hand. Immediate action is imperative. Unless action is taken now, death, craziness, blindness, being over-whelmed, becoming a blithering idiot, etc., will happen next.

An example:

From a woman who panicked while on her loft bed at home and whose panic followed upon weeks of anxiety: Anxiety was okay because nothing was going to happen to me. Anxiety doesn't go away but it doesn't _do_ anything. I can take

tremendous amounts of anxiety...But then when
it looked as if the anxiety itself was going to
go whomming on into something else and carry me
with it, that's when I panicked because I no
longer had control over the situation or thought
I didn't...I got off the bed where I was. It
takes concentration to climb down the loft
ladder from the bed so that got me together
again but I was still freaked out. It's like
the world ended. It was all over. Pictorially,
it would be like buildings crashing down and
yet they weren't quite affecting me that much.
The panic involved thinking, "If this is awful,
what would happen if it got worse? If the buildings are crashing down and I'm still alive,
just think how much pain would be involved in
doing away with me completely."...I couldn't
have done a thing. The only thing I could do
was say "OUT!" Get OUT of this!" That was the
only thought I had. Just: "Get OUT of here!
OUT! OUT!" Just crazy. No thought of how to
get out or anything that made sense. Out of
the state I was in but there was nothing to
get out of; it was me. That made it more
difficult, of course. If there was something
in the room, I could have run out. In climbing
down the ladder; that took my mind off it but
as soon as I got on the floor, as I hit the
floor, IT HIT again!...It was OUT! OUT! without
thinking of how to get out. The only projection
I could make for the future was walking around
thinking I had to get OUT.

Most of those interviewed shared the perception of
the woman just quoted that she had to "get out of
state I was in but there was nothing to get out of;
it was me." These people did not recognize any
cause for the panic, aside from that presented by
other aspects of the experience -- such as the
buffeting by waves of chaotic energy, the occasional
disintegration of body boundaries, the disorganization
of mental functioning and the sense of self as being
on the verge of being overwhelmed by an "it," "a not
me," a "potentially me." A few of those interviewed,
however, did ascribe their panic to a cause which

they later called either "phobic" or "hallucinatory."

The Life Circumstance:
The Possibility of Becoming What One MUST NOT Become

The previous discussion of the essential structure of the life circumstances which accompany anxiety was based largely on the research partners' description of what was in their awareness. This cannot be done with panic because, on the face of it, panic appears to be a senseless event that comes out of the blue. There is nothing in awareness that the person believes can account for the chaotic physical sensations, the disorganization of mental functioning and the experience that the self is on the verge of disintegration.

However, inferences about the essential structure of the life circumstances which accompany panic were drawn on the basis of a composite picture formed from the following sorts of evidence:

1. Interviews with research partners who chose to do what they called "go with the panic" at the time of panicking. This decision ended the panic and led to a series of immediately subsequent events which were experienced as novel happenings by the person. The people who chose to go with the panic assert with some certainty that they know why they panicked and say they base their certainty on the connection they intuitively experience between the panic and the immediately subsequent event.

2. Interviews with research partners who, a few hours or days after they panicked, figured out to their satisfaction why they panicked. These people were spurred on in the process of self-examination by a belief that they were responsible for all their behavior and that everything they did could be explained if they tried seriously enough.

3. Interviews with research partners who, a number of years after they panicked, say they understood why in retrospect. Most of these people had had psychotherapy in the interim.

4. Interviews with research partners who do not know why they panicked but who have some tentative hunches. These hunches were told to me with the specific reservation that the panicking was felt not to be fully understood.

5. Observations of people who panicked, who did not know why they panicked and who did not want to connect the experience up with the moment before, the moment after or with the rest of their lives.

6. Personal introspection, which contains elements of all of the above.

The evidence cited above lacks the weight of evidence based on subjective content reported as contained in the experience. Nonetheless, it seems coherent and consistent enough to warrant making the following inferential statement about the essential structure of the life circumstances which accompany panic and perhaps even to justify the conjecture that they are immanently present in the experience.

Panic, like anxiety, occurs when there is a potentiality for change in who the person is. However, the nature of the potential change differs. In anxiety, the person ruminates on changing his identity along lines he already approves. He mulls over the feasibility of taking the next step toward what he believes he must become in a line of identity development consonant with the hierarchy of values to which he has already committed himself and which he shares with others in his social unit. He is engaged in a working through process which may culminate in a decision about whether he can or cannot meet the criteria for the forthcoming risk he envisages in which it will be determined whether he has become what he believes he must become.[42]

In panic, the person faces the possibility of making a change that would be in a direction unacceptable to the structure of his commitments as currently constituted. The change would drastically alter his line of identity development as he envisages it. There is a real possibility, at the time of

140

panicking, that the person might become what he must not become. From this possibility, the person runs -- literally or figuratively, but instantaneously.

What the person must not become varies with the person; the personal transformation that is taboo to one person is not necessarily so to another. What the various prohibited activities share in common is that they implicitly contain with them a violation of the oughts, the values, the expectation structures of the social unit to which the person belongs. If the person allows himself to develop along the pro- hibited lines of identity development, that is, if he permits what must not become to come into existence -- e.g., if he gets angry in a family that does not permit anger -- he will be forced to change his relationship to his social unit. He will have either to renegotiate the terms of his relationship with that social unit or leave it.

That one must not become something is such a strong prohibition that the thought of what one must not become is ordinarily not allowed into conscious- ness. It is kept out through a secondary unconscious behavior.[43] Should a thought of what one must not become begin to enter consciousness, panic ensues.[44]

The self, the origin in perceived space-time, is subjectively regarded as the responsible agent for all of one's apprehended behaviors. As agent, however, it is construed in terms of various proper- ties which constitute the self-concept concerning which Chein says that "it is largely subconscious, comprising an implicative structure the various parts of which do not become explicit or the objects of scrutiny save under appropriate and special conditions" (1972, p. 215). Of special interest in the present context is one type of constituent which Chein describes as "the proprieties and improprieties that are taken as more or less prescriptive for myself: the kinds of things one feels called upon to do; the activities, roles, garbs, situations with which one feels comfortable and the ones that are not even thinkable" (p. 214). The self-one-must-not- become entails the most unthinkable of the unthinkable

141

-- and so, it is likely to be buried deeply in the subconscious implicative structure of the self-concept, i.e., to be unconscious. In panic, the most unthinkable of the unthinkable seems to be on the verge of emerging, not only as a thought, but as a realized actuality. The possibility devastates.

Experientially, the self, "subjectively, the responsible agent for all of one's apprehended behaviors,"[45] is threatened by an alien, hostile force that the self regards as an "it," a "not me," or, at most, as a "potentially me." The people interviewed who said that they understand, in retrospect, why they panicked report that what they experienced as an alien force at the time of panicking was the unthinkable thought of becoming what they must not become. At the stage of their life when the panicking occurred, they said they believed that they could not assume responsibility for the thought of becoming what they must not become and sought to keep it unconscious. As the unthinkable thought began to surface, they panicked. The people who say they understand, in retrospect, why they panicked also report that they now regard the once prohibited, unthinkable thought as "mine" and have, in many cases, become -- at least, to some extent -- the previously unthinkable person they once believed they must not become.

The change in the status of a thought of what one must not become from the status of a thought belonging to an alien source (part of "it," "not me," or, at most, part of "potentially me") to the status of a thought belonging to "me," involves a change in the structure of an individual's personality.[46] For example, for a timid, conventionally polite person to acknowledge fully a previously panic-provoking angry thought as "mine," means that the person has developed the capacity to assume responsibility for taking as assertive, independent and, possibly abrasive, stand towards other people.

At the time of panicking, a risk situation exists in which the person faces the possibility of actually becoming what he must not become. There is something in the situation which calls forth from him the possibility of acting, speaking, dreaming, wishing, hoping, fantasizing, etc., in a forbidden fashion. There is a real possibility, an actual risk, that the person can become what he must not become and can break, therefore, with his social unit.

This possibility is so unthinkable that the person flees from it without allowing himself to know what it is. That is, at a subconscious level the person perceives the risk but does not allow that perception to enter consciousness. Instead, he panics, fleeing the emergency presented by the possible emergence of the alien thought of what he must not become.

Panicking consists of a struggle between the "I" fighting to retain control over the alien "it," "not me" or "potentially me" which is pushing its way into consciousness. The seesawing of panic can continue for extended periods. It can end with a decision in which the "I" either maintains control over the alien force or in which the "I" yields to the alien force, thus opening the self out towards whatever unknown thing may happen.[47]

Limitations of the Study

Certain limitations should be kept in mind in evaluating this study.

First, it is based largely on observations and interviews of people who had rather special characteristics as a group. The research partners were highly educated, unusually attuned to discriminations of inner psychological experience and very sophisticated in the language available to them to articulate that experience. About two-thirds of those interviewed were engaged in psychodynamically-oriented psychotherapy or had been so in the past. Many of the research partners were imbued with the attitude that one should strive in life towards certain goals and that, once those goals are attained, one should seek out others to attain. Also, many of those interviewed either were in transitional stages of life, e.g., students or young professionals, or were engaged in the sorts of careers in which perfection can never be reached, yet is sought.

That verbal and psychologically introspective people would readily perceive fine distinctions between emotions is not surprising. It is important to remember, however, that other people well might not discriminate between emotions in this fashion and might regard, for example, anxiety, apprehension, guilt, shame, confusion, embarrassment, etc., as just a blur of bad feeling. Also, even if they did discriminate between the emotions experientially, they well might not have the language available to them to articulate the differences in a conventionally recognizable manner.

The people interviewed about the emotion they called anxiety consistently spoke of an experience of confusion regarding what they must become and described the world in terms of risks they saw to the line of identity development they expected of themselves. To some extent, such an account of anxiety experiences may be a function of their membership in that part of contemporary American society in which people are expected to move upward on a ladder of success. The people interviewed live in a world in which the grading system, the publish-or-perish syndrome of university life, production goals, the pressure to maximize profits, the adulation of the masterpiece, the recognition given to individual competitive achievements, the conspicuous-consumption race, popularity contests, etc., are realities of everyday life. People from a traditional society, in which roles were assigned by birthright, in which life was not perceived in terms of striving towards ever-receding goals, and in which children were taught that most of what happens to them is not dependent upon their individual efforts but is a result of the action of fate (of God, of the divine will, etc.), quite possibly might experience anxiety in a different form; or, perhaps, it is more correct to say that they may not experience anxiety but some other

144

emotion that plays an equally important role in their lives and that may not be within the normal range of experiences that occur to such as my respondents.

Also, all of the research partners who felt that they understood what their panicking was about either were or had been in a psychodynamically-oriented psychotherapy in which the "repression paradigm" played a large part in the way they interpreted the world. The statement that panic occurs in life circumstances in which there is a real risk that the person will become what he must not become comes from information supplied by such people. Had either they, or myself, been devout Christians, Tibetan Buddhist monks, South Sea Islanders, or some such, the accounts of the life circumstances accompanying the other experienced aspects of panic might have had quite a different cast.

Finally, my character, personal history and psychodynamically-oriented training as a clinical psychologist obviously influenced what was found.

A test that makes sense in evaluating this study is to compare what is said here with times in your own life when you would say about an experience, "I am anxious" or "I am panicky."

Reference Notes
for Chapter III

1. Cf. Introduction, S. Goodman (1975), de Rivera
    (1966a, 1966b, 1966c, 1976, 1977). The reader
    might find it interesting to contrast the method
    of investigation used with those of Davitz
    (1970) and Fischer (1970, 1974).

2. Cf. Goodman, P. (1971).

3. Zucker (1967).

4. Wolff (1964).

5. Cf. de Rivera's chapter on anger in this book.

6. I mean the term <u>Angst</u> to be understood as a
    general phrase referring to a muddle of unhappy
    emotions, including those meant by the English
    words confusion, fear, apprehension, terror,
    dread, despair, sadness, loneliness, grief,
    guilt, shame, humiliation, and remorse, among
    others.
        Fromm-Reichmann (1959) and Mandler (1968)
    are short, excellent introductions to the
    literature. Overviews of the field, sympathetic
    to psychoanalytic and existential views, are
    Fischer (1970) and May (1951). General works
    which report the experimental literature in
    some detail are Speilberger (1966), Levitt (1968),
    Lader and Marks (1971).
        The theoretical confusion in the field should
    be apparent just from the following: Freud (1933/
    1965) distinguishes between realistic, moral and
    neurotic anxiety, as well as between traumatic
    and signal anxiety. W.R. Reich's (1929/1965,
    1933/1949) patients got "orgasm anxiety."
    Sullivan (1953, 1956, 1964) writes of a range of
    emotions from a "mild anxiety" necessary for
    learning to an "extreme anxiety" that he some-
    times refers to by the words "panic," "terror"
    or "uncanny states." Frieda Fromm-Reichmann
    (1959a, 1959b) follows Sullivan but then adds a

146

plea for the acknowledgement of states of isolation which, she says, are often miscalled anxiety but really belong to a special category. Paul Tillich (1952) speaks of the anxiety of fate and death, the anxiety of guilt and condemnation, which either are or are not aspects of what Martin Heidegger (Gelven, 1970) means by "being facing non-being" or Kierkegaard (1944/1957) by "dread at the possibility of freedom" or R. D. Laing (1960) by "ontological insecurity." In the English school, it takes a true scholar to wade through the terminological confusion of Melanie Klein (1948; Guntrip, 1964), W. R. D. Fairbairn (Guntrip, 1964), Harry Guntrip (1969, 1971), D. W. Winnicott (1965) and Laing (1960). Kurt Goldstein (1940) makes a sharp distinction between anxiety and fear, but the experimental psychologists of the learning or behaviorist persuasions consider the terms to be interchangeable (Levitt, 1969). The operational definitions of the term used by people of the most varied theoretical orientations appear to have little in common.

7. Goldstein's description of the "catastrophic Angst" suffered by his brain-damaged patients is of a different order than his description of the Angst suffered by normal adults. The "catastrophic Angst" resembles, in many ways, the pattern of experiencing characteristic of "panic" as outlined in this paper.

8. Cf. Barrett (1962, p. 221).

9. Cf. Fromm-Reichmann (1959a), Fischer (1970), and Perls (1951).

10. Both the person who is anxious and others observing him can have difficulty determining whether the impaired sense of physical well-being is part of the experience of anxiety or is related to something else. Exhaustion, "coffee nerves," hangovers from whatever causes, muscle strains or other physical injuries,

irregularities in blood sugar metabolism,
infections, neurological problems, etc., may
be accompanied by similar senses of bodily
discomfort.

11. Cf. Fischer (1970), Fromm-Reichmann (1959a),
     May (1951).

12. Cf. Small (1973).

13. Exhaustion, "coffee nerves," hangovers, physical
     injury, lowering of the blood sugar level,
     infections, neurological impairments are among
     the other factors that may be related to a
     diminution in the level of intellectual,
     perceptual and motoric functioning usual for
     the person. Both the person who is anxious and
     others observing may have difficulty in telling
     whether the lessening of ability is related to
     these factors or to anxiety. This can lead to
     a certain amount of social difficulty.

14. Compare Erik Erikson's description of the
     subjective sense of psychosocial identity
     quoted later in this chapter.

15. See the discussion of the "life circumstances of
     anxiety" later in this chapter.

16. Cf. Sullivan (1953, 1954, 1956, 1964) and Fischer
     (1970a, 1970b, 1974).
          It is beyond the scope of this paper to
     consider the effects of anxiety on inter-personal
     relations. It should be evident from what has
     already been said, however, that a virtual
     Pandora's box of potential difficulty in inter-
     personal relations exists -- given the different
     ways in which self-criticism is experienced, the
     insubstantial sense of self, the experience of
     impaired physical well-being and of interference
     in intellectual, perceptual and muscular
     functioning. Fights, sulks, withdrawals into
     isolation, stalling, temper tantrums, petty
     fussiness, snotty remarks, contempt, unjust
     criticism, misunderstandings, compliant yielding,

hypochondriacal complaints, etc., etc!, abound.
The interpersonal situation can be further
complicated by the fact that many people while
anxious do not recognize that they are anxious.
Furthermore, they are often not recognized by
others as being anxious. If a number of anxious
people are together, especially if they are
unaware that they are anxious, the social interaction can become quite horrifying (or hilarious,
depending upon your view of human nature).
As a practical matter, I have found it
helpful to regard the increase in the salience
of self-critical assessments, the insubstantial
sense of self, the experience of impaired
physical well-being and the interference in
intellectual, perceptual and muscular functioning, as a "fever" indicating the possible pre-
sense of a certain structure of life circumstances that accompanies anxiety. If I turn my
attention in a therapeutic interview to the
structure of the life circumstances and deal
with that first, the "fever" often abates. I
have, for example, been impressed by how often a
discussion of such things as the ins-and-outs of
presenting a paper at a seminar, inviting certain people for dinner, getting a new apartment,
opening an office, playing in a basketball
championship game, etc. -- all matters which can
be associated with anxiety -- seems to cure
people who are burning with fevers composed of
bodily discomforts, the tireds, the stupids, the
self-attacks or the picking fights.

17. Dr. Chein (personal communication, June 1974)
suggested this word, pointing out that a person
cannot fully experience in the present who he
will be in the future; the future experience is
more of an abstractly conceived what than of a
concretely felt who. The issue of the difference
between the actual and the imagined crops up
again in the discussion of "criteria" later in
this chapter.

18. With some people, the scare images diminish con-
siderably once the connection is made between
their appearance and the life circumstance of

149

being concerned with who or what one might become
in the future. For example, a case of lockjaw
became merely a muscle tension in the jaw once
the connection between the muscular spasm and a
forthcoming examination crucial for her future
was pointed out to one girl.

19. Also, see Erikson (1968b), pp. 22-23, 50, 211.

20. Cf. Karen Horney's (1950) discussion of what she
    calls "the tyranny of the should."

21. Cf. Heider's chapter on "Ought and Value," in
    The Psychology of Interpersonal Relations (1958).

22. Cf. the following from Fischer's (1970) account
    of the experience of anxiety felt by a student
    about to take an examination crucial for his
    career: "The exam is not simply experienced as
    such -- that is, it is not conceptualized as an
    event in itself. It is not an isolated thought
    that presents itself as being unrelated to the
    individual's life, as essentially extrinsic to
    his general concerns. It is not something that
    occurs and is then forgotten. Instead, as the
    young man states, 'so much depends on it.' The
    meaning of this 'so much' reveals itself to be
    a complex network of relationships (to parents,
    to girlfriend, to peers, etc.), projects
    (graduating, securing the job, paying for the
    car) and identities (being somebody). The
    meaning of his possible performance on the exam
    -- it is this to which he is, in fact oriented
    -- points not only toward an anticipated future,
    but also it illuminates a past, a context of
    relations (with parents, girlfriends, peers) in
    which plans were made and promises enacted.
    There is a continuity, an unfolding, which is at
    stake here. In other words, the experienced
    meaning of the to-be-encountered exam is that of
    a hurdle or milestone. If it is passed, then
    the door is open to a world of "being somebody,"
    a world that has already been envisioned and
    experienced. If it proves to be insurmountable,
    this lived-and-planned-for-world vanishes into

meaningless oblivion; the past goes nowhere; the
future is being nobody..."
　　　"What we are suggesting here is that the
motivational component of this experience is a
must. The individual's life, as it has been
lived, demands successful performance on the
exam; it demands that the world that has been
lived-for-and-toward, the identity with which
he is at home, be sustained. There is no
question of mere preference, of an 'I'd like
this to happen but my life doesn't depend on it.'
Nor is it a case of 'I ought to pass and
graduate because if I don't, I'll feel guilty
and people might not like me.' Instead, it is
a must; there is no alternative, at least none
that is thinkable..."
　　　"Both the particular world that the person
lives-for-and-toward, as well as the identity
that is expressed as either affirming or negat-
ing that world, reveal, in the condition of
anxiety, the presence of musts. In other words,
when an individual is anxious, it appears that
the network of relations and projects that have
been and continue to be constitutive of both his
world and his identity emerge as demanding to be
sustained. This demanding does not have the
character of a want or even an ought. Rather,
it is experienced as a question of necessity, an
absolute requirement of life. There are no
conceivable alternatives or, to put the matter
differently, the alternatives all involve not-
being-myself. Further, although the questionable
milestones-to-be achieved may involve doing
certain deeds or acquiring certain possessions,
their significance lies in their implications
for the person's being. That is to say, passing
an exam and graduating from college or eliciting
expressions of sexual affirmation and thereby
feeling one's self to be an attractive woman are
deeds and acquisitions in the service of continu-
ing to live one's world and identity." (pp. 123-
125)
　　　The nuances of Fischer's discussion of "must"
and mine of "must become" are somewhat different;
otherwise my analysis of the relation between

151

"must" and "identity" is substantially the same as his.

23. Heider defines "can" to mean that the power of the person is greater than the difficulty posed by the opposing environmental forces (1958, p. 86).

24. I disagree with Leslie Farber's (1966) formulation that "anxiety attends that range of distress which attends willing what cannot be willed" (p. 42). It seems to me that people both believe that they can become what they will while anxious and, in fact, often do become what they will -- precisely because they held the belief that they "can" become what they will.

25. See discussion of the relationship between panic and "must not become," on pp. 63-67 of this paper.

26. Cf. Fischer's discussion of "milestones-to-be-achieved" and "uncertain ability" (1970, pp. 129 ff.).

27. Cf. Schachtel's discussion of "embeddedness" and anxiety (1959, pp. 44 ff.).

28. These factors tend to be ignored in discussions of and experiments about "test anxiety."

29. This raises the question of what are the relations between anxiety and those phenomena referred to in the psychological literature by such terms as defense, security operations, symptom, character, identification, resistance, role, etc. The issues are problematic and beyond the scope of this essay.

30. Cf. Alfred Adler's views on the striving for superiority (Ansbacher, 1956, 1974).

31. The question of the relationship between creativity and anxiety (or, for that matter, between neurosis and creativity) is far beyond the scope of this study. I think that neither

May in the concluding section of his The Meaning
of Anxiety (1951) nor Horney in her Neurosis and
Human Growth (1950) begins to grasp the complex-
ities of the issues involved.

32. Cf. Sullivan (1953, 1954, 1956, 1964).

33. It is important in talking with an anxious person to be aware of his remarkable vulnerability
to the opinions of others and his readiness to
feel criticized. Otherwise, one can find oneself in the predicament of having one's remarks
taken as devastatingly critical onslaughts, when
they would not ordinarily be so regarded by the
person were he not anxious.

34. I am grateful to Dr. Louis Cassotta (personal
communication, December 1973) who, after reading
an earlier version of this manuscript, pointed
out this alternative to me.

35. I have a dourer view of the nature of man's
potentialities than do, say, May (1951), Maslow
(1962) or Schachtel (1959) -- all of whom, it
seems to me, ignore the real limitations on what
can be achieved by man in favor of a glorifi-
cation of the "creative and productive personality," the "self-actualizing personality" or the
personality that can surmount "embeddedness."

36. Cf. earlier discussion of Erickson's concept of
identity.

37. I am not fully satisfied in my own mind with
respect to the point at which the identity
change occurs. As de Rivera (personal communication, February 12, 1975) pointed out to me,
it looks as if the point of the decision to
meet the risk, rather than the person's performance at the actual risk situation itself, is the
point at which the identity change occurs.
However, there are problems with this formulation. For example, does a person still feel an
identity change if he, in fact, fails in the
risk situation which he decided to meet? Is not
the confirmation of another, given in a cultur-

ally significant form, required for an identity change to occur?

38. Gay Wilson Allen, in his biography, William James, cites James' son, Henry, as saying that the passage quoted above was an actual experience had by his father in the spring of 1870. Allen points out the similarity to the "vastation" of William James' father, Henry Sr., eighteen years before (1967, p. 17).

39. See Chein's (1972) definition of the self, the discussion of "being myself" and of the self while anxious on pp. 6-8 of this paper.

40. To a Buddhist, of course, it might not be, for the disintegration of the self might be viewed as an acceptable part of a progress towards serenity.

41. The following discussion possibly does not apply to the use of the word panic when a person is in extreme physical danger -- such as that indicated by the sentence, "I panicked when I thought I was drowning." I lack satisfactory interviews on this experience.

42. See the discussion on the "Life Circumstances of Anxiety" above for the meaning of the terms in quotations.

43. Cf. Chein (1972), p. 108.

44. Cf. Freud (1933/1965, 1936/1963) and Brenner (1957).

45. Chein (1972, p. 280).

46. Cf. Sullivan (1953, 1956, 1964) and Rogers (1959).

47. I also conducted a preliminary investigation into the emotions of apprehension, fear, and

terror. The following was found:
The experience of apprehension is characterized by tense waiting, a slight improvement in
functioning and an intact sense of self. In
apprehension there is a gradual surmise that a
situation might become dangerous in the future.
People can become apprehensive prior to occasions
in which they become anxious, panicked, afraid,
relieved, etc.
The experience of fear is characterized by
a remarkable ability to function in a way
appropriate to the situation. In fear, people
experience the self as powerful, centered and
present in the body. Afterwards, and sometimes
before, people feel weak. Fear occurs when a
person finds that something is dangerous to him
physically and that danger is believed to be
clear, in the immediate present and from a
specific source external to the person. The
person tacitly defines the situation as one in
which he can do something to affect the outcome.
The experience of terror occurs when a
person believes he can do nothing about a clear
and present danger to his life. Immobility, a
paralysis of thought and a sense of immense
isolation were mentioned. The self was described
as present in the body but about to become "Not."
An experience in which the self is located
outside of the body was also noted.
There appear to be a number of different
experiential referents for the words "fear" and
"terror" which would require extended research
for full explication. Additional aspects of
the confusion in the psychological literature
surrounding the term anxiety (Angst) could
probably be clarified were this done.

References
for Chapter III

Allen, G. W. *William James.* New York: Viking, 1967.

Ansbacher, H. L., & Rowena R. (Eds.). *The individual-psychology of Alfred Adler.* New York: Basic Books, 1956.

Ansbacher, H. L. Goal-oriented individual psychology: Alfred Adler's theory. In Burton, A. (Ed.), *Operational theories of personality.* New York: Bruner/Mazel, 1974.

Barrett, W. *Irrational man: A study in existential psychology.* Garden City, N.Y.: Doubleday Anchor, 1962.

Basescu, S. Human nature and psychotherapy: An existential view. *Review of Existential Psychology and Psychiatry,* 1962, $\underline{2}$, 149-158.

Brenner, C. *An elementary textbook of psychoanalysis.* Garden City, N.Y.: Doubleday Anchor, 1957.

Chein, I. *The science of behavior and the image of man.* New York: Basic Books, 1972.

Davitz, J. R. *The language of emotion.* New York: Academic Press, 1970.

de Rivera, J. H. An alternative discipline. Unpublished manuscript, 1966(a). (Available from 142 Woodland Street, Worcester, Massachusetts 01610).

de Rivera, J. H. The semantics of inter-personal process. Unpublished manuscript, 1966(b). (Available from 142 Woodland Street, Worcester, Massachusetts 01610).

de Rivera, J. H. Psychological mathematics. Unpublished manuscript, 1966(c). (Available from

142 Woodland Street, Worcester, Massachusetts
01610).

de Rivera, J. H. Field theory as human-science:
Contributions by Lewin's Berlin group. New York:
Gardner Press, 1976.

de Rivera, J. H. A structural theory of the emotions.
Psychological Issues, 1, no. 4. New York:
International Universities Press, 1977.

Erikson, E. Identity: Psychosocial. In International Encyclopedia of the Social Sciences.
New York: Macmillan & Free Press, 1968(a).

Erikson, E. Identity: Youth and crisis. New York:
Norton, 1968(b).

Farber, L. The ways of the will. New York: Basic
Books, 1966.

Fischer, W. Theories of anxiety. New York: Harper
& Row, 1970(a).

Fischer, W. The faces of anxiety. Journal of
Phenomenological Psychology, 1970(b), 1, 1,
31-49.

Fischer, W. On the phenomenological mode of
researching "being anxious." Journal of
Phenomenological Psychology, 1974, 4, 2,
405-423.

Freud, S. New introductory lectures in psychoanalysis. (J. Strachey, Ed. and Trans.).
New York: Norton, 1965. (Originally published,
1933).

Freud, S. The problem of anxiety. (H.A. Bunker,
Trans.). New York: Norton, 1963. (Originally
published, 1936).

Fromm-Reichmann, F. Psychiatric aspects of anxiety.
In Bullard, D. (Ed.), Psychoanalysis and
psychotherapy: Selected papers of Frieda

157

Fromm-Reichmann. Chicago: University of
Chicago Press, 1959(a).

Fromm-Reichmann, F. On loneliness. In Bullard, D.
(Ed.), Psychoanalysis and psychotherapy:
Selected papers of Frieda Fromm-Reichmann.
Chicago: University of Chicago Press, 1959(b).

Gelven, M. A commentary on Heidegger's "being and
time." New York: Harper Torchbooks, 1970.

Gendlin, E. A theory of personality change. In
Worchel, P., & Byrne, D. (Eds.). Personality
change. New York: Wiley, 1964.

Goldstein, K. Human nature in the light of psychopathology. Cambridge: Harvard University Press,
1940.

Goodman, P. Speaking and language: A defense of
poetry. New York: Random House, 1971.

Goodman, S. A clinically-oriented phenomenological
investigation of the experiential referent of
the word "anxiety" as distinguished first from
the experiential referents of the words
"apprehension," "fear," and "terror." Unpublished Doctoral Dissertation. New York
University, New York, N.Y., 1975.

Guntrip, H. Personality structure and human
interaction. New York: International
Universities Press, 1964.

Guntrip, H. Schizoid phenomena, object-relations
and the self. New York: International
Universities Press, 1969.

Guntrip, H. Psychoanalytic theory, therapy and the
self. New York: Basic Books, 1971.

Heider, F. The psychology of interpersonal
relations. New York: Wiley, 1958.

Horney, K. The neurotic personality of our time.

158

New York: Norton, 1937.

Horney, K. Neurosis and human growth. New York: Norton, 1950.

James, W. The varieties of religious experience. New York: Modern Library, 1947. (Originally published, 1902).

Kierkegaard, S. The concept of dread. (W. Lowrie, Trans.) Princeton: Princeton University Press, 1957. (Originally published, 1844).

Klein, M. Contributions to psychoanalysis, 1921-1945. London: Hogarth Press, 1948.

Lader, M., & Marks, I. Clinical anxiety. New York: Grune & Stratton, 1971.

Laing, R. D. The divided self. Chicago: Quadrangle, 1960.

Levitt, E. E. The psychology of anxiety. London: Staples Press, 1968.

Lowrie, W. A short life of Kierkegaard. Princeton: Princeton University Press, 1942.

Mandler, G. Anxiety. In International Encyclopedia of the Social Sciences. New York: Macmillan & Free Press, 1968.

Maslow, A. H. Toward a psychology of being. Princeton: Van Nostrand, 1962.

May, R. The meaning of anxiety. New York: Ronald Press, 1961.

May, R., & Basescu, S. Psychology: Existential psychology. In International Encyclopedia of the Social Sciences. New York: Macmillan & Free Press, 1968.

Perls, F. S., Hefferline, R. F., & Goodman, P. Gestalt therapy. New York: Dell, 1951.

159

Reich, W. The function of the orgasm. (2nd Ed.)
New York: Strauss & Giroux, 1965. (Originally
published, 1927).

Reich, W. Character analysis. New York: Noonday,
1949. (Originally published, 1933).

Rogers, C. R. Client-centered therapy. Boston:
Houghton-Mifflin, 1951.

Rogers, C. R. On becoming a person. Boston:
Houghton-Mifflin, 1961.

Rogers, C. R. A theory of therapy, personality and
interpersonal relationships, as developed in
the client-centered framework. In S. Koch
(Ed.), Psychology: A study of a science (Vol.3).
New York: McGraw-Hill, 1959.

Schachtel, E. G. Metamorphosis. New York: Basic
Books, 1959.

Small, L. Neuropsychodiagnosis in psychotherapy.
New York: Bruner/Mazel, 1973.

Spielberger, C. D. (Ed.). Anxiety and behavior.
New York: Academic Press, 1966.

Sullivan, H. S. The interpersonal theory of
psychiatry. New York: Norton, 1953.

Sullivan, H. S. The psychiatric interview. New
York: Norton, 1954.

Sullivan, H. S. Clinical studies in psychiatry.
New York: Norton, 1956.

Sullivan, H. S. The fusion of psychiatry and social
science. New York: Norton, 1964.

Tillich, P. The courage to be. New Haven: Yale
University Press, 1952.

Winnicott, D. W. The maturational processes and the
facilitating environment. New York:

International Universities Press, 1965.

Wolff, K. H. On "surrender." In Bennis, W. G.
    et al. (Eds.), Interpersonal dynamics.
    Homewood, Ill.: Dorsey Press, 1964.

Zucker, H. Problems of psychotherapy. New York:
    Free Press, 1967.

IV

ELATION, GLADNESS, AND JOY

Janice Lindsay-Hartz

Understanding the role of positive emotions in our lives is as essential as understanding the role of negative emotions. There are as many words for positive emotions as for negative ones, and any useful theory of emotion must be based on a knowledge of both (de Rivera, 1977). Yet, despite the importance of positive emotions, their study has been generally neglected.

I set out to explore positive emotions by studying experiences of elation, gladness, and joy. These emotions had been judged by research partners, in a 1974 study by Lau, to be close neighbors along several different dimensions. Studying a group of neighboring emotions appeared to have certain advantages over studying a single emotion. It was assumed that the perceived affinity of these emotions would encourage research partners to be more thoughtful when asked to select specific experiences to exemplify each emotion and would hopefully result in a more sensitive differentiation of these emotions. Further, it was assumed that analysis of experiences of these emotions would result in the specification of a unique structure for each that could be used to illuminate individual examples and to understand their distinctive functions in our lives.

The Method of Conceptual Encounter

I used the method of conceptual encounter to develop descriptions of the unique structures of

163

joy, elation, and gladness. A total of thirty persons, were interviewed during two studies. Each person was told that I was interested in understanding elation, gladness, and joy and distinguishing these emotions from each other and from all other positive emotions. They were asked to think of specific unambiguous experiences of which "elation," "gladness," or "joy" were the best labels. After taking some time to recall and consider experiences, the research partners were asked to describe and help analyze the example which they selected. Some literary examples of these emotions were also analyzed.

In a first study in which eighteen research partners participated, I integrated Goodman's and de Rivera's methods of interviewing.[1] In the first phase of the interviews, I asked the research partners to describe specific experiences of elation, gladness, and joy. I incorporated Goodman's style of patient and involved listening, posing questions only toward the end of this phase. The research partners responded by giving extensive, uninterrupted descriptions of their experiences. In a second phase, like Goodman, I inquired about several different aspects of these experiences using a check list of items as a guide. In a third phase, I employed de Rivera's technique of engaging the research partners in an exercise of imaginatively varying components of their experiences in order to determine what was essential and what accidental. A fourth phase was modeled after de Rivera's more confrontational style. I gave the research partners my conceptualization of the structure of their experiences and asked them to examine the fit between the proposed structure and their particular experiences. I sometimes argued for a reinterpretation of their experiences in light of the proposed structure. They sometimes rejected my conceptualizations and told me exactly why they did not fit.

The final descriptions of the structures of elation, gladness, and joy were the product of the interviews with the research partners, dialogues

164

with other researchers, and my own analyses of the transcribed interviews and the literary examples which were collected. In a second study, I further developed the method of conceptual encounter by creating a method to test the validity of these structural descriptions.

The Results of the First Study

The structural descriptions of elation, gladness, and joy will be presented below. The structure of each emotion can be divided into four parts or aspects. The four aspects when combined together in a specific way form the whole emotion, just as the features of the face form a face.

For each emotion, the four aspects which will be described are similar in nature to those described by de Rivera (see Chapter II) and Funk (see Chapter V). The first aspect, the situation, is a transaction between the person and the environment involving a number of choices which give meaning to whatever occurs. The situation is, in other words, the meaning of the central events for the person. The second aspect is the transformation of our way of being in the world. There is a change in our relationship to things that are not essential to the emotion but are necessary to our being in the world. For example, our perception of space and time may change. The bodily expression, the third aspect, includes not only the manifestation of the emotion in the body and in bodily action, but also the meaning of this manifestation. It is the meaning expressed by particular movements or actions in a certain situation that is of significance. The fourth aspect, the function, is the role that the emotion plays in furthering our goals or values.

The Structure of Elation

The Situation of Elation

Analysis of the interviews revealed that we feel elated when a wish involving ourselves is fulfilled. In all of the research partners' examples of elation, something happened which was central to the experience, such as getting into the college of one's choice or falling in love for the first time; and that central event could always be characterized as the fulfillment of a wish involving the self. When we are elated, it is as if a dream has come true.

A look at three examples of elation will acquaint us with some of the concrete experiences reported by the research partners that led to this conceptualization of the situation.

One key example which suggested a connection between elation and the fulfillment of wishes was described by a research partner who, with her husband, bought a grandfather clock. Both came from poor backgrounds. When they were first married, they dreamed of someday owning nice things and making a home together. The incident described below happened thirty years later while they were on vacation. The research partner gave this incident as an instance of elation. While she occasionally used the word "happy" in her description of this experience, upon inquiry she stated that "elation" was really the best label for her feeling.

A grandfather clock is something that Paul and I had always talked about and wanted. We both were like two kids. We were elated over the fact that we finally saw it and just decided we were going to get it.

We were just looking at them. We never gave a thought that we were even going to buy one. They happened to be on special. Paul was looking at them, and he seemed very, very interested in them. He had the little girl come over and wait on us and was asking her all these questions. And then all of a sudden, he took hold of my hand; and he said, "How much would it cost to ship it?" And I said to him, "You going to buy one?!" He said, "Yeah, don't you want one?" I said, "Yes." I'd say then

166

the feeling started.

Paul took hold of my hand and squeezed it. We were both just happy. Just he and I, just sharing happiness together. It was sort of like we were by ourselves, I suppose. Everything else was gone. (My hearing) got foggy. We were so intense on what was happening, we couldn't be aware of anything else.

(The clock was) kind of like a dream come true, a wish or something. Like Paul said, we looked at them when we were married and always wanted a grandfather clock, especially something we could pass on as a heritage.

The research partner is so caught up by the elation when her wish is fulfilled that she goes out of touch with the rest of her environment.

A second example centers around a research partner's being accepted into college and is typical of many of the examples involving being accepted into schools or special programs, winning awards, or being recognized for one's achievement.

I had applied to a school early decision, and I hadn't gotten in. And all the schools that I applied to were pretty tough to get into. I was beginning to worry that maybe I wouldn't get into any. I was downtown, and I called my home. My brother answered the phone. He said, "You got an envelope from Clark today. It looks pretty fat." I said, "Open it up!"

I figured if I didn't get into here, it was all over. So my brother opens it up and he says, "Dear Mr. D. We are pleased to announce-" And with that I just started screaming...in the phone booth in the middle of Washington. I was with a friend. I said, "I got into Clark."

From there to walking back to where his car was, I just kept talking about how great it was that I got in. If I had known any of the

167

people that were walking by, I would have said
to them, "I just got into Clark!" Then I kept
telling him why Clark would be such a great
place to go, how it fits in perfectly with
what I want do do. Every good thing about the
place popped right into my mind. So I started
telling him about that and telling him why it
was so important to me that I got into Clark.
I associate elation with talking about the
feeling that you're experiencing.

(Getting into college) meant a lot because my
parents had been pushing for this ever since
seventh grade. I guess it was important to me
because all throughout my life when people
asked me what I wanted to do, I was talking
about professional jobs. The first thing I
can remember I wanted to be was a paleontol-
ogist. Somebody must have said to me, "Well,
if you're going to do that, then you have to
go to college." In twelveth grade I took a
psychology course in high school. I took
that, and I really liked the course, and that's
when I started thinking, maybe I'll go into
psychology in some form. But I knew you have
to go to some kind of grad school. So that's
why I thought it was pretty important that I
got into a good school. Plus, for my own self
pride because I always had thought of myself
as a good student. After switching to the
suburban school system, I realized how much
less than spectacular I really was. So I
needed some kind of a boost to tell me that I
wasn't as bad as I was looking like I was.

In this example, the student is elated not so
much over the achievement of being accepted but
over what his acceptance means in terms of all that
he can now do. The student's behavior consists
primarily of eagerly announcing the fulfillment of
his wish. He is focused on the thought of the
fulfillment of his dream and is thinking of little
else.

A third example of elation was described by a

168

research partner who fell in love with a woman for the first time. He had spent years fantasizing what it would be like to fall in love and wondering if it would ever happen to him. When he felt elated, the thought "Hey, I'm in love!" was dominant. As was true of the previous examples, the central event, in this case falling in love, was perceived as the fulfillment of a wish or fantasy; and the elated person was focused on the thought of this fulfillment.

While we all have some intuitive notion of what is meant by "the fulfillment of a wish involving the self," the terms will now be more explicitly defined.

The act of wishing that is part of elation must be understood in its own right and in distinction from similar actions such as hoping and desiring. In a study of the acts of wishing and hoping, Marcel (1967) characterized wishing as a "consciousness to obtain an anticipated satisfaction, when the possibility of obtaining this satisfaction is lacking." For Marcel, the essence of wishing is captured in the phrase, "How I should like to..." There is a dream-like quality to it. Wishing implies a gap between a certain actual situation and the idea of an imagined satisfaction. However, the possibility of obtaining this imagined satisfaction is lacking or at least is not central in our awareness. That is, we may be focused on possibilities that are small steps toward the imagined satisfaction (e.g., we may be filling out college applications when our dream is to go to college and to become a renowned professional), but there is a gap between the actual possibilities focused on and the more extensive imagined satisfaction. We allow ourselves to dream beyond what we consider realistically possible at the moment. Marcel points out that wishing is transformed to desiring if we perceive that the imagined or anticipated satisfaction can be fulfilled. Desire belongs to the realm of having and impatience.

Wishing is distinct from hoping in that only hoping involves a commitment to waiting, with patience and with some confidence that a certain event will occur" (Marcel, 1967). We see a possibility (not necessarily a probability) of the hope's being fulfilled, and we focus on such possibilities in the present moment. Yet being also aware of the possibilities of the hope's not being fulfilled in any particular situation, we experience uncertainty in the present when we hope. Often this uncertainty is manifested in the form of doubt or worry. In contrast, wishing does not involve doubt or worry as we are not focused on the possibilities of the fulfillment of the wish in any particular situation. It does not concern us if the wish remains a fantasy in the present moment.

Since we do not focus on possibilities of fulfillment when we wish, we are not prepared for the wish actually to be fulfilled in the present. Hence, the fulfillment is always unexpected and elating moments necessarily involve an element of surprise. The fulfillment can be unexpected in timing; that is, we were not expecting the event to happen when it did. Or, the fulfillment can be unexpected in degree; that is, the change is greater than we had expected. In addition, the particular form of the fulfillment may be unexpected. For example, one may dream of falling in love but never have imagined it would come in the particular form it did.

The interviews indicate that the wish involved in elating experiences is more specifically a wish that involves the self. It may be a wish to be able to do something or a wish that others will see us in a certain desired way or both. Wishing to be able to do something may involve: (a) wishing to achieve some goal, like executing a perfect dance step if we are an aspiring dancer, or writing a good paper if we value such activities, or (b) wishing to be able to actualize some fantasy, like falling in love. If we wish that others will see us in a certain desired way, their view of ourselves must be congruent with our own. Some examples of such wishes are a wish to be seen as intelligent or lovable or powerful.

The fulfillment of such a wish, while experienced as realized when we feel elated, is not necessarily an actual fulfillment. Later we often realize that the central event represented only one step toward the fulfillment of our wish but was taken to be the complete fulfillment. For example, one research partner wished to be a good director of plays and to be recognized as one by others. He directed one play which was well-received and got good reviews. Upon hearing the audience's applause and also upon reading the critics' reviews, he felt elated and was swept up with the thought that he "could direct." He was a director. Yet later he realized that one play did not make him a director forever and that his successful direction of that play was only one step toward becoming a good director. Similarly, our being accepted into the college of our choice may in part fulfill our wish to be a student at that school, pursuing a life we imagine to be desirable; but being accepted only opens the possibility of our going. With the acceptance we are not actually there, but we may focus on the imagined complete fulfillment.

The research partners perceived a variety of events to be the fulfillment of their wishes. These events can be grouped into three classes. First, according to the research partners' descriptions, an announcement by another may fulfill our wish; there may be an announcement that we can do something or that another has seen us in a desired way. An example of this type of announcement is the actor's reading the reviews of the play he had directed and his taking them to be a declaration that he was a good director. Second, our own personal performance may fulfill our wish. In this case feedback from others is not necessary; our performance is a private announcement to ourselves. For example, one research partner performed a perfect dance movement with no audience present, and she knew from the feel of the movement that it was perfect and that she was a good dancer. "There was no question but that I was in the right way." Third, an event which enables us to see ourselves in a way that realizes a prior fantasy may serve as the fulfillment. For example, the case of the woman's having her dream (of owning a grandfather clock and being able to pass it on as a heritage) come true arose out of a situation which enabled her to own a grandfather clock.

The theme of another's announcing that one has achieved something seemed so important to many of the examples collected that achievement was, at first, thought to be an essential part of the situation of elation. However, a few research partners resisted interpreting the central event of their experiences as an achievement, and some examples clearly had nothing at all to do with achievement. These research partners and their counter-examples forced a reconceptualization of the situation. It was found that each example of elation could be more aptly characterized as the fulfillment of a wish. Even when achievement was present, the particular achievement always fulfilled a wish.

In summary, we feel elated when an event is perceived to fulfill a wish which involves ourselves. Our wish is realized as we take one event to be evidence of the total fulfillment. Our dream has come true.

The Transformation of Elation

Moments of elation transform our way of being in the world. Analysis of the interviews revealed two interrelated qualities which characterize this transformation. First, we are psychologically lifted. Some of the research partners' descriptions of this experience follow.

I just feel sort of like I'm floating. I feel very light.

I felt released from earthly constraints, like I was flying. It's more of a hyper state. I feel on top of the world and bouncy.

I felt lifted, like I was floating down the

172

hall, up in the air.

Second, we are not psychologically grounded; that is,
we are "lifted off the ground." We are in some ways
distant from other things or persons, slightly out
of touch with the world. Research partners described
this experience as follows.

> I was kind of numb to the whole rest of the
> world. It's just that I was up on cloud nine,
> and I was being very irrational. If somebody
> had come along and said, "World War III started,"
> I would have said, "I don't give a shit!"
> (laugh)

> It was sort of like we were by ourselves, I
> suppose. Everything else was gone. We were
> so intent on what was happening, we couldn't
> be aware of anything else.

> It wasn't so much that I was radiating out to
> people around me but that I was hung up in
> sort of revolving around an idea of what I had
> just done, or what I was doing, since it was
> still going on. I was kind of putting the
> idea in people's heads and wasn't really too
> concerned with what they were saying. When
> my friends came over to talk to me during the
> intermission, I really wasn't too concerned
> with them; but everything was directed toward
> the play. I didn't want to really stick
> around and talk much.

> I didn't notice other people or what sur-
> rounded me. I was sort of closed off from the
> rest of the world, just thinking about what he
> had said.

In order to make this description of the transformation more understandable, it may be helpful to
explain the phrase, "lifted off the ground," in a
less metaphorical way. First, the "lifted" aspect
includes both a suddenness and an "up" vector. The
suddenness is related to the element of surprise
described in the previous section. Several factors

seem to contribute to the "up" vector. The feeling is positive and persons report being "on top of the world." Positive feelings are typically represented as being "up" in relation to negative feelings. Also, the research partners frequently described a sense of freedom and a sense of increased ability or mastery. Several times, persons said, "Look what I can now do." Certainly this sense of increased ability contributes to the "upness" of the experience.

Most importantly, wishes and fantasies are on the level of unreality; and this level is metaphorically represented as "up" (Lewin, 1935). Fantasies and dreams are lighter, less serious. When elated, we are "lifted up" to realize the fulfillment of our wish. We "go up" rather than bring the wish "down" into the level of reality because there is still an element of unreality in the total fulfillment. To realize the total fulfillment, one event is taken as evidence that our wish has come true, and the realization is completed by imagination or fantasy.

The second aspect, "not being grounded," involves the loss of a firm contact with the situation at hand. As one research partner said, "It lifts you out of reality." This lack of "grounding" is related to the realized fulfillment of our wish. When elated, we are often focused almost exclusively on the thought of having the whole imagined satisfaction, when actually only one step toward fulfillment has been taken. As long as we are focused on the thought of fulfillment, we are not particularly attending to anything else in our environment. We are "off in another world." One research partner, who felt elated when the first draft of his thesis was evaluated as the best his advisor had ever read, described this experience as follows.

So I couldn't help but go over this in my mind for the rest of the day. I went over in my mind various possibilities, what that meant. And there were periods of fantasy about getting

an article published. The whole general tone
of turning over things like that in one's mind.
I was very much enclosed on myself.

Sometimes the lack of grounding involves a
confusion in that we are so focused on the thought
of the fulfillment that other thoughts and perceptions are lost. One research partner said, "Nothing
matters. I lose track of everything, really, even
the thought." Another said, "I could have walked
past my best friends and not have noticed them."

Sartre (1962, p. 72) relates an example of a
realization that a wish is fulfilled which nicely
illustrates the person's being swept up to the
level of fantasy and magic while focused on the
thought of the fulfillment.[3] He describes a "man
to whom a woman has just said that she loves him."
Sartre says about the man,

> (He) may begin to dance and sing. In so doing
> he turns his mind away from prudent and dif-
> ficult behavior he will have to maintain if
> he is to deserve this love and increase it, to
> gain possession of it through countless details
> (smiles, little attentions, etc.). He turns
> away even from the woman herself as the living
> reality representative of all those delicate
> procedures.[4] Those he will attend later...
> For the moment, he is possessing the object
> by magic, the dance mimes his possession of it.

In this example, the words of the woman do not
totally fulfill the man's wish or desire to possess
her in a love relationship. The words are only one
step toward the fulfillment, but he is swept up
with the fantasy of total fulfillment.

When we feel elated and find ourselves focused
on the thought of the fulfillment, the interviews
indicate that the passage of time is one particular
aspect of our environment to which we do not attend.
Most of the research partners made observations
about their experience of the passage of time
similar to the following.

175

I forgot all about Christmas, and finally I
started hearing Christmas music, and I started
thinking, "Oh, my God, it's going to be
Christmas in about a week or two." So that's
kind of where I was at.

I lost (time). We just looked at each other a
lot. And it must have been for hours.

Being "lifted off the ground" creates a certain
distance between ourselves and our environment.
Analysis of the interviews indicated that two of the
three types of psychological distance described by
Kreilkamp (see Chapter VI) are characteristic of
elation and serve to form a protective barrier
around us when we feel elated. The first type of
distance involves our failure to take into account
the effects of our actions on others. The second
type of distance involves our failure to understand
and consider the viewpoints of others. If either of
these types of distance are not present, then the
feeling of elation ends. For example, if we begin
seriously to take other persons or things into
account or begin to take the view of an other, then
we can no longer be focused solely on the idea of
the elating fulfillment. The feeling is then
temporarily or permanently ended. The third type
of distance described by Kreilkamp involves our not
being in a unit with an other person. This type is
not essential to experiences of elation as several
counter examples were described by the research
partners. For example, when one research partner
described being elated over falling in love, the
feeling of elation was dependent upon the presence
of the woman he was with and upon his commitment to
her during the moment.

Sometimes feelings of elation just fade away.
However, the protective barrier formed by the
distance between ourselves and others can be broken
through rather suddenly, as if our "bubble were
popped." In fact, feelings of elation are frequently experienced as rather transitory and can be
easily ended. An example in which a feeling of
elation was suddenly ended was described by one

research partner who had been a D student but dreamed of being a good student. Suddenly, "like magic," she got an A. She was expecting a C on one exam. When she got her first A ever, on that exam, she "went waving it around," saying, "Look what I got," and feeling very elated. However, she ended up "feeling foolish." One person said, "So what? Grades aren't important." And that "deflated me, made me feel ridiculous - angry at her and annoyed with myself for not being more discrete." Thus, when she took another person's view into account (that grades were not that important) and when she took account of the effects of her actions on others (that she was bragging indiscretely and annoying others), the feelings of elation ended abruptly.

The Expression of Elation

Research partners frequently reported vivid bodily and behavioral manifestations of elation. It seems that elating moments often bring "ear-to-ear" smiles that can not be restrained. Usually, there is increased activity, for example, jumping up and down and running around, and an increased speed of movement. There is a tendency for the elated person to announce verbally to others, sometimes even to strangers, what has happened. The elated person may seek out others to whom to announce the happening. For example, research partners reported calling friends or going to visit people in order to tell them.

While there is a cluster of common bodily and behavioral manifestations, no one manifestation is essential to the experience of elation. Rather, it is only the meaning of these manifestations that remains constant across all the examples. Given that the situation of elation involves the fulfillment of a wish to see ourselves in a certain way or to be in a certain desired situation, all of the manifestations seem to have the meaning of an announcement of our new position in relationship to this wish. When elated, we announce that we can now do (or be) what we wished to do (or be). The announcement may be directed at an audience or at

177

ourselves.

Since feelings of disbelief usually are part
of the experience of elation, announcing our new
position helps to confirm the realization of the
wish in the face of any disbelief and thus helps
maintain the feeling. One research partner described this well. She said:

> When it (the feeling of elation) starts abat-
> ing, I tell somebody about it. I would say
> something like, "Well, that's what my super-
> visor told me (that I'm a good therapist).
> Do you really think she meant it or was she
> just kidding?" Just so I get a chance to
> repeat what happened. I do that very con-
> sciously in order to try to recapture the
> moment.

The Function of Elation

The role that an emotion plays in furthering
our goals or values is the function of the emotion.
These goals or values must be present in order for
the emotion to exist. Given that the situation of
elation involves the fulfillment of a wish, elation
seems to function to allow us to believe that our
wish has been realized. The belief in the realization of fantasy must be present in order for there
to be elation, and feelings of elation further
support such a belief. Elation allows us to realize
our wish by taking one event as evidence of total
fulfillment. Both the bodily expression and the
transformation, which are aspects of elation, serve
this function. Specifically, being lifted up to the
level of unreality frees us to believe the evidence,
and being out of touch with our environment prevents
us from taking any contradictory evidence into
account. The announcement of our new position con-
firms the realization in the face of any disbelief.

With the realization we believe that we can do
(or be) what we have wished to do (or be), and we
are thus able to try.[5] For example, we can direct
plays; we can go to the college of our choice; or we

178

can be loved; and we are free to continue to try to
bring such things about. Our self-image is raised
or reconfirmed. Although our wish is not totally
fulfilled, if we believe it to be realized and try
to act accordingly, we may bring about further
realization and continue the feeling.

Summary

When integrated together, the four aspects just
described form the structure of elation. This
structure can be summarized as follows, with each
line representing a different aspect of the
structure.

Expression: When elated, we announce

Function: the realization of our new
                 position

Transformation: that comes as we are lifted
                 off the ground

Situation: by the fulfillment of our wish.

The Structure of Gladness

The Situation of Gladness

Analysis of the interviews revealed that we
feel glad when a hope is fulfilled. The meaning of
hope will be clarified below. In every case described by the research partners, something happened
which was central to the experience, such as the
arrival of a friend, the acceptance by others, or
a brother's finding a job; and that central event
always was experienced as the fulfillment of a hope.
A concrete example of gladness described by one
research partner nicely illustrates this.

This research partner had plans to visit a
half-way house. One of his college professors had
recommended he involve himself by regularly visiting
there and talking with the boys who lived there.
He described his experience going to the house for

179

the first time as follows.

Going there, I'd developed anticipations. I
was totally unprepared. I was really unaware
as to what I should expect. I didn't know
what I was going to be doing when I got there.
Dr. Sand (his professor) just kept saying
things like, "Well, you know, you'll get a
feel for it and fit in." That told me nothing.
I was walking in wondering, "What exactly is
this all? What am I doing here for? You get
the fear, is this going to be a power experience? Are these people going to reject me?"
Things like this. "Is it going to be good?
Bad? What?"

I was anxious for it all to happen. Of course,
I was hoping that it all would be something
good. To me that meant simply that the kids
would accept me as somebody that was not there
to sit there and study them but just accept me
as somebody who was coming to do what I can.
To learn from them, to get something from them
and them get something from me, like a mutual
experience. I was just hoping the kids would
respond positively to my being there. And I
was hoping I could relate to the situation.
That's what being good would have meant for me.
Because I was just unsure if I would fit in,
in a situation like that. For it to be good,
it just meant that the kids could relate to me.

I got there, and I just felt comfortable for
some reason, just being in the environment.
Initially, the person who runs the house sat
down and had a long discussion with us (just
the couple of kids and Dr. Sand, who went). I
felt I had a good grasp of what he was saying.
I started to feel comfortable there. I was
beginning to understand what this whole situation was all about, the idea of the house and
the kids and all that.

The kids came in. Their openness, their
friendliness, made me feel at home. Also, it

180

turned into a really good experience. I was
open with them. They were open in return. I
could see how I could fit myself in. It was a
good experience, and I got something out of it.
I feel that it was positive all around, with
the kids and myself.

In this example, the research partner has a hope
about which there is much uncertainty and doubt.
Certain events are experienced as the fulfillment
of this hope, as described in the last two paragraphs.

While we all probably have some implicit understanding of what is meant by the phrase, "the fulfillment of a hope," it may be helpful to articulate
the meaning of this phrase more explicitly. Given
this task, Marcel's (1967) analysis of hoping and
wishing will again be found helpful. In addition,
some of the research partners' descriptions reveal
much about the act of hoping and the relation between hoping and gladness.

According to Marcel (1967), hoping differs
from wishing in at least two respects. First, it
involves a commitment to waiting, with patience and
with some confidence that the hope will be fulfilled.
There is some confidence because we are focused on
the possibilities of the hope's being fulfilled.
In contrast, wishing does not involve patient or
confident waiting. Second, whereas wishing involves
focusing on the end that is wished for rather than
on the possible means of getting there, hoping
entails focusing on the means and being aware of the
possibilities of the hope's not being fulfilled in
any particular situation. Because of this latter
awareness, hoping involves uncertainty in the present, usually manifested in the form of doubt or
worry.

Research partners' descriptions indicate that
hoping is also characterized by a positive dependency. We are helpless to bring about the total
fulfillment of a hope all by ourselves; we must
also depend on something other. We cannot control

or cause the event that brings fulfillment, although
we do take an active part in the sense that we must
remain open to possibilities of the event's happening and in the sense that we may sometimes take
steps to bring about the hoped-for event.

Depending on something other necessitates a
commitment to waiting. For example, if we hope for
rain, we depend on Nature (e.g., clouds, a particular combination of warm and cold fronts) and we
must wait for Nature to take its course. If we hope
for friendship, we may take steps toward developing
a friendship with another person, but we are
dependent on and must wait for the other's response.
In contrast, when we wish, we are not depending on
anything else because we are not looking for the
wish to come true in any particular situation.

While hoping and wishing are qualitatively
different, in actual experiences there may be a
mixture of both. For example, we may be hoping to
get accepted by a certain college. That is, we may
be focused on possibilities of our getting accepted.
At the same time we may have a wish to be a sophisticated college student, living away from home,
going to football games, and having a well-decorated
room in the dorms. That is, we may have a fantasy
of what being a college student would be like. Inasmuch as there is a wish which we take to be fulfilled, we feel elated. Inasmuch as there is a
fulfillment of a hope, we feel glad. If an event
fulfills both a hope and a wish, then we feel both
glad and elated.

An experience described by one research partner illustrates such a mixture of feelings. This
man was learning to fly airplanes and was trying a
solo take-off and landing. Once he was up in the
air, he found that unexpected and unusual weather
conditions made the maneuvers extremely difficult.
He strongly hoped he could manage each maneuver
and could land safely. At the same time, he wished
to be able to fly planes expertly and to become an
excellent pilot. When he landed safely on the
ground, he experienced alternating feelings of

182

gladness and elation. He connected the feeling of
gladness with relief that he had landed safely;
hence it was tied to the hope that he be able to
make each maneuver and land safely. He connected
the feeling of elation with the thought that he was
now a good pilot. This feeling was dependent on
his instructor's acknowledgment that he had expertly
handled a tricky landing and his thought that his
landing performance meant that he was a good pilot.
His wish to become a good pilot had been a fantasy,
however. During the flight, he was not focused on
the possibilities of becoming a good pilot. Rather,
he was focused on the possibilities of landing
safely and was hoping to accomplish this.

Hoping can also be contrasted with the act of
expecting. When we expect something to happen, we
know it will happen and we count on it. There is
no awareness of possibilities of its not happening.
Unlike hoping, expecting does not involve dependency
or uncertainty, although expecting can involve
waiting for what we know will happen.

The interviews indicate that hopes and moments
of gladness range from very small, mundane things
to special, important things. They can be very
concrete and totally fulfilled by the happening.
Two examples of this follow. These examples also
illustrate the presence of dependency.

One man described feeling glad when his brother
got a job.

Gladness is a more superficial feeling, feeling
good about somebody else being in good shape or
having done something successfully or something.
Just recently my brother was going through a
bad time, as far as getting jobs was concerned.
He's six months older than me. He took time
off and was traveling around. He got this shit
job driving a taxi. Things were working out
very badly; he was living in a bad section of
town. Finally he got a job at a publishing
company. I was really very glad for him.

I was thinking that he was not satisfied, that he was going nowhere. When he finally happened upon something which at least had some prospect of being interesting or challenging, it just made me feel good that here was a change of fortune for him. I didn't think about it a tremendous amount. Whenever I would think of my brother, I would think, "D.'s in bad straits, I hope things work out."

In this example, it is clear the research partner has a specific hope that "things work out" for his brother. His brother's getting a potentially interesting job clearly fulfills this hope. Although the brother may have been taking steps to find a job, there was also a dependency on something else, such that good or bad fortune seemed to be involved.

A second example which involves a concrete hope was described by a research partner who belonged to a women's club. She was asked to help find a committee that would put out some advertising flyers.

I was glad the other day when Ann called me up and asked me if I would get five women to help on getting out the flyers January 3. All I could think of was the work and all that involvement, right after New Years - and five women to line up and everything. I told her then that we were going to be out of town, and I didn't know that I'd have much time to do it. She was going to be out of town too. She's the kind of person that kind of pushes things off on you. But she said, "I think I'll call up a couple of women and I'll call you back." She called me back and told me that she got two of them, and that she'd help herself. I thought, "Oh, I'm so glad." Then I had to get only two more people.

I was glad the second time when she called and said she had two women. I was thinking of the pressure of working that in with all the things I had to do, getting ready for the holidays. I had decided that I would do it, but finding

184

five people was an awful lot to have to do in that short period of time when everyone is so busy.

I had hoped the two women that she mentioned would do it. I kept hoping after she hung up that she would get them because I knew that it was going to mean an awful lot of calling to get five people. It's hard to do.

When she called me back and said, "Well, I've got Harriet and Pam." Right that moment, I was glad. The burden of thinking of having to find five people was relieved.

In this example, the research partner hoped specifically that the caller would be able to enlist two women. She was dependent on the caller's phoning these other women and on the response received. The hope was specifically fulfilled when the caller informed her that she had enlisted two other women.

In these two examples the research partners' hopes are concretely and specifically fulfilled. A man hopes his brother will get a good job, and it takes little interpretation of the situation to realize that he has one. The moments of gladness described differ little from relief and are relatively unintense. However, hopes involved with moments of gladness may also be more abstract, generalized hopes. Frequently these more abstract hopes are fulfilled for the moment but are hoped for again. For example, we might have a hope for friendship and then feel glad during an evening spent with a new acquaintance because we felt a friendship was established. Yet we may then repeatedly hope for the continuance of this friendship and the establishment of further ones.

As hopes become more abstract, they are necessarily more symbolically fulfilled. For example, in order to see that a hope for friendship is fulfilled, we must interpret certain gestures and exchanges to mean that a friendship is being established. We do not see friendship per se. In

185

contrast, it takes little interpretation to realize
that a brother has a job, or to realize that it is
not raining if one has hoped for a clear day on
which to go on a picnic. An example follows that
illustrates a moment of gladness that involves a
more abstract hope. The presence of dependency is
again evident.

There's one very specific situation. I was
home a couple of weeks ago, after I had my
operation. My younger sister took off from
school one day, and we drove to the beach.
We sat on the beach for awhile. It was comfortable. Then we took a walk along a canal.
We just walked along and made up stories about
what we were encountering as we walked along.

I felt very close to both the physical space
and my sister and very good about everything.
It was a sort of smooth, flowing feeling of
long duration and hours. The feeling stayed
with me for weeks. That one experience triggered my closeness to her. I felt like I was
making good contact with both the place and
the person.

She had decided to stay out of school in order
to spend some time with me. We both knew we
weren't seeing each other for a long time after
that day. So we both were feeling like it was
going to be important that we made contact.
Part of what's a problem when you go away from
people that you love is that you grow in different directions. And you don't always take
a chance to make sure that you still have some
common ground. What happened that day in a lot
of different ways is that we realized how much
common ground we still had and in what similar
directions we were moving.

We really changed a lot while not being in the
presence of each other. And yet we discoverd
how similar things stand for us. Even though
they're different in degree, there's nothing
incompatible about us. Having realized that

by spending the day together and by doing
things together; having realized how really
compatible we are.

She's in some very basic ways very different
from me. I think that being on the beach
brought us closer. Certain things happened
where we shared some common ground. If that
hadn't happened, and it hasn't happened before
when I've been home - like this summer, we had
no event like that. I was very concerned about
it in the beginning of the summer, very concerned that we really seemed very, very far
apart. You can be in the same situation without the thing happening. It takes a certain
openness and a certain movement toward that in
order for it to happen.

By this example, it can be seen that the research
partner describes a specific hope for something
rather abstract. She hopes that she and her sister
share "some common ground" and make "contact."
Throughout the example, the research partner describes how she took certain events to be the fulfillment of her hope. It is clear that the fulfillment of the hope involves a dependency on something
else; the research partner feels that she cannot
simply bring about the event all by herself.

In contrast to the two preceding examples
where the hopes were for something very specific
and concrete, in this last example the hope is for
something more abstract and the feeling of gladness
is more intense. However, whether feelings of
gladness are superficial or intense, they are always
tied to the fulfillment of a hope.

Two events provide further confirmation of this
description of the situation of gladness. First,
one research partner described an example of gladness but was puzzled by her feeling. She felt glad
when she and her fiance had made a visit to the home
of one of his old friends. Yet she was uncertain
how her feeling of gladness related to this event.
This research partner was then told that gladness

187

was thought to involve the fulfillment of a hope and was asked if she had been hoping for anything. In a moment of insight, she excitedly raised her voice and answered that indeed she had been hoping that the visit would turn out well. Prior to the visit, she had worried that she would prevent her fiance and his friend from having a good visit. She hoped that she would be accepted and that the visit would be a warm one. In the interview she then realized that she felt glad during the visit when certain happenings indicated to her that her hope was fulfilled. Thus, the description of the situation of gladness enabled her to gain insight into a previously puzzling experience.

A second event also supports the idea that gladness involves the fulfillment of a hope. In Abrams (1973) study of the relationship of dependency, one woman whom she interviewed described the following example of gladness.[6]

Don is the woman's boyfriend.

If I was hungry and it was late, I could hope that dinner would be on the table or cooking, or that whatever had to be done was done, or that Don would be in a good mood and be able to do that for me, rub off his good mood. But if dinner wasn't cooked, I could cook it. Then if I got home, and he was making dinner, or dinner was ready and the guests were there, I would be glad that things were rolling along smoothly. Everything was happening. No upsets.

This woman described herself as dependent on Don. It is notable that many of her hopes, for example the one described above, depend in part on Don for their fulfillment; and when they are fulfilled, she feels glad. This example illustrates nicely the connection between dependency, hoping, and feeling glad. Other interviews from Abrams' study contain more illustrations of the same phenomenon and hence provide further independent confirmation of the claim that the situation of gladness involves the fulfillment of a hope.

The Transformation of Gladness

When we feel glad, there is a change in our way of being in the world. Analysis of the interviews indicated that this change includes feeling more relaxed and open to things and having a clearer, brighter view of our surroundings.

Some research partners' descriptions of this phenomenon will serve as illustration. The research partner who visited a half-way house and hoped the experience would be a good one stated:

And I started to feel comfortable there. I could see how I could fit myself in. It was an open conversation, and I was part of it. I felt like I was an active participant in the group. When I was leaving and felt glad I would say I was very perceptive; I was very observant of everything in the house itself, of the situation of the house. I was paying a lot of attention to that. I just became more observant.

Another research partner said, "Things brightened up around the place." The research partner who felt glad when she shared some "common ground" with her sister said:

I felt more relaxed. I felt very relaxed, in spite of the fact that we were under a lot of time pressure. We were very much in tune to the way the environment was affecting us.

A fourth research partner described feelings of expanding and being more open to things.

Normally you're kind of waiting for some problem to come up, and then I'd just look around and nothing would come up. I'd be able to kind of expand a bit and kind of blend in with the ground of just everything being a nice day and so on. This is not a kind of mystical expansion. It's more just a matter of feeling like just another part of a nice day. The

189

sun's shining and I feel sunshiny. I don't
feel like I'm communing with the sun or anything like that.

In this last example the research partner distinguishes his feelings of gladness from more mystical
feelings of closeness with the sun. This kind of
closeness will be shown to be characteristic of joy
but is not an essential characteristic of gladness.
Instead, the transformation that comes with gladness
involves feeling more open and having a clearer view
of the situation and one's surroundings.

This transformation is related to the situation
of gladness. With the act of hoping that is implied
by gladness, we wait and we hold back, looking for
something to happen. Then with the fulfillment of
our hope, we relax as the uncertainty -- the possibility of the hope's remaining unfulfilled -- is
removed. We no longer hold back with some antici-
pation but rather we let go and open up to the
situation at hand. This results in a heightened
awareness of our surroundings which comes in the
form of a clearer, brighter view. One might liken
this phenomenon to the view one has to mountains in
the distance on a clear, bright day, compared to the
view on a dull, hazy day. The fulfillment of the
hope, which removes the possibility of the hope's
remaining unfulfilled, is like a cloud's being
lifted. Everything becomes more distinct and
bright.[7]

The Bodily Expression of Gladness

Many research partners reported feeling relaxed
and moving more freely when they felt glad, but no
other bodily responses distinctive of gladness were
described. Consequently, the analysis of the bodily
expression relied primarily on interpretive dialogues involving the researchers. We focused on our
observations of glad persons and asked, "What bodily
expressions communicate that a person is glad?" We
concluded that we usually know others are glad
because their faces brighten up; persons smile and
their eyes sparkle. Glad persons move more freely

and easily; they let go rather than hold back. All
of these bodily manifestations seem to express a
welcoming. The glad person welcomes the event that
fulfills the hope.

The Function of Gladness

The interviews indicate that gladness functions
to illuminate the positive value of dependency and
the value of the event that fulfills our hope. It
also allows us to reconfirm the commitment to whatever we were depending upon while hoping. In other
words, when feeling glad, we accept our dependency
in the particular situation and place a positive
value on this dependency. Our trust in other persons and things and our commitment to them is
strengthened. For example, the research partner who
hoped that his brother would get a good job had to
depend upon his brother's abilities and resourceful-
ness and the availability of jobs. When his brother
finally got a job and he felt glad, the dependabil-
ity of his brother and the job marked was highlighted, and his trust in these things was strengthened. His glad feelings also functioned to
illuminate the value of his brother's getting a
good job.

One research partner reported seldom feeling
glad and this absence of gladness illustrates how
its function is an essential part of the emotion.
She had had some very negative experiences with
other persons during her life and felt that it was
foolish ever to hope, to trust others, or to depend
on others. She was caught in a circle of negative
expectations. Without valuing dependency she was
unable to hope and, hence, could not experience
gladness.

Summary

When integrated together, the four aspects
just described form the structure of gladness.
This structure can be summarized as follows, with
each line representing a different aspect of the
structure.

191

Expression:	When glad, we welcome
Situation:	an event that fulfills our hope,
Expression:	thus relieving the helplessness of our situation, brightening our view
Function:	and reconfirming our commitment to whatever we were depending upon.

The Structure of Joy

The Situation of Joy

The central event of experiences of joy can be characterized as a meeting between the person and not just another person or object but the presence of another person or object. In all the examples described by the research partners, the joyous persons encountered either another person, some natural object, or a diffuse spiritual presence to which they felt close. The following examples illustrate some concrete details of such meetings.

In the first example, a young man describes a joyous meeting with another person.

I was home. A girl called me up that I knew when I was in high school. We're kind of close. We went out, took a long walk. We were just talking. We weren't even talking a lot of the time. It was totally quiet out too. It was just really peaceful. There was no one else around. And we were just walking and laughing and making funny comments and throwing each other in the snow. Doing things like that. We went over by the lake, and we were sitting, asking each other ridiculous things, playing on trees and stuff like that. It was just so nice just to be out there with her, feeling really close to her and kind of in a special sense, not like in a love relationship or anything,

but in a kind of special sense. And I could
tell she was feeling that too. She was responding to it, and we were just really sharing some
incredible moments there.

This was a temporary experience, to just have
and share. We were sharing in each other's
personal lives, and we were responding to each
other. See, in one way I don't think people
respond harmoniously. I think people put up
defenses. Maybe they're even just little
defenses. You're just not really completely
open to people. This experience I would have
to say, I was completely open. It's the kind
of thing where I didn't have to use words. It
could be non-verbal, using her facial expressions, just perceiving them as giving off some
kind of good vibrations.

It was her giving to me, and my being receptive
to her. My giving to her and she, being
receptive to me. Working together. I think
I want to use the word harmony. And it was
just feeling her as being a very warm, sincere,
concerned person, especially about me. Feeling
that she cared what I was saying, that there
was a love there of a certain kind, of a
special kind. A lot of this I often get just
from feeling and from non-verbal stuff, like
maybe looking at her eyes, looking at her, how
she is responding physically, things like that.

In this example, it is important that the research
partner distinguishes this feeling from one of
romantic love. He describes several significant
characteristics of the joyous meeting with his
friend. First, he describes how close he feels to
his friend, and this closeness is characterized by
an openness and a lack of defensiveness. A second
characteristic is the mutuality of the meeting;
there is a mutual attending and responding. Third,
he experiences a sense of harmony and peacefulness.
Finally, it can be seen how the other is a presence
for the research partner; he experiences her as a
whole person and not as an object.

While the other central to experiences of joy was frequently a person, the research partner who described the following example experienced a meeting with the presence of a natural object.

I was walking to work feeling very down. The city was ugly and blah. Suddenly a small flower in a tiny garden arrested me. There wasn't much else living around. It was almost as if I was drawn to it; as if two invisible arms had reached out and forced me to stop and look at it. For a moment the flower and I met. It was the center of my world. I saw only it, and yet I saw everything else reflected in its light. My whole being said, "Yes, yes, yes, life is good. Yes." It was an amazingly strong feeling of affirmation. It sort of rose up in me, as if a dormant seed had suddenly sprouted and flowered. That sounds a little corny, but it burst forth, yet in slow motion. It was bursting, yet not an explosive bursting, but more of a radiating bursting. It filled my whole being and flowed out to my whole surroundings. The saying, "My cup overfloweth" fits the feeling well. It was as if I flowed out to meet everything.

The actual moment with the flower probably lasted only for a few seconds; yet for the moment it was as if there was no time for me and no distance between the flower and me. But it was physically 15 or 20 feet away. I'd say the meeting with the flower was a moment of joy. It lasted only a second and yet it lasted forever.

I continued on my way. There was maybe a brief moment, tinged with sadness at leaving the flower. But then I was joyous. It was like I was filled with tremendous waves of affirmation. "Yes, yes, yes. Life is beautiful." I felt like embracing the whole world. Before I had been trudging along, and now it was a pleasure to walk. I felt that my whole being was smiling, rosy all over. Almost a feeling of a

rush; life stirred in every element of me.
Everything I looked at said, "Yes." Like, not
verbally of course; I just felt it. Everything
seemed to answer back. I think I smiled and
looked at the people that I passed. "Yes, it's
good to be alive. Yes." They smiled back. I
think they felt it too, although I didn't even
say hello. I just felt like embracing the
whole world.

In addition to illustrating the mutuality and closeness of the joyous meeting, which we have already
observed in the first example, this example illustrates the experience of timelessness, the feeling
of affirmation, and the desire to embrace others,
which are all characteristic of joy.

In a third example, a research partner described experiencing the presence of an other; but
for him the presence was diffuse and not clearly
located anywhere.

I walked down to the beach, and the sun was
just rising. It was a steel-blue sky. The
sun was piercing, very golden. It shone over
everything and gave everything a soft light.
Just like that (snaps his fingers), for no
reason, I just felt drunk with the sense of
beauty. But it was a less sensuous thing
because I was also drunk with the thought of
the possibilities that life presented for me.
Possibilities of discovering new things and
having more experiences like the one I was just
realizing. All of a sudden, I thought that
God, the world really is beautiful, and I just
don't notice it.

I started walking along the beach. See, it
was just as much an intellectual experience as
it was a physical sense of beauty. That's why
I find it hard to talk about. I was walking
along and just looking, with the sensation of
looking with new eyes at the world. Peering
at everything, the sea and the sun, the sky,
the trees. Further down about half a mile I

saw a boat shoot out from the land, and there
were a couple of people in it, a small rowboat
with a motor at the end. And I suppose they
were going out fishing or something like that.
And that struck me, as it wouldn't usually
strike me, because if I wasn't feeling the same
sensation of beauty, I would just see the rowboat and those people striking out for the sea.
Somehow it's almost as if it doesn't really
penetrate. There's a veil between me and seeing whatever is seen. Whether it's the rowboat or the sun or anything. For that moment
it was as if the veil came down. There was
nothing between me and whatever I saw. So that
I really took in everything. I felt that I was
taking in the significance of their going out
and really seeing - there were a couple of
people who were going out fishing. I just had
a much sharper perception of it.

That something else there was some kind of
current in the world. All of a sudden I had
the sense of it. It pervaded everything. And
that's the sense in which it was sensual. It's
almost in the sense that beauty means to me.
When I see something that's beautiful, you feel
its presence. You feel the uniqueness of whatever it is that you perceive as beautiful.
It's almost a living presence. You see things
in a different light. It's almost a tangible
thing which exists in the world, a current
which pervades everything. I don't know how
to speak of it any more than that.

As well as illustrating the closeness characteristic
of joyous meetings, several new characteristics are
described in this example. First, this research
partner experiences the presence of a diffuse and
yet unique other. Second, while the research partner's way of being in the world is a new one for him,
it is experienced as the "really" real and as significant. Third, there is a sense of closeness to
everything and he feels in touch with his surroundings. Finally, he describes a sense of possibilities.

The above three examples are in many ways quite different from each other. Certainly, of the three emotions studied, joy was the most elusive and the hardest to describe in any essential way. Yet, in all the examples collected, a mutual meeting between the person and the presence of some other was always central to the experience of joy. The examples seem varied because the "other" can be a person, a felt presence in some natural object, or a diffuse presence, which religious research partners sometimes called God.

It should be noted that the words "meeting" and "presence" are being used in this description in a special way. While the above examples provide some illustration of what is meant by these words, the following explanation will help articulate further their meaning.

A meeting[8] is an encounter that occurs between ourselves and an other. We experience ourselves as part of a larger whole. That is, while we are still a separate being who is not fused with the other, our meeting with the other forms a whole, larger than simply the sum of the two parties. We are close to the other, connected with the other. One research partner described this experience as follows:

> A group of people have merged, or two people have merged. Some contact has been made. In that contact, you're different. It is something greater than either of you. As much as I'm still an integral whole, there's still something else that's neither me nor the other person, that's both of us.

Furthermore, the meeting of joy is mutual in that we are attending and responding to the other, and the other is attending and responding to us. Both parties to the meeting are on an equal level in that neither party is placed above the other; for example, no one is worshipped. Of course, we may feel joyous in a relationship when we feel understood by an other or accepted by an other.

While these relationships may seem skewed in that one person is giving and the other is receiving, a moment of joy transforms such a relationship into one characterized by sharing and mutuality. Neither party is seen as the sole giver, or as the greater or more powerful one.

The meeting essential to a moment of joy is also characterized by a spontaneous beginning. We cannot cause it to happen and need not have been looking or hoping for it to happen. Rather, it is given like a gift. We must be open to such a meeting and responsive. In this sense, we must give something of ourselves. But the other must also give.

One research partner described very well the mutuality of this kind of meeting. In his example, he and the other are clearly on an equal level, and his openness to the meeting is evident.

I stopped, touching a tree. It just really feels wonderful. You go up and feel a tree and it takes on like a new meaning for you. Whereas normally I might experience something in a desacrilized (sic) manner, that it's just there. It's kind of sacrilizing everything; and everything becomes magnificent and wonderful in itself. I don't lessen myself to it. I don't think I would deify it in the sense of, "Wow, that's incredible, almighty, wonderful." I see it as being, but incredible and magnificent in itself.

It involves me being an active part in it, but it's also nature as the instigator of it. As bringing out feelings in me. It's two way. My active part is being aware of it, which means in a way being open for it, should the experience begin to manifest itself, being receptive toward it.

Another identifying characteristic of joy is that we encounter not simply an other but the presence of an other. The presence of an other is

198

that through which the other is known, that through which the other reveals itself. As the phrase is used here, "encountering the presence of an other" means that we experience the wholeness and uniqueness of the other. In contrast, we may experience an other as one object among many; we may focus on individual qualities or aspects and label the other or parts of the other. When we encounter the presence of an other, however, we encounter the whole other, without judging and without labeling. Characteristically, we are aware that this encounter involves a different perception of the other. As the research partner who felt joyous at the beach said, he was "looking with new eyes at the world."

One research partner described the presence of the other as follows.

I was with a girl. I slept with her, and I remember looking into her eyes for a long time without talking. She looked beautiful to me and mysterious. But I was seeing her in a unique way, not seeing her as a personality. I usually put people into slots, even if I say they're a wonderful person, I'm defining them. But I wasn't doing this to her. It was a magical thing...Not looking at (her) as an object.

As the meeting is mutual, not only is the other a presence for us, but we are a presence for the other. "Being a presence" is characterized by a sense of personal wholeness and unity. In other words, we do not experience any part of ourselves as split off from the rest. As the research partner who felt joyous at the beach said, it is an intellectual experience as well as a physical and sensual one. Another research partner expressed the sense of personal wholeness as follows.

For one thing, it's very much rooted in my body. That is, I feel my body, not as an object. I feel as a body. I feel very whole, in other words, very, very whole. It wasn't this divorced feeling as if I were a mind

separate from a body. There's that instant
where there's nothing really happening except
I just am.

Since many research partners reported difficulty describing in words the experience of joy, I
found that poets' and novelists' descriptions of
such moments were among the examples that most
clearly illuminated the experience. Two of these
examples are presented here because they describe
so well the mutual meeting with the presence of an
other that is central to the experience of joy. In
a passage from "Lines: Composed a Few Miles above
Tintern Abbey," Wordsworth (1904) describes an
encounter with a diffuse presence.

> For I have learned
> To look on nature, not as in the hour
> Of thoughtless youth; but hearing oftentimes
> The still, sad music of humanity,
> Nor harsh nor grating, though of ample power
> To chasten and subdue. And I have felt
> A presence that disturbs me with the joy
> Of elevated thoughts; a sense sublime
> Of something far more deeply interfused,
> Whose dwelling is the light of setting suns,
> And the round ocean and the living air,
> And the blue sky, and in the mind of man;
> A motion and a spirit, that impels
> All thinking things, all objects of all thought.
> And rolls through all things. Therefore I am
>   still
> A lover of the meadows and the woods,
> And mountains; and of all that we behold
> From this green earth; of all the mighty world
> Of eye, and ear, -- both what they half create,
> And what perceive; well pleared to recognize
> In nature and the language of the sense
> The anchor of my purest thought, the nurse,
> The guide, the guardian of my heart, and soul
> Of all my moral being.

Joyce (1964, pp. 171-172), in Portrait of the
Artist as a Young Man, describes a meeting with
another person.

200

He was alone. He was unheeded, happy, and near
to the wildheart of life...

A girl stood before him in midstream: alone and
still, gazing out to sea. She seemed like one
whom magic had changed into the likeness of a
strange and beautiful seabird... But her long
fair hair was girlish: and girlish, and touched
with the wonder of mortal beauty, her face.

She was alone and still, gazing out to sea; and
when she felt his presence and the worship of
his eyes her eyes turned to him in quiet suf-
ference of his gaze, without shame or wanton-
ness. Long, long she suffered his gaze and
then quietly withdrew her eyes from his and
bent them towards the stream gently stirring
the water with her foot hither and thither.

The first faint noise of gently moving water
broke the silence, low and faint and whispering,
faint as the bells of sleep: hither and thither,
hither and thither: and a faint flame trembled
on her cheek.

--Heavenly God! cried Stephen's soul, in an
outburst of profane joy.--

He turned away from her suddenly and set off
across the strand. His cheeks were aflame;
his body was aglow; his limbs were trembling.
On and on and on and on he strode, far out over
the sands, singing wildly to the sea, crying
to greet the advent of the life that had
cried to him.

The encounter of joy need not respect our
logical sense of a space-time continuum. The pre-
sense of an other need not be physically embodied
but may be encountered also through such things as
letter, poems, gifts, or paintings. For example,
one research partner had received a poem from his
daughter. He described his feeling of joy upon
reading it.

It was a real occasion to get the thing.
Something unexpected, something with real deep
feeling in it. I read the verse on the card.
I'd never gotten anything like this from her
before. It showed the depth of her feelings.
And it related to me; it touched me. It put
her right next to me then, even though she
was 1500 miles away, she was right with me.
She was on the paper. It made her a part of
me at that time. I mean it warmed me very
much to get this from her.

There was a very closeness, to the point of
almost bringing tears. I mean, it's a choked
up feeling, getting something like that. I
envisioned her writing that and her thinking
of me. In other words, our thoughts joined
across thousands of miles. Although I wasn't
aware of it at the time she did it. I had to
wait to get it from her. I felt a very closeness at that point, at the point she wrote it.
There was a closeness, but I didn't realize it.

The Transformation of Joy

Moments of joy transform our way of being in
the world and our experience of our surroundings.
The interviews indicate that when joyous, we feel
totally close to everything; and we are grounded,
or in touch with things. This transformation
affects our experience of other persons and objects
in our environment, our experience of ourselves,
and our experience of space and time.

The closeness we experience is total because
it involves a collapse of all kinds of psychological
distance.[9] As one research partner said, there is
"a mystical feeling of wholeness and oneness with
the world -- not being separated from the world,
completely part of it." This total closeness does
not, however, involve a fusion with the other.
Three research partners described this experience
as follows:

...seeing myself as part of that, just being

202

part of this wonderfulness, and the magnificentness, and saying that, "My God! I'm part of this! And this is me!"

...realizing my uniqueness, but as part of everything. Seeing that I am a unique being. I'm still a part of everything.

This is not what I would call a blending into each other. I don't think I'd lose my boundaries in a joyful situation. I really define my boundaries.

The closeness characteristic of joy contains no conflict or discord. Rather, there is a sense of harmony and peacefulness. Typically, research partners described this feeling as a vibrant, active harmony between self and other. Note that it is not as if the world were in harmony with us and everything were suddenly going our way. We and the other are in harmony together.

Our transformed way of being in the world includes not only closeness to others but also a sense of being grounded. Being grounded means we feel in touch with things and in firm contact with the other and with the situation at hand. We are rooted in the moment. Maycroff (1971) has created a technical term, "in-place," to describe an aspect of this same phenomenon. He says:

In-place is in contrast with being "out of place." ...Something fundamentally new has occurred in our lives... Place is not something I have, as if it were a possession. Rather I am in-place because of the way I relate to others. And place must be continually renewed and reaffirmed; it is not assured once and for all. (pp. 54-55)

When we are grounded and in-place, all of our senses seem more acute, and we experience space as infinite and full. Our perception of time is similar to our perception of space in that we experience the infinity of the moment and are not

203

aware that time is divided into units or is passing.
Research partners described this experience in
varied ways.

During joy, there's certainly a crack (in time)
in the sense that time seems still for awhile.

My senses just kind of opened up. I paid
attention to the sounds around me, the space
around me. It looked very beautiful, as if
it always was, but I never bothered to pay
attention to it. Then I just started listening
to everything, including my footsteps. The
sensations are different; they're more acute.

I had been looking at everything with new
eyes, at other people, at nature, at people's
faces, at colors. All seemed so striking and
so new. It was a very sensual experience.
Everything struck me sensually - colors, forms,
shapes, things in nature. My senses were
heightened.

I often notice detail a great deal more. I
take pleasure in it, the exquisite detail of
everything. I'm much more aware of the
fantasmagoria of objects around me; they're
just so many. The world's so full. It's just
infinite. Smells are sometimes heightened.
They're not so much heightened as I probably
notice them, whereas I usually ignore them.

Joy is a much more universal experience (than
elation or gladness), infinite, yet somehow
very close, close and infinite. That is,
close in the sense that it's personal, it's
very personal space and friendly. But it's
universal in its extent and depth. I'm very
much aware of looking at the sky, thinking
that it goes on forever. And at the same
time, how things nearest to me, the bushes and
the plants, are very close.

Being grounded also means that our experience
is understood to be a perception of reality, or as

204

one research partner said, "really seeing...the way
things really are." While the level of unreality
and fantasy is metaphorically represented as "up,"
(Lewin, 1935) reality can be metaphorically represented as "being on the ground." The interviews
show that when we feel joyous, we understand our
transformed view of the world to be the real one.
Everything else has been only appearance. Research
partners typically said things such as:

> It was more of a realization that this is
> the real nature.

> I'm still convinced of the accuracy of my
> perception and I think I saw into the true
> nature of the world. This is a strong state-
> ment but I mean it.

Wordsworth (1904) also very clearly describes
this experience:

> While with an eye made quiet by the power
>   Of harmony, and the deep power of joy
>   We see into the life of things. (under-
> lining added)

While I have separated the experience of
closeness and the experience of being grounded for
my own purposes, in the actual experience of joy
they are intertwined. Three research partners'
descriptions of their transformed way of being in
the world illustrate nicely the unitary sense of
closeness and of being grounded.

> Usually there's a veil between me and what-
> ever is seen. For that moment it was as if
> the veil came down and there was nothing
> between me and whatever I saw.

> I felt like embracing the world. The world
> was fine and I was fine, and all had a place.

> I can remember a particular instance of just
> being-in-the-woods. I guess it was just the
> aspect of feeling a sense of harmony, experi-

encing myself <u>in</u> with everything. It just
seemed to fit <u>so</u> nice. I just start feeling
myself in harmony with everything. It feels
so incredibly wonderful. I don't feel it all
the time. I felt in place with it (nature).
I felt <u>totally</u> comfortable there, like <u>being</u>.
It's a <u>feeling</u> of having a perfect relationship,
that you're just understanding <u>how</u> you are a
part of it, and understanding <u>that</u> you are a
part of it in a positive sense. There is
nature and <u>that is me</u>. I am a <u>part of it</u>, and
there is a <u>oneness</u>. Everything working together, beautiful. That would be being in
place, being in harmony.

The Bodily Expression of Joy

The research partners described a variety of
bodily responses during joyous moments, including
sitting quietly, walking around smiling at everyone,
and leaping and dancing. When we feel joyous, it
seems that we do not behave in any single, uniform
way that can be used to identify the emotion joy.
However, the interviews indicate that all the varied
expressive behaviors that we exhibit when joyous
have the meaning of a <u>celebration</u>. We celebrate the
meeting with the other and the resulting feelings of
closeness and affirmation.[10] The joyous feelings
overflow and are made public and celebrated as we
meet the presence of an other. Typically, there is
a desire to embrace others and to include them in
the joy. It is as if we were saying, "Life is good.
This moment is wonderful!"

A description given by one research partner
provides an illustration of such a celebration.
This research partner had spent an evening with
three friends, eating dinner together and then
dancing at a nightclub. She described several
joyous moments that occurred during this evening.
All the friends felt very close to each other.
Their dancing had a quality of celebration. Eventually,

the whole place got into group dancing - a

206

lot of people whom we didn't know, and we
didn't talk to. We just really enjoyed the
idea that there was some unity in a lot of
people dancing together. I felt like there
was a lot of physical contact because we
danced together in large circles. It was
just a really good feeling, not only to feel
so good together but to draw a lot of people
into it.

In this example, the celebration literally made
public the joyous feelings and the sense of affirmation. Several strangers were drawn into the dance
of celebration.

The Function of Joy

Joy plays a very important role in our lives.
All the research partners concurred that it serves
to affirm meaning. Moments of joy do not necessarily answer the question, "What is the meaning
of life?" but they do affirm that there is a meaning.
Furthermore, nothing about the moment seems illusory
or meaningless. Joy is a very solid feeling, unlike
elation. The sense of being grounded highlights the
significance and the "realness" of the moment. We
realize that there is meaning, and this realization
lasts long after the joy is gone. Most of the
research partners said that without experiencing
moments of joy, they could not live.

The affirmation that comes with joy involves
a sense of expansive possibilities. We become
aware of the possibilities of this way of being and
may become aware of possibilities of self-growth
and self-realization arising out of this way of
being.

Three different research partners described
their sense of affirmation as follows:

Here was a sense of everything making sense.
I could think anything I might think of, and
I'd be able to fit it into a framework of
meaning. It was more of a realization that

this is the real nature and a determination
to cut through what's blocking the realization
of the real nature. The real nature of things
is this mysteriousness and the beauty of the
world.

It involved having him confirm my identity.
Do I have a place? A direction? Am I part of
the stream of life or floating in space? He
was confirming something already there. It was
a growing experience, opening me up to relating
to other people. It served to encourage openness, instead of retreat and seclusion.

It was as if I were filled with tremendous
waves of affirmation. "Yes, yes, yes, life is
beautiful. Yes, it's good to be alive, yes."

Discussion

Thus far, we have focused on specifying the
essential structures of elation, gladness and joy.
We can now ask what the results of this analysis
can tell us about some of the more variant features
of these emotions. For example, how is it that for
some persons, feelings of gladness are described as
being very intense and deep, while for others gladness is experienced as more superficial and mundane?
Even the same person can have different experiences
of gladness which vary tremendously in their intensity. Also, how can we account for some persons'
preferring feelings of elation to feelings of joy,
while others prefer joy?

Consider first, the varying intensity of
feelings of gladness. According to the research
partners' descriptions, while feelings of elation
and joy can also vary in intensity, they have much
less extreme range of variability than do feelings
of gladness. The situation and the function of
gladness provide clues that assist in understanding
this extreme variability of intensity. We have
already encountered the explanation that less
intense feelings of gladness seem to be connected
with the fulfillment of small and concrete hopes

208

while more intense feelings seem to be connected with the more symbolic fulfillment of abstract hopes. In addition, since dependency is characteristic of hoping and feeling glad, the value we place on dependency seems to affect the experienced intensity of feelings of gladness.

Given the stress on independence in the Western World and the negative value often placed on dependency, our language may reflect this bias. In support of this, it is notable that there is an inadequate language of dependency in English, whereas in Japanese there are several words related to the Japanese "amae" whose meanings have to do with a positive dependency (Doi, 1973). We can speculate that if our culture made it difficult for us to place a positive value on depending on something other, then feelings of gladness would seldom exist. This occurrence might lead to a situation where the word "gladness" would begin to lose its original meaning, leaving behind only a stylized use of the word in social situations. In fact, the etymology of "gladness" supports the idea of such a transition. At one point in history, "glad" meant something very similar to joy (Onions, 1966). It was a strongly felt emotion. Presently, it can also refer to very low-intensity feelings of being pleased or willing, as in "I'm glad to do it" (Guralnick, 1957); and the earlier meaning of the word seems to be disappearing. This shift in meaning may reflect a shift in the structuring of our experience that is a result of a devaluation of dependency.

The structural descriptions can also assist in understanding persons' preferences for one emotion over another. The research partners frequently reported preferring one emotion to another, and even sometimes reported shying away from certain of these emotions.

According to the analysis of elation, in order to feel elated, it is essential that we believe in the realization of fantasy. Persons who enjoy fantasizing seem fully to enjoy feelings of elation.

209

In contrast, persons who place a negative value on fantasies or who are afraid of them do not always welcome or prefer the feeling of elation. For example, some research partners who preferred joy to elation reported being afraid to dream of positive things, thinking that then such dreams would never come true. Others feared the intensity of fantasies colored by anger or hatefulness and defensively avoided fantasy altogether. They also found the "out-of-touchness" that is part of fantasizing and experiencing elation to be an uncomfortable or even a frightening experience. Ironically, these reasons for shying away from feelings of elation include fears based on misconceptions. Elation can actually serve to further the realization of our wishes; reveling in fantasies of positive happenings does not necessarily open a Pandora's box of hateful and angry fantasies.

Based on the analysis of joy, we can see that persons who prefer joy to elation seem to prefer to remain in touch with reality and desire the affirmation and closeness that come with joy. Those who avoid feeling joyous seem to be more frightened of intimacy. There may also be a fear of fusion with an other and a resulting loss of self. Or, persons may avoid closeness with others to avoid the pain which they think will accompany the loss of such closeness. Again, these fears are ironically based on misconceptions. Moments of joy do not involve a fusion with the other, and the conclusion of a joyous encounter seems to be more affirmative than painful.

The above discussion illustrates how the structural descriptions can assist in understanding the various ways in which elation, gladness and joy can have an impact on our lives. Understanding the structures of these emotions provides a guide to personal experiences that may be helpful in revealing personality differences. In a therapeutic setting, it may be useful in exposing misconceptions and sensitizing persons to positive, new experiences.

The Second Study

The descriptions of elation, gladness, and joy just presented were developed to describe the essential structures of experiences of each of these emotions. Attainment of this goal obviously necessitates demonstrating the intersubjective validity of these descriptions.

To some degree the validity of the structural descriptions was confirmed during the first study. In the early part of the study, the research partners participated in the formation of the structural descriptions. Toward the end of the study, when the descriptions were for the most part completed, I judged that the descriptions captured the essence of the research partners' experiences, and several research partners confirmed this judgment when they expressed surprise at the accuracy of these descriptions. Additionally, when asked, these research partners could not think of any experience of these emotions which did not fit the structural descriptions. Nevertheless, the degree of validation obtained in the first study is debatable. Perhaps as I became attached to some of the ideas in the descriptions, I inadvertently led others in the first study to interpret their experiences in terms of these ideas. Or, perhaps the research partners were fooling themselves and simply trying to please me, the researcher.

In an attempt to minimize some of the problems encountered in the first study when the validity of the descriptions was tested, a second study was designed to test the validity of the statements in a more rigorous and formalized manner. The purpose of this second study was to determine whether the structural descriptions standing alone, without further interpretation, could be understood and whether research partners could match these structural descriptions with their experiences. The second study also provided more information about the three emotions.

The method that was used in the second study is

211

a development of the method of conceptual encounter which incorporates some of the characteristics of the experimental method. Research partners were asked to describe two specific experiences of elation, gladness or joy. They were then shown several sets of statements consisting of three descriptive statements each. For each specific experience, they were asked if they could select the one statement from each set which most accurately described the experience. They were also given the option of reporting that none of the statements described the specific experience, if this was the case.

Giving the research partners the task of selecting statements that describe their experiences creates results that are measurable in an objective and quantifiable manner and extends the method of conceptual encounter. It permits the use of statistical analysis in order to help determine whether the statements are a valid description of persons' experiences.

The Method of the Second Study

Research Partners

Twelve persons volunteered to participate in the second study as research partners. They learned about the study through posted advertisements or word of mouth and were not paid for their participation. These research partners ranged in age from 20 to 35; five were male and seven were female. None of them had any knowledge of the first study.

Materials

The structural descriptions of elation, gladness, and joy previously presented in this chapter were given to the research partners in summary form. These summaries were brief and contained no illustrations.

For each emotion, the summary description was divided into statements describing the situation,

the transformation and the function.[11] Thus, there
was a total of nine statements. These statements
were arranged in three sets consisting of three
statements each. The first set contained the statements describing the situations of elation, gladness,
and joy. The second set contained the statements
describing the transformations; and the third set
contained the function statements.

Procedure

        Each of the research partners participated in
an individual interview. In contrast to the more
open-ended style of interviewing employed in the
first study, the interviews in the second study
followed a pre-set script. This script dictated
all of the instructions and responses that I, as
the researcher, gave; and it was followed rigidly
in order to avoid leading the research partners to
interpret or structure their experiences in any
special ways.

        In the first phase of the interviews all
research partners were asked to describe specific
experiences of two of the three emotions of interest here. Four described experiences of elation
and gladness, four described experiences of elation
and joy, and four described experiences of gladness
and joy. Research partners were encouraged to talk
for 20 to 30 minutes about each experience. Following the description of each experience, the
researcher asked, "What were the most important
things about this experience that made it an
experience of elation (or gladness or joy) and not
something else?" The researcher then asked the
research partners to tell more about each thing
that they listed and to explain what meaning these
things had for them.

        In the last phase of the interviews, the
research partners were asked to read the nine
statements being tested. They were told that the
researcher wanted their opinions of these statements. They were informed that the statements
might or might not apply to their experiences and

213

that several probably needed revising. For each
experience described, the research partners were
asked to review the three sets of statements describing elation, gladness, and joy and to select
the one statement from each set which most accurately described that experience. In other words,
they were asked to select a situation statement, a
transformation statement, and a function statement
for each experience. Each research partner made
selections for two specific experiences. They were
allowed to select the same statement to describe two
different experiences or to report that none of the
statements described an experience, if either of
these was the case. It was emphasized that a
selection was to be made only if the entire statement applied to the experience and made sense of it.
After each selection, the research partners were
asked to explain why they made the selection which
they did and to comment on the accuracy of the
statements.

The Results of the Second Study

The research partners' selection of statements
created a series of matches between specific
experiences and selected statements. These matches
were analyzed both statistically and qualitatively.

It was expected that the research partners
would match the three statements describing elation
with their experiences of elation, the three
statements describing gladness with their experiences of gladness, and the three statements describing joy with their experiences of joy. Overall,
the matches made conformed well to this expected
pattern of matches. The specific matches made by
the research partners are summarized in Table 1.
For the eight research partners who described
experiences of elation, two-thirds of the statements
selected to describe their experiences were the
statements describing the situation, the transformation, and the function of elation. Similarly, for
experiences of gladness, two-thirds of the statements selected were the statements describing the
different aspects of gladness. For experiences of

214

joy, three-fourths of the statements selected were the statements describing the different aspects of joy. Overall, most of the unexpected matches involved the function statements. Most of the research partners expressed surprise at the accuracy of the descriptions.

An exact randomization test, similar to those described by Edgington (1964), was used to determine if the pattern of matches obtained could have resulted from chance selections of statements.[12] First, the overall pattern of matches created when the research partners selected situation statements to describe their experiences of elation, gladness, and joy was examined. Considering all of the emotions at once, the pattern obtained was found to be significant, as the probability of obtaining such a pattern of matches, or one more closely approximating the expected pattern, was .006. Likewise, the overall pattern of matches created when the research partners selected transformation statements to describe their experiences of the three emotions was examined and was found to be significant (p = .002). The pattern of matches made with the function statements was also found to be significant (p = .032).

Using the exact randomization test, it was possible to refine further the analysis of the results in order to determine the significance of the pattern of matches created when the research partners selected statements from one specific set of statements (e.g., the situation statements) to describe one particular emotional experience (e.g., elation). The following matches were all found to be significant at the .06 level or less -- experiences of elation matches with the situation statement, experiences of joy matched with the situation statement, experiences of elation matched with the transformation statement, experiences of gladness matched with the transformation statement, experiences of joy matched with the transformation statement, and experiences of joy matched with the function statement. Three matches were found not to be statistically significant -- experiences of

215

gladness matched with the situation statement, and experiences of elation matched with the function statement.

A qualitative analysis of the research partners' explanations of why they made their selections as they did suggested that the non-significance of the pattern of matches between the experiences of gladness and the situation statement reflected an unrelability in the use of the word "glad." The results would most likely be significant with a larger n.

While the overall pattern of matches with the function statements was significant, there were strong indications that the non-significance of the matches between the specific experiences of elation and gladness and the respective function statements reflected the inadequacy of these two function statements. These statements seemed to be fair descriptions of the two functions, but they did not accurately capture the essence of each function.

Since the elation and gladness function statements were found to be inadequate, all research partners' descriptions of these emotions were examined and analyzed. New descriptions of the functions of these emotions were developed. The descriptions which were presented earlier in this chapter are these revised descriptions. These descriptions appear to capture more adequately the essence of the function of each emotion, although the validity of these new descriptions has not yet been tested.

Discussion

The results of this second study demonstrate that research partners can match most of the descriptions of the different aspects of elation, gladness, and joy presented in this chapter with their personal experiences of such emotions in a consensual manner. Persons have judged most parts of these descriptions to be accurate and inform- ative, and such a judgment is one confirmation of the validity of these descriptions.

Table 1

Summary of the number of matches made with the nine statements
and probabilities that these matches were due to chance

	Joy Situation Statement	Elation Situation Statement	Gladness Situation Statement	Specific Exact Randomization Test Probability	Overall Exact Randomization Test Probability
Experiences of Joy	6	0	2	.06	
Experiences of Elation	1	6	1	.015	.006
Experiences of Gladness	2	0	6	.11	

Table 1
(continued)

	Joy Trans- formation Statement	Elation Trans- formation Statement	Gladness Trans- formation Statement	No state- ment	Specific Exact Randomi- zation Test Probability	Overall Exact Randomi- zation Test Probability
Experiences of Joy	6	2	0	0	.03	
Experiences of Elation	1	6	0	1	.06	.002
Experiences of Gladness	1	0	6	1	.015	

Table 1
(continued)

	Joy Function Statement	Elation Function Statement	Gladness Function Statement	No statement	Specific Exact Randomization Test Probability	Overall Exact Randomization Test Probability
Experiences of Joy	6	0	1	1	.06	
Experiences of Elation	1	4	2	1	.18	.032
Experiences of Gladness	2	1	4	1	.10	

Reference Notes
for Chapter IV

1. See Lindsay (1975) for a more detailed description of the method.

2. This technique was originally introduced by Husserl (1962) and has been developed by de Rivera (1977).

3. In the English translation, the experience described is labeled "joy." Sartre's analysis is included in this section on elation because it clearly relates to the structural description of elation and clearly does not relate to the structural description of joy yet to be presented. Since Sartre was writing in French, he probably used the French word "joie," which was translated as "joy." One cannot assume that the word "joie" means the same thing in French that "joy" does in English. In support of this assumption, the English word "elation" is often translated as "joie." Thus, "elation" and "joy" do not appear to have any one-to-one translations into French. In this case Sartre's example would have been more accurately rendered had the translation used the word elated.

4. It is this sentence in particular, describing the man's distance from the woman, which indicates that this example clearly does not relate to the description of joyous phenomena presented here.

5. See Heider (1958) for an analysis of the relation between the concepts "can," "try" and "success." According to his analysis, if we see that we are able to do something and wish to succeed, then we are free to commit ourselves to trying to do what we wish.

6. I am indebted for this example to Iris Abrams, who conducted an unpublished study of dependency as a project for Dr. Tamara Dembo at Clark University.

221

7. The word "glad" originally meant bright, shining (Onions, 1966; Shipley, 1945). To gladden something was to brighten it. Only gradually has the meaning shifted to refer to a feeling of a person.

8. This term is used in the same sense that Martin Buber (1970) uses it in his book I and Thou.

9. See Chapter VI for a description of the three basic types of psychological distance.

10. See the following section, The Function of Joy, for a description of the sense of affirmation characteristic of joy.

11. See Lindsay (1975) for a more detailed description of the method. The descriptions of bodily expression were not tested as they were not completed at the time the second study was conducted.

12. See Lindsay (1975) for a more detailed description of the statistical analysis.

References
for Chapter IV

Abrams, I. A study of dependency. Unpublished
    study conducted for Dr. Tamara Dembo, 1973.
    Available from Dr. Tamara Dembo, Clark
    University, Worcester, Massachusetts.

Buber, M. I and thou. New York: Scribner's, 1970.

de Rivera, J. A structural theory of the emotions.
    Psychological Issues, X (4), Monograph 40,
    1977.

Edgington, E. S. Randomization tests. The Journal
    of Psychology, 57: 445-449, 1964.

Heider, F. The psychology of interpersonal rela-
    tions. New York: Wiley and Sons, 1958.

Husserl, E. Ideas. New York: Macmillan, 1962.

Joyce, J. A portrait of the artist as a young man.
    New York: Viking Press, 1964.

Lau, J. A phenomenological investigation of a group
    of positive emotions. Unpublished Master's
    Thesis, Clark University, Worcester, Massachu-
    setts, 1974.

Lewin, K. A dynamic theory of personality. New
    York: McGraw-Hill, 1935.

Lindsay, J. A phenomenological investigation of
    elation, gladness and joy. Unpublished Master's
    Thesis, Clark University, Worcester, Massachu-
    setts, 1975.

Marcel, G. Desire and hope. In N. Lawrence and D.
    O'Connor (Eds.), Readings in existential
    phenomenology. Englewood Cliffs, New Jersey:
    Prentice-Hall, 1967.

Mayeroff, M. On caring. New York: Harper and Row,
    1971.

Onions, C. T. (Ed.) The Oxford dictionary of
     English etymology. Oxford: The Clarendon
     Press, 1966.

Sartre, J. P. Sketch for a theory of the emotions.
     London: Methuen, 1962.

Shipley, J. T. Dictionary of word origins. New
     York: Philosophical Library, 1945.

Wordsworth, W. The complete poetical works of
     William Wordsworth. New York: Houghton-
     Mifflin, 1904.

V

LAUGHTER

Joel Funk

"If there were no laughter,
the Tao would not be what it is"
-- Lao Tzu

It seems odd indeed that of all possible human
qualities and capacities, Lao Tzu chose something
as ordinary as laughter to indicate the essential
nature of the Tao. I will endeavor to show, however,
that Lao Tzu's comments are not as odd as might
appear. As we shall see, laughter shares certain
commonalities with both the extreme highs and lows
of experience: satori (liberation in Zen terminology)
and schizophrenia. Furthermore, a fuller understanding of laughter will radically alter our apprehension
of the entire scope of human existence, high, low,
and ordinary. Here is another, perhaps more mundane
puzzle: look closely at the bodily movements that
accompany a good belly laugh. Is there any sense to
the bizarre facial expressions, the raucous peals of
noise, the aimless rocking back and forth of the
solar plexus? Their meaning is certainly far less
obvious than the more transparent expressive movements of, say, anger.[1]

Despite this elusive quality of laughter, there
are some theorists who maintain that laughter is
simply the outward expression of certain emotions,
or combinations of emotions (Keith-Spiegel, 1972).
It is my contention that laughter is not reducible
to emotions and that it is a distinct affective
behavior, deserving of analysis in its own right.

225

Laughter structures our mode of being-in-the world
in a unique manner; it transforms our world quite
differently than does any other affect.

The structure of laughter can be revealed
through the process of conceptual encounter. Now
the methodology used in this study was rather unusual
in several ways. First, I did not engage in extensive interviewing as a first step towards elucidat-
ing the underlying structure of laughter. Rather, I
focused intensively on one personal example,
employing conceptual encounter as a form of inner
dialogue between concept and experience. After I
had intuited a tentative structure based on this
example, I extended my investigation by examining
numerous other occasions of laughter, some again
based on personal experience, some observed, some
obtained through interviews, a few gleaned from
cases presented in the literature. The initially
formulated structure was thus checked against other
experiences for goodness of fit and to some degree
modified.

Second, I did not, as in classical phenomenology, base my analysis solely on the things themselves, i.e., concrete experience. Indeed, I admit
to building on the theories of Koestler (1964),
Plessner (1970), Piaget (Flavell, 1963), and others.
In conceptual encounter the important issue is not
the starting point but the fact of dialogue between
the conceptual and the experiential.

Finally, I did not restrict my data to verbal
report. Given the aforementioned riddle of
laughter's unique mode of bodily expression, the
nonverbal aspects of laughter were deemed too
crucial to omit (Plessner, 1970).

I would like to share with the reader my personal conceptual encounter with laughter. I will
then test the analysis by examining its usefulness
in accounting for any laughter situation. Towards
this end, I will discuss eight fundamentally distinct categories of laughter, pointing out the
underlying unity structuring each, as well as the

subtle yet important differences among the numerous
varieties. Finally, the relationship between laughing and crying will be explored briefly.

I

Let me now present my example, in my own words,
just as if I were being interviewed by another
person. Although in some sense every case is unique,
this example should reflect the essential structures
that underly all laughter experiences. Though
particular, it is also universal.

The incident was a rather simple event, a
funny face made inadvertently by my wife:

My wife and I went to a party at a friend's
house one Saturday night and, as it turned out,
there were not many people there whom I knew.
After an hour or so of the usual party banter,
I felt somewhat bored; the situation was com-
pounded by the fact that there was a piano in
the other room, simply begging to be played.
As I am almost always in the mood for impro-
vising I casually sat down and played -- for
almost two hours! The prospect of talk seemed
dull in contrast to the near-ecstasy of musical
expression, yet I felt that, after all, I
should return to the party. Reluctantly I went
into the living room and tried to find some
conversation to participate in. As I glanced
around the room I noticed my wife smiling,
perhaps out of politeness to whomever she was
talking to. It struck me that this was not her
ordinary smile; there was something odd about
it. Almost immediately a new meaning had
appeared in her smile; I realized (without
actually thinking so in words) that her facial
expression was identical to a smile I had seen
as a boy in an old Mad Comic! The cartoon face
in question belonged to a character named
Batboy, a spoof of Batman I think, drawn as a
short, tough, impish looking figure. It was
most probably the exaggerated smugness and
impishness of Batboy's face that allowed me to

227

remember it after so many years. And just then and there, for a moment, my wife had unknowingly captured this same odd expression in her smile!

I realized all this in a flash. I did not have to think about or imagine Batboy as a separate entity. No, I simply recognized (re-cognized) all at once the Batboyness of my wife's expression, at the same time being aware that she was of course simply my wife smiling at a party.

At the point where this double meaning was appreciated, I began to laugh, although not for more than a second or two. I remember really enjoying this newfound relationship and I teased my wife about it afterwards. Anyway, after laughing briefly I noticed that her expression had changed; Batboy was no more and the whole incident would have passed, except that something new had been created and added to my world, something enjoyable, laughable.

We can now examine this simply example in detail, attempting to grasp the four parts of the structure of laughter embodied in this case: the conditions for the appearance of the laughter, the instructional transformation involved, the means of executing this transformation, and the function served by the laughter (as described in de Rivera's chapter on Anger, this volume). Keep in mind that these four aspects are only artificially segregated; they implicate each other and should not be seen as links in a causal chain.

Conditions for the Appearance of Laughter

It is unanimously agreed in the literature that the condition for laughter involves some sort of paradox, incongruity, collision of ideas, or ambibuity (Wilson, 1979). It is also clear that some such incongruity exists in the example just presented. But consider: the resemblance of my wife

228

to a cartoon character is not in itself necessarily laughable. In fact, it might more likely be considered shocking! Laughter then must involve more than the noting of an incongruity.

What else is required? Note that one meaning, my wife as a woman smiling, is appropriate to one's normal expectations about the world; the second meaning, my wife as an exaggeratedly smug "Batboy" is, in contrast, inappropriate. In scientific theorizing, there is a similar collision of frames of reference, only there both meanings are appropriate (Koestler, 1964). Thus an incongruous conjunction produces laughter, which is why new scientific inventions, like Fulton's steamboat are often derided at first.[2]

The one who laughs has no appropriate cognitive framework to give sense to the laughable event. The situation is, as Plessner (1970) puts it "unanswerable," yet, the need to answer the situation is still present, for one's reality has been challenged. I could not accept my wife as Batboy, nor could I reject the resemblance, since it was manifestly there; nor could I dismiss the whole matter. In short, I was in a situation which demanded a response while simultaneously prohibiting any normally effective means of response!

The paradoxical nature of the laughable event has much in common with the Zen Koan (riddle) and the double-bind, thought to be a cause of schizophrenia (Watts, 1961; Bateson, 1972). Instead of going crazy, fortunately, I took an alternative route, one strangely reminiscent of the satori experience that liberates the Zen adept from the koan.

The Instructional Transformation of Laughter

Is there then some way out of the impossible situation just described? Several "second order" responses or "meta-responses" can be imagined, all of them operating by moving to a higher level than the one in which the paradox has been posed. If

the condition for laughter is unanswerable paradox,
the instructional transformation may well be to
answer anyway (!) by disengaging or "leaving the
field."

One might do this, first of all, by trying to
be scientific and objective, stepping back,
"accommodating one's schemes" to include the new
incongruity.[3] I might have chosen this avenue,
telling myself in effect, "Apparently then my wife
does resemble a smug, impish cartoon character.
So be it." This rather detached solution was hardly
likely, for mixing the human with the fictional this
way is simply too threatening to one's existence.
I recall one episode late at night when a roommate
of mine did begin to take on a cartoon-like quality
and it was a terrifying, not a laughable experience.

Another option, mentioned above, would be to
go crazy or at least fall prey to panic and confusion (see Goodman's analysis in chapter III).
Perhaps this is the solution "chosen" by the schiso-
phrenic caught in the double-bind. While this is
hardly a satisfactory choice it is a possible one
and it is of interest that in my example I did not
go crazy! The feeling of going mad did perhaps
begin to encroach on me in the instance with my
roommate. Yet, with my wife I merely laughed.

A third meta-response might be to break down
and cry. I will return to this solution later, but
I should note that this was indeed present as an
option. When I was about eleven, a friend of mine
pointed to a rather funny looking boy in the schoolyard and commented that he looked like a cartoon
character. I remember feeling rather sad for this
boy, although I did not actually cry.

The three meta-responses above share the
quality of accepting the situation as presented,
i.e., as serious and demanding a serious response,
some drastic accommodation perhaps. A fourth
possibility exists, however, which operates by a
totally different process. In laughter, the
instructional transformation is to deflate the

seriousness of the situation as presented. In other words, in perceiving a situation as laughable, one is perceiving it as not needing to be dealt with at all. Not only can one do nothing in response, one need do nothing; the paradox evaporates.

What allows a person to choose this particular instructional transformation, given a paradoxical situation or event? What was it about the wife/Batboy resemblance that allowed laughter to ensue rather than one of the other three solutions?

1. <u>Transience</u>. My wife's resembling a cartoon character was perceived by me as a passing relationship; I fully expected that in a moment she would appear as her usual self again. This was not the case for the funny looking boy in the schoolyard, whose comical appearance was essentially permanent. Another example: when watching the Roadrunner cartoons, we laugh because although the coyote falls on a cliff in scene one, he is back in one piece in scene two. Thus impermanence is one guarantee that the situation need not be dealt with.

2. <u>Insignificance</u>. Even when a situation is permanent, it can still be laughable if it is insignificant, non-threatening to one's world. If the inappropriateness observed involves only a minor part of an otherwise sound appearance or personality, one can treat it as not serious. Even if my wife did permanently have a Batboylike impishness, this would not have been cause for alarm. Such a "defect," if it sould be so labeled, might even make her more endearing. When my roommate began to look cartoony, however, it seemed to involve his entire being; he seemed like a three-dimensional puppet, something out of Disneyland. This was not an insignificant incongruity and was therefore not laughable.

3. <u>Dehumanization</u>. A third, less attractive possibility exists. One can still choose to see the situation as laughable even where the inappropriate element is both permanent and significant, but only, I feel, at the cost of distancing or dehumanizing

231

the other (see Kreilkamp, chapter VI). When children make fun of a stutterer, for example, they are failing to appreciate the difficulties this affliction imposes and are thus treating stuttering as if it were of the same nature as a minor or transient defect. Thus one can laugh at another by not viewing them in their full humanness.

In all three perceptions what is crucial is that, at least in the eyes of the laugher, the consequences of the incongruity or inappropriateness are, well, inconsequential!

The Means of Transformation in Laughter

Thus far, I have been treating the laughter rather casually. Laughter seems like an ordinary, nay, simple technique for getting out of otherwise impossible situations. When we examine the "how" of laughter, the means of executing the simple transformation described above, it becomes clear that matters are no longer so simple. For it is in its particular means of transformation that the uniqueness of laughter is revealed.

A full analysis of the means of transformation of laughter requires examining it from four mutually related perspectives (van den Berg, 1972): the relationship between the experiencing subject (or self) and the world, the relationship between the self and time, the relationship between the self and the body, and the relationship between the self and others. Of course, we would expect that all four relationships would be structurally homologous. For example, in depression the world is heavy, gray, and featureless, time is slow, ponderous, and unchanging, social relationships are unenjoyable and avoided, and the body slumps lethargically.

Self and World

What is so unique about the means by which laughter fulfills the instruction to "not take events as serious?" To jump ahead a bit, laughter succeeds through a type of "levitation" -- no levity

232

intended! In order to understand levitation and
levity, it is useful to first comprehend its
opposite: gravity. The term "gravity" has an
everyday usage not unlike its use here, but we
will employ it in a more rigorously defined sense.

It is an established dictum that people maintain a more or less stable conception of the world
(Berger and Luckmann, 1966; Flavell, 1963). Despite
varying contents, every culture and every individual
has some sense of normality against which all events
are weighed. Analogous to the feeling of physical
gravity, ever present yet rarely noticed directly,
I believe it is fruitful to speak of a "psychological gravity" attached to all events in one's
world. Just as gravity represents a relationship
between earth and another body, psychological gravity
can be considered a relationship between some event
or idea and the structures (or "schemata" in Piaget's
terminology) of one's normal psychological world.
If this gravity is rarely noticed, it is most
probably due to its obviousness. Only when our
equilibrium is severely disturbed, i.e., when events
are of high gravity, are we usually aware of the
"gravitational relationship" that exists between
world and event.

Now, there is undoubtedly a sense of normal
gravity attached to most everyday experiences. That
someone wrote this paper is a fact of normal gravity
-- it fit's one's ideas about the nature of human
beings. In Piaget's language, one can easily
assimilate this fact. If the reader were told, however, that this essay was produced by a computer or
an ape pecking randomly at a typewriter, this would
immediately be of high gravity; it would challenge
your whole notion of the way things are. Or, you
might assume (correctly) that I was joking; you
would treat my statement about the origins of this
paper as if it were of low gravity.

To return to my example, in laughing I was
treating my wife's resemblance to Batboy as a low
gravity event, presumably due to its transience and
insignificance. But what was the fate of this

laughable incongruity? It did not simply pass away; if it was neither accepted nor rejected, neither assimilated nor accomodated to, what did I do with it?

It seems fruitful to conceive of this and all laughable incongruities as removed somehow from one's normal gravity world, as being levitated to an entirely separate region of the world, a region of low gravity.[4] Applying this idea to my example may clarify it. My wife's resembling a cartoon character, if taken as a normal or high gravity event, would most likely have been shocking, not laughable. In laughing, though, I was indicating that the relationship was of low gravity, that it belonged to a region outside my normal gravity world. I would most certainly have chosen to construe the situation quite differently had I discovered, say, a facial scar.

The logic of the low gravity region is distinct from the logic of the normal. For example, it makes normal gravity sense to state that members of the same class, e.g. people, can share similar properties. My wife resembling her sister is not particularly laughable. My wife resembling an extremely smug cartoon character, i.e., revealing a property that does not belong to the class "normal people's qualities," is laughable. What then occurred when I laughed? Rather than revising my rules of logic (accommodating), I applied a special subset of rules to the situation. In low gravity logic it is possible for a person to exhibit the exaggerated properties of a cartoon character. In short, the essential logic of the low gravity region is paradox; this is why we can assimilate apparently impossible situations through laughter. They are impossible only from the standpoint of normal gravity logic. Thus, in laughing, we are liberated from paradox by levitating above paradox, to a region of experience in which paradox itself is the ruling logic![5] And, as should by now be clear, it takes the complexity of human being-in-the-world, to inhabit such a region. The simple solution "it need not be dealt with" is not so simple after all!

Note: low gravity does not mean no gravity. I did not dismiss my wife's resemblance to Batboy as some error; rather it was assimilated, accepted as fact, but with conditions namely that the resemblance has only a limited validity, such that it does not interfere with my normal gravity conceptions of my wife.

To sum up: laughter is unique in that it is the only response to events that does not meet the situation head on, but rather undermines it.[6] All other affective and cognitive transformations operate within normal (or high) gravity region(s), betraying some involvement within the boundaries of the situation as given. Laughter, however, indicates that a person has stepped outside the bounds, by means of what I have called levitation. As Plessner (1970) put it, while emotions are responses within a situation, laughter is directed to a situation, meaning that one is already outside it. In an odd way, laughter, like grace, allows a person to be in the world, but not of it! As Herman Hesse observed, "To live in the world as though it were not the world...it is in the power of humor alone to make efficacious" (Hesse, 1963, p. 65). In levitation one is in the world (of normal gravity) but is momentarily not of it, having abandoned it through levitation. Were it not for the power of humor, all paradoxes and incongruities would immediately be construed as having high gravity, requiring drastic accommodations of the schemata that constitute the normal.

The levitation of laughter is akin to the liberation in Zen. Watts (1961) describes a typical scenario in which Master double-binds student. The student is told that he will be hit with a stick if he says something and he will likewise be hit with the same stick if he says nothing. In this damned if you do, damned if you don't situation, the student is likely to suffer many a sore shoulder until he finally becomes liberated enough to step outside the bounds as given by the Master and simply reach up and grab the stick!

235

Thus both laughter and liberation employ dialectical logic, i.e., they negate both A and not-A by forming a higher synthesis. In laughter one neither accepts nor rejects outright; instead one assimilates the incongruity using the paradoxical logic of the low gravity region.[7] Even schizophrenia may be seen as a largely unsuccessful attempt at solving the impossible by moving to a new level. Trapped by contradictions in the social nexus, many schizophrenics leave the field, by withdrawal, delusion, ideas of reference, etc., as a means of avoiding an insoluble dilemma altogether (Laing and Esterson, 1970). Seen thus, schizophrenia is transcendence failed.

Let us take a closer look at the concept of levitation. The word used to designate anti-gravity, in the physical sense, is levity, as in levitation. But levity also connotes laughter and mirth, metaphorically. In a children's book, The Light Princess (MacDonald, 1962), a princess who weighed less than air had to be tied down to keep from floating away. While in this state of levity she could not take anything seriously, laughing at the most pitiable sights. Only when she cries does she return to earth and normal gravity!

This story suggests a limitation of my formulation, in that I have described laughter exclusively in the negative, as a denial of gravity, whereas it could be viewed more positively, as a positive expression of the force of levity. After all, there is something quite enjoyable aobut setting aside the normal rules of logic and exploring a region which has greater flexibility. How else explain the universal appeal of jokes, play, and the ubiquitious pie-in-the-face? Is laughter always merely a release, a sort of noisy sign of relief? It is probable that people often find themselves in a light, i.e., low gravity, mood, much like the princess, searching for or receptive to novel situations. Incongruities thus encountered already possess low gravity. The success of a good comedy is based to a large degree on the ability of the plot and characters to maintain this attitude in

the audience, even when nothing particularly funny
is happening. Thus, there appears to be an energiz-
ing factor to levitation; all the conditions for
laughter can be present, but if sufficient energy
to break the gravity barrier is not present, one
will only nod in amusement, not laugh. Conversely,
as we shall see later, sometimes the energy of
levitation alone is sufficient for laughter, even
when nothing especially funny has transpired.

Self and Time

    The transition from normal to low gravity and
back again is reflected in the unique temporal
character of laughter. Just as we possess a set of
mental structures that constitute our normal world,
we also have a normal experience of time, although
obviously the nature of this experience may vary
widely among cultures. Before laughing at my wife's
smile, for example, I had been "flowing along with
the present in my own private world." As events
moved along, I moved along with them.

    This normal flow was disrupted when I stopped
playing the piano, rejoined others and had to
adjust my private reality to accommodate others.
When the resemblance to Batboy was noted I was
stopped short by the incongruity of this event.[8]
Time felt blocked -- I seemed unable to move on
temporally. While laughing I was stuck at one point
in time, the point at which I had chosen to construe
the incongruity as being of low gravity. In G.
Stanley Hall's phrase (Hall and Allin, 1897), I was
"transfixed on the point of the jest," transfixed
in the immediate past. Thus, in addition to breaking the normal relationship to the world, laughter
breaks one's relationship to ongoing time.

    This feeling of being transfixed should not
be conceptualized as statis; it is still dynamic
in nature, although in an unusual way. While,
temporally speaking, I appeared to be stationary,
I was moving, but moving in place. To give an
analogy: the blocking of time by an incongruity is
like the sudden braking of a car at high speed. The

237

car will stall unless the clutch is depressed, thus
disengaging the engine from the gears. If the
clutch is depressed, the engine will keep rocking
until the proper gear is re-engaged. Laughter is
the clutch that disengages one from the flow of time.
Although no forward movement in time (or in space)
is possible during laughter, laughter is a form of
stationary movement, like the rocking of the car
engine, which allows the possibility of continued
movement one back in gear.

The timelessness of laughter has been compared
to the eternity of the mystic. As Hesse wrote
(1963, p. 244):

Seriousness...is an accident of time...In
eternity, however, there is no time...Eternity
is a mere moment, just long enough for a joke.

Self and Body

The stationary movement in time mentioned
above is reflected in the curious bodily expression
of laughter. As mentioned at the start, the facial
and bodily convulsions of laughter appear quite
senseless. Whereas the assertiveness of anger is
stamped in its mode of expression -- the clenched
fist, loud voice, red face -- the movements of
laughter seem unintelligible. There appears to be
no purpose or goal-direction in the expressive movements of laughter, yet laughter surely serves some
function for the self. Once again an examination
of the normal relation of self to body will be
helpful in comprehending its disturbance by laughter.

Normally a person responds through the body to
effect some change in the world. This may take the
course of action of will, or the course of passion,
i.e., emotion, which seems to emerge from beyond the
will. In addition to producing changes in the
world, many emotions effect changes in the self
(de Rivera, 1977). When I laughed at my wife's
smile, I in essence chose not to change either my
world or myself. In other words, laughter is an
abdication of the use of the body, a temporary

238

letting go of the body as an instrument of change.
Note: letting go does not mean doing nothing at all;
if that were the case, we would expect no bodily
response at all, clearly not the case in laughter.

Faced with the potential shock of my wife looking like a cartoon character, I no doubt prepared to
mobilize will or emotion. By laughing, however, I
was releasing myself from the need to effect change.
In other words, laughter indicates (as we have seen)
that one does not have to do anything since the
potentially disrupting event has been assimilated
into the low gravity region. This state of pre-
paredness must be released, though, and, in keeping
with the discontinuous nature of laughter (as a
sudden breaking of normal gravity and time), it is
released suddenly.

The peculiar rocking movement of laughter and
the vulnerable position displayed by the laugher,
i.e., head thrown back, person buffeted about help-
lessly, are the bodily echo of this letting go of
the readiness to act. The diaphragmatic movements
in particular are analogous to the movements of a
spring when pulled beyond its resting point. When
let go suddenly, the built up tension does not
simply restore the spring to the initial resting
position but overshoots it. The spring begins
oscillating back and forth until damped out by
internal friction. The short "ha" bursts of
laughter represent the dominant expiratory or outward phase of the oscillation, which alternates
with the silent inward phase. The stomach area as
the "center of gravity" of the person (Durckheim,
1962) is the suitable locus for expressing a
complete letting go.

Thus, the lack of apparent goal, the diffuse-
ness, and the opacity of laughter are precisely
what are essential to its meaning. In their
apparent functionlessness, they indicate that the
person has relinquished his hold over the body as
a means to change the world. Although the person
appears to be helpless (and is momentarily), he
is, by his very willingness to lay down arms,

asserting himself (or at least preserving himself).
That is, laughter can be seen as a controlled loss
of control (see Plessner, 1970).

Thus far we have described the expressive form
of laughter as a negation of will and emotion. But
laughter itself is a positive behavior, and we
would like to ascertain precisely what it indicates
about what one is doing. If laughter is not goal-
directed, it can be viewed as consumatory. The
(belly) laugh can be considered a form of digestion,
in which an object is torn apart and resynthesized.
This is exactly what laughter does in restructuring
an event so that it subsequently belongs to a different level of gravity![9] In doing nothing actively,
laughter is still doing something for the person,
in reorganizing that person's world.

What of the fact that laughter is audible,
that it peals explosively for all to hear? Undoubtedly the cause is social; we almost always
laugh in groups, and even when alone the norms of
our reference group are still present. As has been
noted,[10] laughter is a means of reinforcing group
ties, strengthening group agreement on what is
acceptable and what is not. The need for social
verification, then, is probably one root of laughter.

Self and Others

By now the reader may well anticipate the
analysis from this final vantage point. Along with
a normal world, normal time, and normal use of the
body, there is a relationship to others that can be
labeled normal. Actually all four normal relationships are one and the same, for our basic notions
of reality are socially constructed (Berger and
Luckmann, 1966). Thus even to have a normal gravity
world is simply another way of stating that one
belongs to some group(s) to which one refers one's
norms. As members of a group we expect that others
will share the same beliefs and structures that
constitute our own world. Anger, for example,
insists that the other obey a suprapersonal "ought"
applicable to all members of the group.

240

Numerous theories explain the interpersonal relationships in laughter, usually seeing them as manifestations of aggression, sueriority, or surprisingly, sympathy (Keith-Spiegel, 1972). As suggestive as these views are, I feel that a more fruitful concept is that of identification, which can solve the mystery of why laughter can be both aggressive and sympathetic!

Briefly, identification means that two people are fused; what the other experiences is taken to be a part of one's own experience, and one's own experience is taken as belonging also to the other (Scheler, 1970). This is not the same as sympathy, which requires a degree of distance between self and other. Identification signifies precisely a lack of distance and thus precludes sympathy.

Now to some degree we identify with all other human beings, and possibly even with all organic life, as Scheler has suggested. To a greater degree we identify with members of our reference groups, and to an even stronger degree with the people to whom we are close: friends, spouses and children.

My wife, in manifesting a cartoon-like smug-ness, was violating the norms of our reference group, which, had I chosen to view the situation as of normal gravity, would have meant her explusion from the group. I would have been compelled to de-identify from her, which I did not wish to do. In assigning her resemblance to Batboy to the low gravity region, however, I was able to avoid having to expel her from the group and was allowed to maintain my identification with her. In effect, my laughter was saying, "This is not really you" -- although, remember, in the low gravity region it simultaneously affirmed, "This is you." Another way of phrasing the interpersonal function of laughter is to say that it differentiates between an action by or minor characterological flaw in the other and the other as a whole.

I believe that this view can resolve the dispute as to whether laughter is an expression of aggression or sympathy. The Batboy example, insofar as my wife was still perceived as a person with whom I remained identified, is a sympathetic example. The situation is quite different, however, in the case of mocking or insulting laughter. If I laugh gleefully when another, say, slips in the mud, I am thereby not differentiating the other from his act. The other is left totally in the role of outcast kicked out of the group, and de-identified from myself. In a sense the other is placed entirely within the low gravity region, up in the air.[11]

We can understand why being laughed at aggressively can be such a humiliating experience. We derive stability, worth, and self-comprehension from the norms of our reference group(s). To the person who wishes to abide by the group's norms, being the victim of another's laughter can be quite frustrating. It is probably akin to the frustration a child must feel when, in attempting to fight a larger opponent, he is held up in the air. On the ground some form of footing and thus movement is possible; away from gravity one has no grounding, no position from which to assert oneself.

In short, the sympathy or aggression present in any instance of laughter depends on whether or not the other is perceived as still belonging to one's reference group, the source of the normal. If I de-identify from the other, pushing him into the outcast role, then my laughter is aggressive; if I remain identified and allow the other to stay in the group, the laughter is sympathetic.[12]

The Function of Laughter

The function of laughter has been implicit throughout the preceding discussion. In assimilating an unanswerable situation into the region and logic of low gravity, laughter gains a person a three-fold freedom. First there is the freedom from the situation as it presents itself, from the drastic accommodation that would be necessitated by, say, seeing one's wife as impossibly smug. There is also the corollary freedom _to_ continue one's normal world undisturbed, indeed refreshed. Finally there is the freedom in treating the situation lightly, the buoyant feeling that accompanies levitation to a region where the rules of logic don't exist. This can be seen in the teasing of my wife afterwards, as mentioned in my example.

Freedom from the demands of a situation is invaluable as a brake on will, emotion, and cognitive reorganization. Without laughter a person would have to deal with every small incongruity as if it possessed normal or high gravity.[13] This state of affairs is often found in schizophrenics who have lost their ability to metaphorize. When asked if an aide had "gotten into his hair," one unfortunate patient began searching wildly through his hair, as if the person in question might actually be there.[14] Laughter is thus a "second line of defense" behind the front line systems of emotion, action, and normal gravity cognition.

In a sense, laughter does nothing at all. After laughing one's world remains unchanged; but this is essentially laughter's function, to preserve the world intact. In Piagetian terminology, laughter is a conservation process: the world appears altered, but in reality it remains the same. In another sense, however, since an incongruity has been assimilated into the low gravity region, it is phenomenally not the same world.[15]

What of the rest of the world? While laughter is busy dealing with the incongruity, the rest of the world is momentarily forgotten; the laughter is disengaged from the normal. When a person breaks up laughing, his ordinary relation to the world is indeed broken. It is only in being thrust past the confines of the normal gravity world that one can enter the region of low gravity, as if breaking through a gravitational barrier. In denying gravity, laughter also denies the entire world of gravity, albeit momentarily.

It may seem paradoxical that laughter, which

243

stabilizes one's world in the long run, produces a momentary break with that world. It is analogous to digesting a meal: energy is being provided for action and thought, but while digesting, it is difficult to act or think. Thus dis-engagement is the means for re-engagement.

A similar process is mirrored in the relations between the self and time, the body, and others. When discussing the disturbance of temporal flow in laughter, I compared laughter to a clutch mechanism; again there is the paradox of disengagement from the nromal in order to facilitate an easy return to this very normality. Likewise, in the analysis of the form of bodily expression of laughter, I described laughter as a digestive process in much the same manner as above. Finally, in the interpersonal realm, laughter allows one to maintain one's identifications via a process of dis-identification. Formally, all four domains exhibit identical processes.

II

Thus far, I have derived my conclusions from a single instance of laughter. It is necessary now to examine more rigorously the entire spectrum of laughter, as a means of testing the adequacy of the proposed structure. In considering each type of laughter, I will emphasize both the points of identity with and difference from the formulation presented above.

The Batboy example belongs, as we shall see, to the category of comedy. In addition to comedy at least seven major classes of laughter have been observed: wit, playful laughter, laughter arising from joy or a positive emotion, laughter arising from a negative emotional situation, laughter produced by tickling or sensory stimulation, laughter at oneself (or one's norms), and the laughter of disorganization.

It might be helpful to explain how these eight categories were established. There existed, at the

244

time of writing, many schemas for classifying laughter. Harlow (1969), for example, constructed a scale of eight degrees of laughter, ranging along the dimension of cognitive development, practical jokes being the lowest and dry wit the highest. Eysenck (1942, 1947) and Freud (1905) divided laughter into conative, cognitive, and affective varieties.

As valuable as these systemizations are, they do not accord with the methodology of conceptual encounter. There is no a priori reason, for example, to arrange types of laughter along the dimension of cognitive development. Furthermore, as we have seen, any occasion of laughter reveals conative, cognitive, and affective aspects.

What is required in conceptual encounter is that the investigator abandon preconceived strategies of classification and go instead to the experiences themselves. Any conceptual schema will have to emerge after rather than before the descriptive analyses have been completed. It took several years, in point of fact, before the varieties of laughter organized themselves into a coherent framework. See Funk (1974) for a fuller discussion.

Comedy

As mentioned above, the Batboy example fits this category. The source of comic tension lay in the fusion of two meanings -- one appropriate, one not -- in a single image. Unlike wit, which is abstract, comedy is concrete; the realm of the comic is the realm of observed events. There is always a relation to the senses, primarily the senses of greatest distance, most often vision and occasionally, as in musical jokes, audition. It is not merely the appearance of things that makes them laughable, but, as we have seen, the incongruous meaning of that appearance. That is, an event is comic only when contrasted with the structures of the normal; gravity always involves two objects.

Some familiar examples of comedy: a man

slipping on a banana peel, a clown being hit with a
slapstick, a team of men putting forth great effort
to no result (as when trying to move a piano in
opposite directions), a speaker getting tangled in
a tongue-twister, a musical note blatantly out of
key, the coyote missing the roadrunner yet once more
and hurtling over a cliff, or a drawing of a gro-
tesque animal, such as one with heads on both ends.[16]
One can even laugh comically at one's own situation,
as did one interviewee who found himself wedged in
a stairway while trying to move a sofa!

Generally stupidity, clumsiness, or inferiority
incline people to laugh more than do skill or
superiority. Most norms establish minimally acceptable behavior and are likely to be violated on the
side of deficiency. While a person exceeding one's
norms or expectations normally arouses admiration,
if he is too good he may also appear somewhat laughable. I remember laughing at Phil Silvers'
character Sgt. Bilko, who was as impossibly persuasive with his tongue as he was skillful with a
deck of cards.

What is crucial is that in each case events
appear simultaneously appropriate and amiss. My
wife is a real woman, yet also a smug Batboy; the
clown is not superhuman, yet is the victim of an
inordinately violent attack; the musical note is
part of the piece it disrupts; the coyote is limited
by the laws of nature (in falling), yet allowed to
transcend them, recovering instantly by scene two.
Comic laughter denies full gravity to the incongruous
event and restores the laughter to normality.[17]

Wit

The realm of wit is the realm of language and
symbolic meaning, not of concrete events. The most
common form is the verbal joke, although a political
cartoon also illustrates wit, as long as the message
rather than the image provokes the laughter.[18]

Consider the following example:

I was at the wedding reception of two good
friends of mine. They were a normal, well-
matched couple. At the reception a guest
brought a gift to the bride and remarked,
"This is something you can use later." The
bride, deducing the contents from the shape
and the guest's hint said, "It's a wedding
cake knife!" Instantly some onlooker piped,
"no, it's a whip!" Uproarious laughter
followed.

The above example is similar to the Batboy case
in that there is an incompatibility of meanings
built into the witty remark: "It's a whip" does fit
the logical requirements of the situation; after all
it is the right size and is "something to be used
later." Yet the notion that the whip would actually
be used was of course outside the value structure
(norms) of the listeners.

As with comedy, the solution lies in seeing
the whip as a possibility within the region of low
gravity; thus, the problem dissolves as it appears.
Obviously this would not be the case if such a remark
were made at a gathering of sado-masochists, where
it would actually fit the norms of the group!

The lascivious interest aroused by the remark
"It's a whip" existed momentarily as a normal
gravity possibility, but as everyone laughed it
instantly disappeared. Laughter reassured the group
that they and the couple involved were normal, i.e.,
abiding by the group's norms. The lascivious in-
sinuation was simultaneously denied in the normal
gravity region while enjoyed as a play of possibilities in the low gravity region. In a sense then,
laughter allowed the listeners to have their cake
and eat it too.[19]

With regard to the various identifications
restructured in wit, the pattern is much the same
as comedy, only in comedy there are often only two
people involved, a victim and an observer, while
in wit there are usually three, a teller, an
audience, and a victim, often absent or even

fictional. Teller and audience share an identification, feel part of the group, while the victim is,
at some point in the joke, portrayed as an outcast.
In the whip joke, the outcast role was that of
"whipper," although no actual person filled this
role. Momentarily bride and groom were postured as
if filling this role, but they were immediately de-
identified from it and were allowed to rejoin the
group (of non-whippers), joining in the laughter
themselves. Where the victim of the joke cannot
de-identify from the outcast role, he will feel
insulted. Thus, as with comedy, a witty remark can
be either "sympathetic" or aggressive depending on
the alignment of identifications. We can laugh
with or at.

   The distinctions between comedy and wit can
now be explored in greater detail. A comic event
is funny in itself, in its concretely overstepping
the bounds of the normal. There is no reason why
it is funny. There is no point in retelling a comic
event; essentially you had to be there to appreciate
it. In wit, on the other hand, the event, e.g., the
whipping, must not be seen or even envisioned.
Rather it must be alluded to (Plessner, 1970), so
that the intended meaning is grasped without any
sensory cues. In wit, all the tension is condensed
into a single point, the point at which two meanings intersect. While comedy is obvious, wit leaves
something hidden from the listener who must put in
some mental effort to get the point. There is thus
a logic to wit, a reason for laughter that can be
explained to another (although explaining a joke,
as everyone knows, ruins it. Jokes must be understood all at once, not in linear, logical form[20]).

   Thus the focus of wit is sharper; more is trans-
mitted in the punch line of a joke than in a comic
mishap, and, by the same token, more is required of
the audience. Among the many techniques used to
achieve a density of meaning are: condensation (as
in puns), omissions, suggestions, internal contradictions (as in "This sentence is a lie"), double-
entendres, and so on. A formal analysis of the

248

techniques of wit would reveal much about the underlying paradoxical logic of low gravity (see Wilson,
1979).

Wit provides a great variety of ways in which
to be knotted and set free. The fact that the teller, and through collusion the audience, have a good
deal of control over and distance from the thrust of
the joke and are able to play with an infinite
number of ludicrous low gravity possibilities may
account in part for the great popularity of jokes
and joke tellers. It may also account for differences in personal preference -- one probably chooses
to joke about those areas in which getting trapped
and released affords the most pleasure.[21] Being a
scientist, for example, I tend to like jokes with
logical twists, jokes that seem to threaten the
very facric of reason. One favorite: the sign of a
true scholar is that he is able to debate both sides
of an issue equally well. On the other hand...

Play

Despite some important similarities, the
experiences of play and laughter are distinct (see
footnote 6). One can play without laughing, and
laughing is not a form of play, although it can
arise from playful activity. Again an example will
help:

> Two children, a boy aged three and a girl aged
> five, sat at a table playing with plastic
> animals. They pretended the animals were real,
> moved them with their hands, spoke for them,
> and tried to stick to the appropriate roles for
> each animal, e.g., the larger animals would
> speak with the deeper voices. Then the play
> got wilder. At the point where cows jumped off
> the cliff (table) and began flying, one or the
> other (or both) would laugh, as if indicating
> how silly this idea was.

The object of laughter here is different from
the object in either comedy or wit. The children
did not witness a cow jumping off a cliff and flying,

which would have been comical, and there was clearly no play of abstract meanings. Instead they took an active role in making a cow under their own direction, jump off a cliff.

Observers have previously commented on the ambiguous nature of play, Plessner (1970) referring to it as "controlled capriciousness." This means that while the play region is entered into by one's will, one must still, to some degree, surrender one's will to the rules of the play situation. Once a person has chosen to respond playfully, he finds himself committed to this activity, with the corollary commitment to keep from slipping back into the normal gravity region. In order for the children in the example to relate to the cows within the play region, they had to actively shut out extraneous aspects of the world, such as the rule that animals do not talk. In other words, as relaxed as play looks, it actually requires a constant intentional activity to maintain one's relationship to objects in a playful way, against the larger and more weighty normal gravity region.

In the example above, I believe the children were beginning to slip back into a normal gravity perspective, losing control over the objects of play. The laughter reasserted the playfulness, i.e., low gravity, of the flying cows at a point where the boundaries between play and normality began to blur. That is, the laughter reestablished the boundaries between potentially merging regions, thus reasserting the children's mastery over the play objects.

Developmentally, playful laughter may be the first to emerge. I have observed laughter arising from, if not active play, at least a playful attitude as early as the third month. When my daughter Rachel was four or five months old, the easiest way to get her to laugh was to pretend to eat her up, making appropriate guttural noises, nibbling gestures, and so on. As the infant's primal fear at this age is that of being swallowed by the other (Wilber, 1978), the laughter arising from mock-swallowing undoubtedly serves to signify for the infant (and for the parent) that what appears to be a threat is in fact not. Even at this early age the ability to differentiate levels of reality is in evidence.

Like comedy, playful laughter emerges from the concrete, but whereas comedy is observed at a distance, playful laughter emerges from action initiated by the person without any mediating distance present. In comedy, the provoking event is out there; playful laughter, in contrast, stems from a relationship between person and environment. One does more than observe in play; one interacts.

Laughter Arising from Positive Emotions

There are occasions when one will laugh out of joy, triumph, or elation. Consider the following example of joyful (and possibly elated) laughter:

> A college student received unexpected news of his election to Phi Beta Kappa at a time when he had a rather low view of his academic work. At first he could not quite believe it. As the truth of the matter sank in, he began to feel joyous and perhaps somewhat elated. His heart beat faster, he felt increasingly alive, his whole being seemed to surge outwards. Overflowing with the good news, he jumped up and down, whooped, and ran to tell everyone he knew. In the midst of the leaping and whooping he laughed briefly several times. There was no joke nor anything comical, yet the laughter was genuine. However, the laugh seemed to come from the heart more than from the belly.

The most striking feature of this example is that, unlike all previous cases, there is no apparent paradox or ambiguity present. The student was entirely wrapped up in joy. Where was the incongruity, supposedly so essential for laughter!

251

The solution lies, I believe, in the particular type of gravity change that accompanies joy. In joy the person remains in the world of normal, or even high gravity. Nevertheless, there is a type of gravity change transpiring. To the joyous person the texture of gravity itself is modified. The normal gravity region begins to take on properties that previously belonged only to the low gravity region, such as ease of overcoming barriers, a certain fluidity, and so on. The normal rules of gravity seem to be suspended. In short, gravity begins to look suspiciously like levity, while retaining all the while its true character. This paradox is usually stated as "It's too good to be true," although one knows that it is indeed true. Thus gravity itself has become ambiguous, partaking of the qualities of gravity and levity simultaneously. The function of joyous laughter then is to reaffirm that the joyous event is in fact possessed of gravity.

Such doubts are usually of small magnitude compared to the sweeping rush of emotion in joy. Thus, the laughter is sporadic, frothy, appearing only at the edges of certainty. Joyous laughter is principally from the heart, not from the belly, the center of gravity (see Reich, 1949). In contrast to other forms of laughter, joyous laughter affords little psychological distance -- none really is required -- and is the least creative in establishing some new relationship of meanings. Nevertheless, joyous laughter is consistent structurally with other occasions of laughter. A similar analysis can be performed on the laughter of triumph and the laughter of elation, essentially the triumph of a wish (see the analysis of Elation by Lindsay in Chapter IV).

Laughter Arising from Negative Emotional Situations

Thus far, all the examples considered have contained a strong element of positive emotion, pleasure, or fun. There are numerous instances, however, when laughter arises from some negative

252

emotion. Can the idea of levitation fit here as well?

Example 1:

A professor was trying to imagine himself laughing fiendishly by picturing himself torturing another person. As he began to get into the role of sadist, he laughed briefly.

Example 2:

A teenage boy was on an overnight with a teen group, which included members of both sexes. He walked out of his tent in the morning, only to be told by a girl that his fly was open. Before he became really embarrassed, a male friend pointed out that it was all right because he had his bathing suit on underneath, rather than underpants. This somewhat alleviated the situation and the boy responded with embarrassed laughter (as he zipped up his fly).

Example 3:

A frontiersman discovered his family massacred by Indians upon returning from the woods. He declared to some friends that this was the funniest thing he had ever seen, whereupon he broke into laughter and eventually died! (Hall and Allin, 1897)

Example 1 is an illustration of what might be termed laughing it off. Note that the professor was not laughing at an other in the world, but at a part of himself. That is, he laughed off his own sense of evil. This type of laughter is more the laughter of relief, of being glad to get back to normal, than of enjoyment; there is little levitation, and we might view laughing it off as an intermediate state between full laughter and horror. The ambiguity lay in the man's view of himself, as

253

fundamentally not evil, while being, in the role of torturer, apparently evil. Laughing off the identification with the role of torturer gained the professor freedom from it. He then felt relieved at not being actually evil -- ... "This is not me."

The laughter in such cases is usually brief, with little letting go; the person sounds as if shaking something off. In contrast, there can be true comic laughter at the self, in which case the person is able to take an outside perspective on one's own situation. Laughing it off takes place within the self.

Example 2 is a case of embarrassed laughter. The laughter of embarrassment is like laughing it off, in that it takes place within the self, but it is less successful. To the degree that the boy was still gripped by embarrassment, was still choosing this particular relationship toward his situation, he was unable to gain distance, de-identify, or let go bodily. He did not achieve the complete transformation of laughing it off, as he still felt embarrassed. Now, there was some freedom gained, but essentially the boy remained right there in the embarrassing situation. Thus, the sound of embarrassed laughter is not full; it even sounds embarrassed.

Example 3 is an example of the laughter of despair. In such cases there is almost no bodily resonance at all; the laughter comes from the head alone, thus sounding "hollow" or insane. The person, unable to find any solution, tries to preserve himself by splitting off from the body, and from the world, thus escaping the iron grip of despair (literally no hope). I would venture that the frontiersman's death was due to the pressure brought on the body, caught in the powerful grip of despair, by the strong oscillations of laughter.

In all cases of negative emotional laughter,[22] the one who laughs is trying to free himself from a situation that seems, for the moment, too bad to be real. One cannot quite believe the situation has

254

the gravity that it appears to, yet, of course, one does still accept the gravity and demands of the situation. Negative emotional laughter does have limited efficacy, but its function is primarily defensive not "digestive," especially in examples 2 and 3. Laughing reveals the often fleeting doubts one has in accepting the gravity of a negative situation. It is structurally identical with joyous laughter, except the "sign" has been changed from positive to negative.

Tickling[23]

Surely tickling provides a challenge to my analysis, as it seems to be little more than a reflex reaction to unwanted stimulation, totally devoid of meaning.

Instead of describing an example, I will ask the reader to remember an appropriate case. The act of being tickled has an ambivalent character; it is simultaneously pleasant and unpleasant. The victim is in conflict, seeking both to remove the stimulus and sharpen the pleasure. It is a mistake to think of pleasure and pain as mere nervous twitches; to conceptual encounter they indicate a fundamental attitude of the person towards an object and are hence meaningful. Pain signifies separation, pleasure unification (Straus, 1963). In tickling both attitudes co-exist, thus meeting the condition of ambiguity. In other words, laughter at tickling is a true form of laughter, exacting what one would expect on the sensory level. If I belabor this point it is only because there is a strong tendency to view sensory processes as mechanical and meaningless.

The function of laughter when one is being tickled is, as before, to restructure a potentially threatening situation by differentiating the levels of gravity involved. Laughter at tickling denies one's own embodiment, source of one's captivity. In a sense, the person is laughing off his own body, tickling being the physical analogue of a negative emotional situation.

Laughing gains the person a certain measure of freedom; however, since the laughter arises from stimulation of an immediate sensory mode, there is little room for psychological distance and the laughter is of limited efficacy. One is too immediately caught in the here and now by the body to be totally freed by laughter. Only cessation of stimulation will bring true release, and at some point the one being tickled is only too glad to have the torture terminated. What a strange vicious circle: trying to laugh off one's embodiment through the body itself!

Laughter at Oneself

Previously I had considered laughter at oneself to be a reflexive form of comedy, but further examination of several cases suggested that this is not always the case. In some instances of laughter at oneself, a person comes to view quite ordinary aspects of the self and/or the world in a novel way, often rather abruptly. There are several levels of novelty, depending on the significance of the re-evaluation.

To begin with a modest example: Aldous Huxley (1956), under the influence of mescaline, reported going into fits of laughter at the most mundane objects and events, i.e., those not laughable by normal gravity standards. At one point he found the streams of shiny metallic cars pouring across the Los Angeles highways extremely hilarious! Huxley was not, I believe, laughing at the appearance of the cars per se, as in comedy; instead, we can see him as laughing at his own former system of norms. Huxley was not observing an incongruity that clashed with his already established world-view; rather, he was expanding the bounds of his former world, creating new norms. The cars, then, provoked laughter only insofar as they served as the locus for the collision of two sets of constructs about the world. The old view was that cars are attractive, sensible, utilitarian, and the backbone of American life. The newly created view -- and it is a creative view for its time -- is that automobiles are little more than

pretentious and even dangerous toys. Against this
broader perspective, Huxley's former view appeared
(and appears) eminently laughable.

This type of laughter indicates, as before, a
restructuring of an event in terms of levels of
gravity, only here it is the old norms which are the
occasion for levity. This is quite distinct from
comic laughter at oneself, wherein one's prior norms
are maintained. Laughter at oneself is the only
type of laughter which proceeds at least partially
via what Piaget calls accommodation rather than
assimilation, for the laugher is willing to modify
his perception of himself and/or his world. This
type of laughter might be considered therapeutic,
an occasion for growth (Boorstein, 1980).

The notion that laughter can be therapeutic is
superbly illustrated in Hesse's (1963) novel
Steppenwolf. The protagonist, Harry Haller, repeatedly clings to then gradually surrenders a falsely
dichotomized conception of his own nature -- as
being part man, part wolf -- ultimately embracing a
far more panoramic view of his life. Before exploring the innumerable facets of his personality, he
must first laugh at the limitations of his previously
held self-image. The goal set Harry by his mentors
is simply to learn to laugh at the absurdities of
life, including those of his own devising.

Occasionally laughter at oneself assumes truly
cosmic proportions and even one's self, the core
of one's sense of identity (to us in the West at
least), may be revealed as a clever sham:

> Basically, my own laughter at myself has some-
> thing to do with the incongruity of such a
> clown being God in disguise, of the "big act"
> called Alan Watts being a manifestation of the
> infinite energy of the universe. For behind
> the scenes you see all the string, tacks, wire,
> and masking tape that prop up the show, and as
> I witness the universe getting away with me I
> wonder what other uprorarious deceptions it
> will perpetrate (Watts, 1973, pp. 260-261).

At its root, I believe, laughter is a manifestation of the divine, of ultimate freedom. Here laughter and liberation merge.

Laughter of Disorganization

From the sublime to the ridiculous, as befits any discussion of laughter, there are certain occasions when laughter occurs without there seeming to be any reason at all. This category includes the laughter of giddiness, of fatigue, pointless or silly laughter (as when two people look at each other and just break up in hysterics), some instances of drug-induced laughter, and the laughter of infection, as when one enters a room full of laughing people and inexplicably is caught up by the force of levity. In all these cases the fundamental conditions for laughter are not met, yet laughter occurs anyway. I believe my analysis is valid here as well, although I am less certain exactly how. In fatigue, giddiness, or infaction, the structure of one's world begins to disintegrate. Gravity fades, the familiar seems odd, and the world seems to be following the logic of levity. The situation is something like that of joyous laughter, but without the sense that the joyous event, beneath it all, is indeed of high gravity. In disorganized states everything simply falls apart and one feels energized, levitated or, as we commonly put it, high. The laughter probably functions to reassure the person(s) that the appearances are not to be taken as having gravity. One is then free to just let go and laugh -- which is oddly reminiscent of cosmic laughter at oneself.

Synthesis

There is a form of laughter appropriate to each mode of human experience: playful laughter in the realm of action, tickling in the immediate sensory mode, laughter arising from positive and negative emotional involvement, comic laughter at events observed via the senses of distance, wit in the domain of abstract thought, and finally laughter at oneself (and perhaps laughter of disorganization) in what might be called the intuitive realm.

Despite the important distinctions noted, the
underlying unity of all categories of laughter is
apparent. To put it succinctly, laughter differentiates between appearance and reality. The function of laughter is to free the person from what
could otherwise be a confusing (literally impossible)
situation, allowing him to continue undisturbed;
the success of the laughter will vary, however, depending on the type. Comedy, wit, and laughter at
oneself are generally more effective than laughter
arising from sensory or emotional involvement. The
laughter also gains the freedom to play with the
incongruity within the region of low gravity, wherein the relationship is true, although this too will
vary. Embarrassed laughter affords much less
flexibility than comedy or wit. To some degree
every type of laughter offers a sense of release
and even pleasure, expressed in the body as a series
of purposeless oscillatory movements. The degree
of letting go will vary depending on the type of
laughter: the laughter of despair sounds hollow,
of joy frothy, of embarrassment embarrassed; a good
comic belly laugh will sound full and free. Finally,
in the extremes of laughter, in joy, despair, or
cosmic laughter at oneself, laughter may blend,
paradoxically, with tears.[24]

Comparison with Elation

In conceptual encounter, one typically sharpens
one's analysis by comparing the intuited structures
of one affect with those of another. Much of what
has been said of laughter, in particular the notion
of levitation, sounds applicable to the emotion of
elation (see Lindsay, Chapter IV), which requires
a similar "lifting" process. Note, however, that
elation presupposes that the provoking event is of
high not low gravity, the person fulfilling a long
held wish. In laughter, too, a person retains his
or her center of gravity, deflating the incongruous
event, while in elation the person's self is lifted,
out of touch with reality to some degree. Finally,
elation is very much in time, while the temporal

flow stops in the timelessness of laughter.[25]

III

We can now use this tentatively complete analysis of laughter as a basis for comprehending its polar opposite: crying.[26] Let us consider briefly some key aspects of these two affects:

1. Laughter obviates the need for emotion, action, or reorganization of thought by levitation, by rising above the situation. One breaks up, momentarily denying gravity. Crying is the inverse. Whereas laughter negates emotion, crying develops from emotion. Gravity increases to the point where the person surrenders to its pull, breaking down in tears. Although not an emotion itself, crying can be seen as an overflow of feeling, emerging at the point where emotion can no longer be contained or expressed.

2. Laughter asserts that while the situation cannot be dealt with, it need not be. One dissolves the problem -- by doing nothing. Crying too arises from situations in which nothing can be done, only in crying one does not deflate or undermine the situation. The person becomes aware of a superior force against which he can do nothing, as in pain, sorrow, impotent range, joy, and even when faced with a work of art or nature. In these instances a basic finitude becomes manifest; the self is overwhelmed by the infinite (Plessner, 1970). The problem does not dissolve as in laughter; rather, the tension develops inwardly, welling to the point where the person dissolves in tears.

3. Laughter erupts suddenly and explosively. Quick inspiratory breaths alternate with a series of short expiratory bursts (Hahahaha!); the major thrust is outward. Koestler speculates that laughter is mediated by the sympathetic nervous system. Crying, in contrast, is rarely sudden. It normally takes time to surrender to the developing inner tension. Crying has a mediated onset, marked

260

by a gradual turning down of the entire visage and an increasing quiver of the jaw and lips. Crying is basically inspiratory (Aaaaaaaah!), long continuous outward cries alternating with short inspiratory bursts. Koestler views it as regulated by the parasympathetic nervous system.

4. Laughter is basically an assertive act. It preserves the self by enhancing the person's autonomy[27] except in those cases where its function is primarily defensive (as in the frontiersman example). Crying preserves the person by a homonomus[27] extension of the self. Instead of asserting against the world, in crying one maintains contact with the situation, often becoming more deeply a part of it. In some cases, however, where crying indicates simply capitulation to an overpowering environmental force, crying expresses heteronomy.[27]

5. The laughter is open to the world, as revealed in the vulnerable posture. Furthermore, the laugher shares his "helplessness" with others by laughing out loud. Laughter is basically conservative, however; the laughter is open to a world basically unchanged. The one who cries is closed to the world, as revealed by the clouded eyes. The tears, as Plessner notes, serve as self-verification, not as a social pronouncement. There is, however, a movement within the self in crying, and when one returns to the world it is usually to a world essentially changed, often broadened or deepened.

Laughing and crying, while in many respects mirror inversions of each other, do share certain features which distinguish them both from emotions. Emotions involve a person within a situation in an immediate sense (de Rivera, 1977) while laughing and crying relate a person to a situation. That is, laughing and crying are meta-responses, indicating that one has overstepped the boundaries imposed by the situation. Laughter is thus qualitatively distinct from, say, amusement, which in de Rivera's (1977) scheme is an emotion, closely related to wonder. Whereas amusement thus embodies some emotional meaning, laughing and crying indicate the

261

opposite -- that no meaningful response is possible -- which is paradoxically the most suitable response. If emotions constitute a first line of reaction to the world, laughing and crying form a second line, highly useful when all else fails. Whereas emotions use the body to take a stance towards the world (as in the aggressive posture of anger), laughing and crying respond by simply letting go, letting the "body answer as body" (Plessner, 1970).

At the risk of being overly metaphorical, I cannot resist the following analogy. Picture emotions as describing a circle with person and other located inside the circle. Laughter makes the circle vanish to a point, freeing the laugher and, depending on circumstances, perhaps the "victim" as well. Crying, on the other hand, seems to expand the circle hyperbolically. The other now appears infinite, or at least overwhelming.

However one attempts to portray them, one thing is clear: laughing and crying, despite interminable analysis still remain as fundamentally mysterious as the human being-in-the-world which brings them into existence. Thus, it is fitting that I end as I began, quoting Lao Tzu:

If there were no laughter, the Tao would not be what it is.

Reference Notes
for Chapter IV

1. Apparently this is true for other simians as
   well. Arnheim (1949) has observed that the
   chimpanzee, normally highly sensitive to the
   subtle nuances of human expression, is unable
   to comprehend the significance of laughter.

2. Whether an event is treated as science or comedy
   depends not so much on the qualities inherent in
   the event itself, but on the attitude of the
   observer. We now laugh at those who laughed at
   Fulton!

3. I am using Piagetian terminology here and will
   do so at points throughout the discussion (see
   Flavell, 1963).

4. I should emphasize that spatial metaphors like
   "gravity" and "region" are just that -- con-
   venient metaphors. They refer not to actual
   spaces and physical movements but to structures
   of one's experience. In this regard, I am
   borrowing from Lewin (1935).

5. Note that although the low gravity region
   possesses a different logic from that of normal
   gravity, it is still a region of reality. In
   this sense laughter is like play and unlike
   dreams and fantasy, which have an unreal
   illogical nature (Dembo, 1931). Paradoxical
   logic is not primary process.

6. Play can rightly be considered another type of
   low gravity activity and its close relation to
   laughter will be discussed below. Play, however, is not a response to a perceived incongruity; rather, it requires a prior attitude --
   a sort of low gravity intentionality -- which
   is used to construct a world in which one then
   acts (see Plessner, 1970). Similarly an ironic
   attitude allows one to treat the world as if

it is not what it claims to be. In fact, Arieti (1976) speaks of it as a "tertiary" process.

7. McGhee (1972), using a Piagetian analysis, refers to this type of assimilation as "fantasy assimilation."

8. There is, in fact, an entire class of theories which base their analyses on just this surprise factor (Keith-Spiegel, 1972).

9. It is amusing to note that the verb to "ruminate," meaning to mull over, is from the same root as "ruminant," which refers to cud-chewing animals. The laugher can be said to be ruminating in both senses!

10. See Martineau (1972) and Wilson (1979) for a complete discussion.

11. Of course it may be difficult for the one being laughed at, or even an unbiased observer, to determine whether the laughter is with or at. Consider the report of Korean children laughing at a blind girl stumbling through the rubble of a war-torn city. Our reaction to this event will differ dramatically, depending on whether we construe the laughter as aggressive or sympathetic (which, surprisingly, it may well have been). In any case, the outcast always retains the option of laughing at himself and thus rejoining the group; this requires, however, a self-objectivity often difficult to achieve.

12. The interested reader will find a thorough discussion of the social uses of laughter, both to strengthen and break down group structures, in Martineau (1972).

13. Here we agree with Freud (1905, 1928) who pointed out how economical laughter is.

14. Reported by Searles (1962). It is interesting to note that the logics underlying laughter and schizophrenia are opposites. In laughter an apparent identity is transformed into a harmless likeness -- my wife is only _like_ such and such. In schizophrenia a resemblance is transformed into an identity (Arieti, 1955). For example, on the basis of a partial similarity between herself and Mary -- both are virgins -- a schizophrenic woman may conclude that she is the Virgin Mary. Laughter differentiates appearance and reality; schizophrenia fuses them.

15. The alteration in one's world is, as mentioned above, something like the liberation of satori. The major difference is that in laughter one's normal world is conserved, the change occuring in the low gravity region. Satori, in contrast, is an alteration in one's being-in-the-world at a fundamental level and is thus of high gravity. Still, laughter can be treated as a satori "in miniature!" Capra (1975) speaking of the intuitive nature of jokes, writes, "In the split second where you understand a joke you experience a moment of enlightenment" (p. 37).

16. Note that comedy can be real, staged (as in the clown act), or a work of art (as in the two-headed figure). We have norms regarding fictional being as well.

17. See Plessner (1970) for a detailed analysis of comedy.

18. There are many sub-varieties of wit, such as humor, "dry" wit (as in puns), satire, sarcasm, the sardonic, etc. (Fowler, 1926). Here we are concerned with the uniformities of these variations.

19. There is debate as to whether laughter extinguishes the original emotional involvement, in

this case lascivious interest, or whether it is in fact merely a disguised outlet for the emotion (Freud, 1905). In the latter view the pleasure of laughter arises from allowing a forbidden impulse expression in a socially acceptable manner. This is a plausible theory; such a "hydraulic," causal model, however, belongs to natural scientific theorizing, not to conceptual encounter, which is concerned only with description.

20. Despite the noted differences between comedy and wit, they can shade into each other. Freud (1905) suggested a laughable situation of intermediate structure, namely laughter at the "naive." Children, for example, will frequently make adults laugh by innocently violating adult norms, as when a child asks "Is God going to the bathroom when it rains?" There is a "point" here, as in wit although there is no intention to be witty, as in comedy.

21. Kris (1938, 1940) suggested that people frequently joke about situations just previously mastered, as a means of maintaining control over the precarious. Note, for example, the "anal" jokes of young children who have only recently graduated from toilet training.

22. Several other varieties of negative emotional laughter have been discovered, but will not be explored. One is fiendish laughter, which is an extreme case of laughing it off. Another is anxious or nervous laughter, which is analogous to embarrassed laughter. Laughter also can be used to "hold off" negative states. One girl reported laughing uncontrollably through the funeral of a friend, not sobbing until afterwards.

23. In addition to tickling, this category includes laughter produced by jogging, as when a child is thrown in the air and caught, roller coaster rides, etc. What is crucial is that the stimulation be exclusively of the senses of

immediate contact -- touch, kinesthesia, and/or the vestibular sense.

24. For example, at the end of one filmed version of Dickens' "A Christmas Carol," Scrooge, following his revelations, is laughing almost to the point of tears. The audience response to his laughter can just easily be tears as laughter; or the two affects may alternate.

25. Laughter is also closely related, surprising as it may seem at first, to the emotions of faith and horror (see Funk, 1974). In differing ways both faith and horror are attempts to deny a potentially negative situation, but unlike laughter, both operate within the high gravity region of reality.

26. Not surprisingly, much less has been written about crying than laughing. For further discussion see Plessner (1970) and Koestler (1964).

27. The terms "autonomy," "homonomy," and "heteronomy" are taken from Angyal (1941). Autonomy and heteronomy refer to the person's dominance over or submission to the environment, while homonomy refers to the person's participation in some larger unit.

References
for Chapter V

Angyal, A. Foundations for a science of personality.
  Cambridge: Harvard University Press, 1941.

Arieti, S. Some aspects of language in schizophrenia.
  In Werner, H. (Ed.) On expressive language.
  Worcester: Clark University Press, 1955, pp.
  53-67.

Arieti, S. Creativity: the magic synthesis. New
  York: Basic Books, 1976.

Arnheim, R. The Gestalt Theory of expression.
  Psychological Review, 56, May 1949.

Bateson, G. Steps to an ecology of mind. New York:
  Ballantine, 1972.

Berger, P. & Luckmann, T. The social construction
  of reality. New York: Doubleday and Co., 1966.

Boorstein, S. Lightheartedness in psychotherapy.
  Journal of Transpersonal Psychology, 12, 1980,
  pp. 105-115.

Capra, F. The Tao of physics. Berkeley: Shambhala,
  1975.

Dembo, T. Der arger als dynamisches problem.
  Psychologische Forschung, 15, 1931, pp. 1-144.

de Rivera, J. A structural theory of the emotions.
  Psychological Issues, Vol. X, No. 4, Monograph
  40, New York: International Universities Press,
  1977.

Durckheim, K. Hara: The vital centre of man. London:
  George Allen and Unwin, 1962.

Eysenck, H. Appreciation of humor -- An experimental
  and theoretical study. British Journal of

268

Psychology, 32, 1942, pp. 295-309.

Eysenck, H. Dimensions of personality. London: Routledge, 1947.

Flavell, J. The developmental psychology of Jean Piaget. New York: Van Nostrand, 1963.

Fowler, H. A dictionary of modern English usage. London: Oxford University Press, 1926.

Freud, S. Jokes and their relation to the unconscious. New York: Norton, 1960 (original 1905).

Freud, S. Humour. International Journal of Psychoanalysis, 9, 1928, pp. 1-6.

Funk, J. A phenomenological analysis of laughter. Unpublished Masters Thesis, Clark University, 1974.

Hall, G., and Allin, A. The psychology of tickling, laughing, and the comic. American Journal of Psychology, 9, 1897, pp. 1-41.

Harlow, H. The anatomy of humor. Impact of Science on Society (UNESCO) Vol. 19, No. 3, 1969.

Hesse, H. Steppenwolf. New York: Bantam, 1963.

Huxley, A. The doors of perception (with Heaven and Hell). New York: Harper and Row, 1954.

Keith-Spiegel, P. Early conceptions of humor: Varieties and issues. In Goldstein, J., and McGhee, P., (Eds.) The psychology of humor. New York: Academic Press, 1972.

Koestler, A. The act of creation. London: Hutchinson, 1964.

Kris, E. Development and the comic. International Journal of Psychoanalysis, 19, 1938, pp. 77-90.

Kris, E. Laughter as an expressive process. International Journal of Psychoanalysis, 21 1940, pp. 314-341.

Laing, R. D., and Esterson, A. Sanity, madness, and the family. Baltimore: Pelican, 1970 (original 1964).

Lewin, K. A dynamic theory of personality. New York: McGraw-Hill, 1935.

MacDonald, G. The light princess. New York: Thomas Crowell and Co., 1962.

Martineau, W. A model of social functions of humor. In Goldstein, J., and McGhee, P. (Eds.) The psychology of humor. New York: Academic Press, 1972.

McGhee, P. On the cognitive origins of incongruity humor: Fantasy assimilation versus reality assimilation. In Goldstein, J. and McGhee, P. (Eds.) The psychology of humor. New York: Academic Press, 1972.

Plessner, H. Laughing and crying: A study of the limits of behavior. Evanston: Northwestern University Press, 1970.

Scheler, M. The nature of sympathy. Hamden, Connecticut: Shoestring, 1970.

Searles, H. Collected papers on schizophrenia and related topics. New York: International University Press, 1962.

Straus, E. The primary world of the senses. New York, Free Press, 1963.

van den Berg, J. A different existence: Principles of phenomenological psychopathology. Pittsburgh: Duquesne University Press, 1972.

Watts, A. Psychotherapy East and West. New York: Mentor, 1961.

Watts, A. In my own way: An autobiography. New York: Vintage Books, 1973 (original 1972).

Wilber, K. Spectrum psychology, Revision, Vol. 1, No. 1, 1978, pp. 5-28.

Wilson, C. Jokes: Form, content, use and function. London: Academic Press, 1979.

VI

PSYCHOLOGICAL DISTANCE

Thomas Kreilkamp

What is psychological distance? This is the
question this chapter will answer. Psychological
distance is especially interesting for a psychologist
because even though many people are familiar with the
experiences related to it -- people feel separated
from one another, they will talk with interest of
barriers and gulfs and walls which intervene between
them and another -- psychologists have not paid much
attention to this realm. Psychological distance is
an aspect of interpersonal relations which although
important and sometimes explicitly discussed by
psychologists has not received sustained attention
and analysis.

Of course this distance concept is a metaphor.
It is a term with a basically geographical meaning --
things can be measurably near or far in space --
which has been extended in use so that now it can
have a psychological meaning. Metaphorical extension
is a very common phenomenon in the development of a
language, and the distance concept has in fact been
extended metaphorically in a number of ways, for
example, in economics and international relations,
as well as in psychology.[1] Metaphors may not be the
most precise way of communicating, but this particular metaphor is useful and even necessary; the
distance terminology is used widely to talk about
interpersonal relations because no better way of
talking about crucial interpersonal events exists.
Present vocabulary may not be the best possible,
but it arises in response to a desire to communicate
about important observable phenomena. Literature,

273

everyday speech, and the more technical communications of psychologists all offer evidence of the usage and importance of the psychological distance, yet it has not been given intensive treatment as a distinct topic.

This notion of a psychological distance between people, not at all a matter of how many feet apart they are standing, but a complex feature of their psychological relation to each other, underlies for example a conversation in which one person mentions a friend of his who has drifted away, who is no longer a close friend. It is implied also, when teachers are told for example to maintain more distance from their pupils; when a young person is spoken of as alienated; or when patients are spoken of by their therapists as being out of touch or not maintaining contact.

In this chapter I will present my theory of psychological distance. Details of this study are available elsewhere (Kreilkamp, 1970); in brief, I gathered examples of psychological distance from three major sources (interviews with research partners, the psychological literature, and fiction), wrote each out on a sheet of paper, and then examined them together and sorted them into groups. The groupings into which the examples were sorted were rough at first and then later became more coherent (see Chapter I of this book for further discussion of this process). After this sorting was concluded, there were eighteen groups of distance examples, each characterized by a label which refers to the essential psychological process involved (for example, "shy" and "respect" and "not belonging" and "exclusion" were four of the eighteen labels used). The labels of psychological processes in this chapter will refer to this group of eighteen processes.

The theory to be presented here arose out of a sustained comparison of these groups of examples and their concomitant psychological processes, both with one another and with the ideas about distance which already exist in the psychological literature (for example, Bogardus' notion of social distance, 1933; 1951; or the discussions of distancing in interpretations of Rorschach tests). The theory attempts to account for all of the collected examples and for all usages of distance terminology in the psychological literature[2] in a systematic coherent understandable fashion. The theory is of interest, I think, not simply because it illuminates the data but also because it generates some ideas about people and their behaviors which I think might be pertinent to the development of psychological theory in general and social psychology in particular.

This chapter will now review the eighteen groups of distance examples, briefly discuss the psychological processes occurring in these groups, and show how, out of a need to account for the kinds of processes occurring in these groups, a theory developed. Not all eighteen groups will be considered in equal detail; the purpose is to illustrate the range and to make the theory clear. For further detail, see Kreilkamp (1970).

The Groups of Distance Examples

Each group is referred to by a label; this label will be used as we proceed to refer to the psychological dynamics (or processes) characteristic of the examples contained in the group.

The first group involves ritual. In order to see the relation between ritual and distance, we must realize that a ritual involves a set of rules by which behavior is governed. In a ritual the emphasis is not on expressing one's own momentary and transient feelings, but rather on fidelity to the rules which govern the behavior; the emphasis is on doing things the right way, as they are supposed to be done; and the reference throughout the behavior is not to the particular human beings who are participating, but to the set of rules being followed.

Ritual becomes connected with distance when

ritual has become a perceptible aspect of interpersonal interaction, but before it has become
fully formulated in an explicit code. That is,
two people who do not perceive the existing
ritualistic aspect of their interaction are in a
different situation psychologically than two people
who just barely apprehend a ritualistic aspect of
their interaction; and these two situations are in
turn different from that of two people partaking in
what both realize is a formal ritual such as a
marriage ceremony. So far as distance is concerned,
we are interested in the situation of two people
one or both of whom realize, more or less dimly,
with a consequent lack of comfort and satisfaction,
that a ritualistic element exists -- not explicitly
formulated, nor desired -- in what they are doing
with each other. We are also interested in an
interaction whose ritualistic nature is fully
realized and accepted by one person but not by the
other. In such situations, the term psychological
distance becomes relevant, for the ritual is to
some extent keeping them apart.

How does ritual keep people apart? Obviously
the carrying out of an act which is culturally
defined as a ritual does not in itself produce
distance; but when an act (shaking hands, saying
"How are you?," etc.) is being performed in a
ritualistic manner, then distance is created. And
a ritualistic manner is when one or both of the
participants is acting not with reference to the
other person directly but with primary reference
to the set of rules underlying the ritual.

An example which illustrates some of these
dynamics is Franz Kafka's account of a conversation
he had with his mother:

> Later she asked me if I was going to write to
> Uncle Alfred -- he deserved to be written to.
> I asked her how he deserved it. He has wired,
> he has written, he means so well by you. Those
> are only outward things, I said, he is a
> complete stranger to me, he misunderstands me
> utterly, and has no idea of what I want and

276

need, I have nothing to do with him. (Brod, 1960, p. 143)

Here Kafka's mother is asking Kafka to participate in exchanging gestures with his uncle, gestures which have a place in a code of manners which she believes important. Kafka is saying that he does not want to extend such gestures; he wants either real communication with a fellow human being who understands him, or no communication at all; he will not send a letter just for the sake of appearance.

Kafka and his mother have different interests in this situation; they each have a valid point, but are not successful in making the validity of their point clear to the other. The mother actually is concerned with the family proprieties; but instead of explicitly saying so, she tries to persuade Kafka to write the letter by talking about the uncle's feeling for Kafka. This is a mistaken approach; for it leads Kafka to emphasize the uncle's lack of understanding of him.

Why is her approach mistaken? If we can understand this, we will understand distance better. We can say that Kafka feels distant from his uncle. As Kafka puts it, talking about his uncle, "He misunderstands me entirely." This concept of understanding became more and more central as we gathered more and more examples. More and more often we were finding, as we looked over the groups of examples, that a central dimension on which the examples could be arrayed involved that of understanding. When people feel they understand each other, they feel closer; when they feel they do not understand one another, they feel more distant. Of course, saying this does not explicate fully the nature of understanding, and as we proceed, this issue will be addressed more directly.

What might Kafka's mother have done in this situation, if she wanted to persuade Kafka to write a letter? The mother might instead have tried to encourage Kafka to show his commitment to the family

277

by talking of his responsibilities as a member of the family unit. If Kafka belongs to the family, he should make certain gestures and participate in certain gestures and participate in certain rituals. The rituals are part of what holds the family together. However, the mother does not make this point; and Kafka adheres to his insistence on the uncle's lack of understanding (which ought to be seen as irrelevant to the issue of whether or not Kafka belongs to the family).

How would this emphasis, on ritual as helping to hold the family together, be different from Kafka's own perception of the formality of letter writing and its irrelevance to his own true nature? Here we have a suggestion that ritual needs to be considered from at least two different angles. One point of view is the one that Kafka adopts. As he points out, his uncle does not understand him. But Kafka need not stop there. Admittedly, a lack of understanding is an impediment to one form of human relation. But why need that be the only relevant dimension? Perhaps there is another form of relation, a form that can be nourished by the kind of ritual which Kafka's mother is trying to promote. This idea will become important later when we consider certain of our categories, such as exclusion and rejection. In those examples the main phenomenon which leads to distance appears to be a keeping out; that is, one person or a group is keeping someone else out of their association. The person being kept out feels distant. Whatever is involved here may be similar to what Kafka is doing, this in more than one way, but certainly part of his "keeping away" action involves making his uncle vividly aware of the lack of unity between them, the lack of connection. Kafka's side of this experience we are aware of: he feels his uncle does not understand him. This is certainly a relevant dimension and it is reflected in many of our examples. But on the uncle's side, if we can imagine how he feels, there must be a feeling of distance also which may be related to a second dimension. The uncle has wired, he has written, he has shown an interest, and yet he gets no response.

278

The lack of responsiveness is part of the problem;
another part of the problem is Kafka's desire not
to have anything to do with his uncle and this
latter dimension has something to do with the
nature of ritual itself. That is, writing a letter
to his uncle would affirm some kind of bond between
Kafka and his uncle, a bond which Kafka does not
feel as important, but which his mother and probably his uncle would find important.

Since we are focusing on distance, our examples
do not center on connections between people, but on
a lack of connection. In the example we have been
considering, Kafka feels a lack of one kind of
connection. This other connection we will refer
to as a "unit" which could be formed here between
Kafka and his uncle. Or more accurately, a unit
(a group) exists by virtue of the family relations
between Kafka and his uncle, but Kafka is trying
to break that connection; he is moving outside that
unit and trying to sever that particular connection
between himself and his uncle.

Another set of examples involves politeness.
Politeness is anchored firmly in the realm of
ritual, but it is also extended further and used
as a synonym for "considerate" behavior. When it
is formal it is similar to ritual; when it is
considerate of the feelings of others it implies
not distance, but closeness. As consideration of
the other's feelings is progressively omitted,
polite behavior evolves more completely into
ritual, or into an attempt to fend the other off,
to keep him away from any kind of accurate comprehension of one's real feelings and desires.

Distance appears in situations where politeness
intervenes between two people in such a way as to
keep them from getting to know each other, from
becoming more fully or closely acquainted. Tomkins
(1965) for example, speaks of the artist Marcel
Duchamp's "impenetrable politeness," and of his
politeness as leading people to "keep themselves
at a distance" (p. 16). And in another example
from a novel:

(Dwight Towers and Moira Davidson are spending
the evening together.) He was absent-minded
that evening. He was pleasant and courteous
to her, but she felt all the time that he was
thinking of other things. She tried several
times during dinner to secure his interest,
but failed. It was the same in the movie
theatre; he went through all the motions of
enjoying it and giving her a good time, but
there was no life in the performance.
(Shute, 1957, p. 185)

This example is interesting because in addition to
the factor of politeness, there is Dwight's absent-
mindedness and the fact that his interest is elsewhere. The concept of "interest" is relevant, since
it draws our attention here to the way in which
people often want to know what the other person's
interests are. Knowing what another person is
interested in helps us know who he is and what kind
of person he is; and politeness, whatever its form,
hampers the acquisition of this kind of knowledge.

Politeness and ritual pay obeisance to a
higher social form. However, there is another kind
of ritual which rests not on social consensus about
rules but upon more private psychological foundations; Freud was very interested in the obsessive
rituals of particular human beings, and he tried
to connect them theoretically with the social
rituals. Such private rituals have the same dynamic
relation with distance as do social rituals; they
conceal one person from another; they prevent any
kind of direct contact or access of the sort which
would enable one person to get to know another
well. They discourage clarity of communication
between individuals about their own fluctuating
feelings and desires. Such private rituals do
however differ from those which are more socially
shared in one way which has important implications
for distance; they will become apparent after we
have introduced another phenomenon.

In considering ritual and the closely related
dynamics of politeness, we have discovered a number

of ideas which have become central to our elaboration of a theory of distance. We have discussed the ways in which politeness and ritual involve, to greater or lesser degrees, some allegiance to formal codes, some investment in a higher social form which stands above the individual, as it were, or in which and through which the individual creates an existence. We have talked about consideration of the feelings of others and interest in another as factors which militate against distance. When consideration and interest are lacking, possibly distance increases. We have talked about comprehension of the other person; Kafka felt his uncle did not understand or comprehend him; this seemed to make for an increase of distance. In addition, there are clearly some factors which frustrate any attempt at understanding. That is, a person may want to understand another, but the other will not let himself be understood. Finally, we mentioned unit formation, or the possibility that ritual may work to create larger social units; and of course there are processes which militate against unit formation, which prevent units from being formed or maintained (and again, Kafka illustrated this in our example).

Now we will turn to another group of examples, which we call closed-off; many of the same ideas will recur. In this phenomenon the lack of apparent response to the other person is accentuated. In polite behavior personal idiosyncratic behavior is underemphasized in favor of socially approved ritualistic behavior. A person being polite restrains his idiosyncrasies; he refrains from expressing any unusual feelings or attitudes. In closed-off behavior, however, there is a real question about the very existence of any personal individual response to what is occurring. One is led to wonder whether the closed-off person has any feelings. Let us look at an example:

(Baby is a drug addict who is in a courtroom in connection with her addiction.) Perhaps because Legal Aid was attractive and soft-spoken, perhaps because he didn't probe too

281

much but made her feel that he believed her
story, he gradually brought Baby back from
wherever she was to reality and the courtroom.
It was at rare intervals like this that Baby
could react with a mixture of remorse and
appreciation. (Samuels, 1967, p. 7)

Notice the explicit statement of a withdrawal from
the reality outside, whose momentary reversal is
indicated by a response to that reality; it is lack
of such an appropriate response which embodies the
closed-off aspect of her behavior.

The clinical concept of the defended person is
relevant here, since such a person has managed, in
one way or another, to close some portion of himself
off from other people; he will not risk developing
new feelings towards others.

This phenomenon is different from what happens
when a person has feelings but manages to prevent
them from dominating his behavior (see the next
process, that of detachment). The closed-off process
further differs from what is happening when a person
is momentarily absorbed in some private train of
thought and thus is not available to others, is not
capable for the moment of paying attention to others
(see the fourth process, that of being "away"). All
of these processes have something to do with distance,
and insofar as they are different, they show us
something about the nature of distance.

The concept of being closed-off implies not
only a lack of ability to develop emotional interest
in outside reality, but also a dearth of self-
knowledge. The closed-off person often has little
knowledge of himself; both inner and outer reality
are in varying degrees inaccessible, and this of
course was one of Freud's points in his discussions
of private obsessive rituals. The next example will
illustrate the withdrawal from inner reality which
occurs when a person closes himself off and will
serve as a bridge to the discussion of the next
phenomenon, that of detachment.

282

Her eyes are brighter, and there is a peculiar
detachment in her voice and manner, as if she
were a little withdrawn from her words and
actions (p. 58). Her expression shows more of
the strange aloofness which seems to stand
apart from her nerves and the anxieties which
harry them. (p. 71) Mary is paler than before,
and her eyes shine with unnatural brilliance.
The strange detachment in her manner has
intensified. She has hidden deeper within
herself and found refuge and release in a
dream where present reality is but an appearance to be accepted and dismissed unfeelingly--
even with a hard cynicism -- or entirely
ignored... (p. 97, all from O'Neill, 1956)

In these excerpts, Mary is portrayed as withdrawn
not only from outside reality, but also from her
own feelings and other behaviors; all this is
included in the process of becoming closed-off.
Bettelheim (1967) makes the same observation in his
studies of autistic children:

Why these children are so unresponsive to
physical pain is difficult to know. It is
the more baffling because they seem to pay so
little attention to the external world and to
direct all their attention to themselves.
Thus if the whole thing were to follow the
laws of logic, they should be more sensitive
to what comes from inside them, including
pain, than are normal people. But actually
the opposite is true. In a strange way, they
are just as alienated from the body and its
normal signals as they are from the external
world; witness the fact that their muscle
coordination is poor, that they walk in
strange ways, and move so differently from
normal children.

I believe what we have here is a concentration
on their defensive system to the exclusion of
all other stimuli, whether coming from their
inside or out. (pp. 58-59)

In these examples of what we are calling closed-off people, we notice first of all an apparent lack of response. This is accompanied by an apparent lack of self-knowledge. The closed-off person not only does not show responsiveness to external reality but appears disconnected from internal reality as well. In such people, there is a very real question about whether they are still, psychologically speaking, to be considered as people. This may seem a paradoxical statement; you might argue that anybody must be always considered a person, so long as he is alive. But in fact we have collected a number of examples which make clear that there is something contingent about personhood; that is, from a psychological point of view, people are not always acting like people, nor are they always treated as people. For example, I can treat another person like a dog, as we say, or like an object. Collecting examples of distance necessitates some consideration of what this kind of example means. We may not be able to understand it fully, but we must at least grapple with the question of what a person is, since so many of our examples seem to imply that not being a person can in some situations create a kind of distance.

One of the examples just considered explicitly mentions the word detachment, which indicates the similarity between being closed-off and detached. However, these are separate phenomena, deserving separate discussion. Closed-off refers to a desire to restrict the development of feelings which are in touch with reality, whereas detachment simply implies that a person is not completely swayed by his feelings about some particular event or situation. A related concept is that of being objective or getting perspective; these phrases refer to a person's capacity to remain undominated by any feelings he may happen to have. There are two interrelated issues underlying these phenomena; one is whether or not there is a willingness to develop feelings which are in touch with reality, and the other is what the person does with his feelings, how he deals with them, whether they sweep over him or remain under his control to some extent.

284

Consideration of the concept of cynicism will perhaps illuminate the distinction between detachment and being so withdrawn as to be closed-off from reality. A person who is cynical has some capacity, however rudimentary it may seem, for concern and involvement with reality; yet he must have at the same time an ability to be detached, to separate himself from his feelings and the reality they are part of. It is by knowing well the kinds of feelings that a person can have towards reality that the cynic is able to develop his cynical remarks. A person with no capacity for involvement with reality, for being in touch with reality, could never be cynical; not knowing the feeling, he could not think up the cynical remark which disparages the feeling.

An example from a novel will serve to illustrate the way in which detachment can turn into being shut off, the way in which one psychological process can change easily into another related one:

> (Dick Diver is a psychiatrist whose wife, Nicole, is a former mental patient of his.) Having gone through unprofessional agonies during her long relapse following (their daughter) Topsy's birth he had, perforce, hardened himself about her, making a cleavage between Nicole sick and Nicole well. This made it difficult now to distinguish between his self-protective professional detachment and some new coldness in his heart. (Fitzgerald, 1934, p. 251)

Dick Diver finds the professional detachment which he had adopted as armor changing into a lack of response to Nicole. When a person's lack of responsiveness enlarges to the point where sizable segments of reality are concerned, then that person is closed off from reality.

Obviously in any given situation this distinction might be difficult to make. That is, we may not be able to know whether a person is detached or closed-off. But that is a separate issue from the

one which we want to make central here. What
interests us is the way in which both of these
processes work towards creating some form of distance. Involvement with people takes different
forms; the closed-off person and the detached
person are not so involved, or do not show their
involvement, as much as other people. Thus we can
see that there is something about involvement,
about developing and showing feelings, which de-
creases distance; or, as our examples show, in
situations involving distance, often feelings are
not being shown. In an earlier discussion of ritual,
we pointed out how a person may not feel understood
and how that may help create distance. We also
suggested that when a person does not want to be
understood, or does not communicate enough so as
to be understood, that may create or maintain
distance. In the examples we have just been considering, of closed-off and detached, there is
similarly some inability or reluctance to express
feelings, to attach feelings to others, to become
involved.

Another group of examples involves not paying
attention, or being what we call away. A person is
said to be away when a situation becomes empty of
interest for him. There are a variety of ways of
not paying attention of course, but one way of
describing a person who is not paying attention is
to say that he is away, the idea being that his
attention is elsewhere. This happens when a person
has been trying to pay attention but is unable to
find anything sufficiently interesting to hold his
attention. For example, in the following we see the
narrator of a novel rising out of his boredom:

And then this small woman happens to look up
and meet my eyes, and opening her teeth in a
little nervous smile, raises her eyes to the
ceiling in mock despair. And I find myself
smiling back. A number of things suddenly
grow and sprout all round and inside me. At
this slight contact with an unknown dark brown
woman, life comes flowing back...now life flows
in and details bud into place. One flicker of

interest -- and everything becomes significant.
(Sansom, 1958, pp. 6-7)

The evocation of his interest in her has suddenly
made life interesting again and his boredom has
ended. Boredom involves finding things insignificant; nothing seems worth paying attention to; and
then when -- as in this example -- boredom terminates,
suddenly life becomes significant again.

The sort of interest in the world which is
lacking in boredom and away behavior can vary from
mere attention to a passionate involvement; in
this discussion, we want to include other psychological processes which similarly reveal a lack of
interest in the world, but which stop short of the
kind of radical inability to become involved with
reality which being closed-off implies.

While talking with someone, you may suddenly
notice that he is far away, as in this example:

Suddenly mist came into his eyes. A trap door
slammed shut. The old man was drifting back
in time, sinking back into the first, the
third, the sixth decade of his life. He was
burying one of his children again. Which one
could it be?...When this mood came over him,
the old man had a blind look. (Boll, 1962,
pp. 10-11)

Goffman discusses this kind of "inward emigration"
and calls it away:

Perhaps the most important kind of away is that
through which the individual relives some past
experience or rehearses some future ones, this
taking the form of what is variously called
reverie, brown study, woolgathering, day-
dreaming, or autistic thinking. (1963, p. 70)

People who are "away" are commonly referred to as
distant by my research partners.

The opposite of being away from the world is

287

being in touch with the world; a person who is open is accessible to influence from the world outside him, is capable of developing feelings which are in touch with that world. An example will make clear the connection between being open and what is called "paying attention" to someone (and it is such attention-paying which is lacking in away processes).

I inquired whether I might call the maid, and be conducted to a bedroom? Mr. Earnshaw vouchsafed no answer. He walked up and down, with his hands in his pockets, apparently quite forgetting my presence; and his abstraction was evidently so deep, and his whole aspect so misanthropical, that I shrank from disturbing him again...I was not sure how openly I grieved, till Earnshaw halted opposite in his measured walk, and gave me a stare of newly awakened surprise. Taking advantage of his recovered attention, I exclaimed... (Bronte, 1847, p. 137)

Being open in the sense of being able to develop feelings which are in touch with the surrounding world must involve much more than a simple capacity to pay attention to others; but unless one has at least that rudimentary capacity, unless one is paying some kind of attention to others, and can thus get involved with others, he is away from them. The example just given shows the relation between being away and not paying attention. Being open to someone includes paying attention to them as well as the capacity for further involvement with them; attention is a kind of minimal involvement and creates the route to greater involvement.

One aspect of the example just given deserves our attention. The narrator wants something from Mr. Earnshaw that he is not able to obtain. This is a dynamic factor which appears in many distance examples. That is, distance is experienced often when one person wants something which is not there. In this case, the narrator wants at least Mr. Earnshaw's attention. He wants a response of some sort, an acknowledgement of his presence. But he gets nothing and he grieves over this loss or absence. Many of our distance examples involve a similar sense that one person wants something which is not there. The wanting may set up a relation in which the distance arises; without some degree of relation, or without some desire for a connection, then perhaps distance does not, in a truly psychollogical sense, occur. This again seems paradoxical; that is, we seem to be saying that two people must be near each other, or together, or involved in some sense, before they can be distant. But in fact, there is some element of truth in this. Some connection, which may take the form of a vector or a desire or a want (whatever word should be used), must exist in order for something else to be felt as missing. When neither person wants nor expects there to be a connection between them, then the two people may be apart but they will not feel themselves as psychologically distant.

Anxiety deserves discussion since it is mentioned so often in connection with distance; however, it is not listed as a separate process since it functions, with respect to distance, to create either of two processes we have already discussed: either the process of being closed-off or that of being away. Anxiety can prevent a person from paying attention to another and thus functions to keep him away from the other, as in the following:

My girlfriend is so afraid of mice and rats that when she actually sees one she becomes panicked. Once we were walking down a street fairly late at night and she saw a small animal she took for a rat. She began screaming immediately and even though I urged her to be quieter (there were residences nearby and people would be alarmed) and pointed out that the animal was clearly a cat. She would not listen to me at all for three or four minutes. It was like beating my head against a brick wall to try to get her to listen; it was hopeless. (from a research partner)

Anxiety can also function to create the process of being closed-off from another. If a person's

anxiety is created by the one he is with, then that
person is involved with the other but in such a way
that he cannot be open to things which the other is
saying or doing. In this situation, the person is
both close to the other -- the other matters enough
to him to make him feel anxious -- and at the same
time, the person is distant from the other; his
anxiety has made him not open. Here we have an
indication that more than one type of distance is
needed to account for the kinds of evidence which
we are discussing.

What appears to be happening here is that part
of P's behavior is oriented towards O or is a
function of O's presence. This is a more abstract
way of saying that O matters to P. One type of
distance must be inherent in this form of relationship, though at this point it is not yet clear how
we should describe that form of distance. This kind
of distance may be related to what happens in ritual,
where -- as we pointed out earlier -- two people are
not so much oriented towards each other as towards
social rules, or a social order which is super-
ordinate to them as individuals. That is, there is
something about being involved with another person
on a level which implicates affects and feelings
which is relevant to distance. Perhaps when a
person wants this kind of engagement and does not
get it, he feels distant. But there must be another
kind of distance, since the person whose feelings
about the other are so intense (like the anxious
person we just discussed) that they interfere with
being related in a different way, must also be
described in terms of distance. That is, the anxious
person we discussed is close in one way -- involved
with the other -- but unable to be close in a second
way. This second way has something to do with
understanding and listening and paying attention.
Our examples of away may also illustrate this process.
Mr. Ernshaw, for example, is not paying attention
and not understanding what his guest wants. However,
in that example, there may again be two distance
processes involved. Mr. Earnshaw is paying no
attention to his guest, and this lack of orientation
towards his guest may be our first form of distance.

But his inaccessibility, the fact that he does not reveal himself at all, does not make clear what is on his mind, may be related to the second form of distance, which may involve the issue of understanding or comprehension. Mr. Earnshaw makes himself incomprehensible by not revealing what is on his mind. He is remote and unavailable. We will be returning to this complex issue of how to differentiate these two types of distance as we proceed through our sets of examples. Let us turn now to the next examples, which involve what we are calling alienation.

A rather profound kind of separation between a person and his environment is implied by the term alienation. Alienation also means that a person lacks positive direction, lacks aims of the sort which would serve to link him with the world. The alienated person lacks perspective from which he can view the world; the world is not in any fixed relation to him. In order to have a perspective or a point of view from which to view the world, one needs a stable fixed position on which to rest; the alienated person lacks such a stable fixed position. For example, Sartre's novel Nausea (1949) portrays such a character:

> It is the reflection of my face. Often in these lost days I study it. I can understand nothing of this face. The faces of others have some sense, some direction. Not mine (p. 27)...I must finally realize that I am subject to these sudden transformations. The thing is that I rarely think; a crowd of small metamorphoses accumulate in me without my noticing it, and then, one fine day, a veritable revolution takes place. This is what has given my life such a jerky, incoherent aspect (p. 12)...And the suspicious transparency of the glass of beer in the Cafe Mably. Suspicious: that's what they were, the sounds, the smells, the tastes...as soon as you held on to them for an instant, this feeling of comfort and security gave way to a deep uneasiness (p. 175)...Nothing happens

while you live. The scenery changes, people
come in and go out, that's all. There are no
beginnings. Days are tacked on to days
without rhyme or reason, an interminable,
monotonous addition (p. 57).

This character sees no stability anywhere in his
own experience (though others seem to him to have
such stability: "the faces of others have some
sense"); he has no point of view from which to see
the world and thus the world lacks all but the most
paltry kind of significance. His own experiences
lack coherence; they do not adhere together ("Days
are tacked on to days without rhyme or reason").
This characteristic formlessness of his own experience is linked with the lack of stability he
experiences, though exactly how is not clear.

Although alienation implies a lack of positive
goals, there is often an abundance of negative
goals: that is, the alienated person often knows
what he does not like about the world, but his
response to the world is withdrawal from it rather
than an attempt to change it. For example, the
main character in Melville's story Bartleby the
Scrivener (1853) works in a lawyer's office as a
clerk, copying important papers for the lawyer; but
Bartleby does not talk at all except to reiterate
his opposition to certain tasks which are asked of
him. "I would prefer not to" is his continual
refrain when his employer asks him to do certain
things. Bartleby seems to know what he does not
want quite well; but such knowledge is not sufficient to link one to the world unless it issues
in a strong desire to change the world. Bartleby
has no such strong desire to change things; he
simply wants things to leave him alone. He does
not take advantage of any of his employer's offers
of help; and he eventually dies.

There are some important features of our
account of alienation which need to be emphasized,
since they become important in our construction of
a theory of psychological distance. The alienated
person in the example from Sartre's novel appears

292

to lack a coherent point of view. He has difficulty
finding a stable position from which to view other
people and events. We can surmise that other
people would find him difficult to understand as
well, just as the employer in Melville's novella
about the clerk would prefer not to find Bartleby
difficult to understand. There may be something
about having a position from which to view things,
having a stable point of view, which nurtures the
process of understanding. To understand another,
perhaps we need both a point of view of our own and
the other person to have a point of view. If either
our own experience or the other's experience is
relatively formless, then perhaps understanding
becomes more difficult. Let us keep this notion in
mind as we continue to discuss the variety of distance examples, since it may become helpful in
constructing a theory of distance.

The next phenomenon, which involves examples
of people who are reserved, implies a lack of
expression of feelings and thoughts, either through
verbal communication or gesture; and in addition,
a reluctance on a person's part to have the other
become involved with him. This reluctance leads
the reserved person to maintain control over his
interaction with others. It does not imply any
lack of capacity to attach feelings to reality
(as in closed-off); nor does it imply any inability
to convey or communicate about such feelings as do
exist (of the sort we will come to when we discuss
shyness). Rather the emphasis is on a lack of
desire to express one's feelings openly and clearly,
and on one's reluctance to have the other become
involved with him.

In one example, Freud is characterized by
someone who knew him as reserved: One always
felt that the relationship was under his control.
His affability and accessibility were there
because he willed it so. One sensed an invisible reserve behind which it would be impertinent
to intrude and no one ever did. (Jones, 1955,
p. 408)

Note that the reserve in this case is spoken of as something "behind which it would be impertinent to intrude" as though reserve -- a lack of full outward expression of a variety of feelings and thoughts, a lack of expression of self, a refusal to let the other come too near -- establishes a kind of barrier between the reserved person and the other. The concept of barrier is very pertinent to our whole investigation, for it arises again and again in interview material which is given in response to questions about distance. The concept of barrier implies that there is something between two people preventing free and easy access; in particular, it refers to any constraints placed upon expressiveness on the part of one person, or upon comprehension of that expressiveness on the part of the other person. For example, lack of a common language between two people is a barrier; or if a person has difficulty in making his point of view clear to another person in a conversation, whether or not he knows precisely what the roots of the difficulty are, he will speak of a barrier. A barrier may exist at either side of the interaction; in the case of a reserved person, he is keeping himself hidden to some extent; he is providing the barrier.

The other interesting aspect of this example is that the speaker says of Freud that one felt that "the relationship was under his control." The word "control" is crucial here, and it is congruent in its implications with what we have said about reserve. The reserved person is controlling himself so that the other person does not become too involved with him; being reserved implies that one is able to control oneself almost without any effort.

The opposite quality would be some kind of natural spontaneity; both reserve and spontaneity have to do with how readily a person expresses his feelings; although neither is completely voluntary -- each comes to a person without his being able to will it easily -- nonetheless there is in neither a complete loss of self-direction, such a loss as is implied in being closed-off on the one hand or impulsive on the other.

Another example of reserve which is slightly
more complex follows:

> (Ethan drove the visitor to the railway
> station each day.) Ethan Frome drove in
> silence, the reins loosely held in his left
> hand...He never turned his face to mine, or
> answered, except in monosyllables, the
> questions I put, or such slight pleasantries
> as I ventured. He seemed a part of the mute
> melancholy landscape, an incarnation of its
> frozen woe, with all that was warm and sentient
> in him fast bound below the surface; but there
> was nothing unfriendly in his silence. I simply
> felt that he lived in a depth of moral iso-
> lation too remote for casual access... (p. 14)

> (On another of their trips, through a heavy
> snowstorm, they detoured out of their usual
> path because it was blocked by a stalled train,
> and on the detour went by Frome's house)...
> as if the mere sight of the house had let me
> too deeply into his confidence for any further
> pretence of reserve, he went on slowly (into
> a speech about his mother)...As we turned into
> the Corbury road the snow began to fall again,
> cutting off our last glimpse of the house;
> and Frome's silence fell with it, letting
> down between us the old veil of reticence.
> (Wharton, 1911, pp. 21-22)

Ethan is still able to emerge from his reserve and
make confidences, and talk with other people; but
the narrator's use of terms like moral isolation
implies that the character is not merely reserved,
or that his reserve is so deeply rooted a habit as
to have frozen over the surface of his personality;
thus this seems a slightly more complex example.

But in all of our examples of reserved behavior and people, there appears this common thread
of difficulty getting to know the reserved person.
Here we should underline a point we originally made
earlier in our discussion of ritual: that P's
reserve will only be felt by person O if O wants

some more extensive contact with P. There has to be a desire for something more in order for the reserve to be felt as a barrier. Here again we have the notion of a force or vector or desire for a relation and this force may provide the context within which the distance can occur and be felt as important.

So what the reserved person is doing, then, is to make himself less accessible. His point of view, whatever it might be -- his experiences, his memories, his feelings -- are not clearly revealed to his companion. Here there is not so much a doubt about whether a point of view exists (such a doubt does exist in the case of the alienated person) though more extreme examples will be presented later in this chapter when we consider examples of treating the other person as an object, or seeing the other as a robot. But with the reserved person, the difficulty is in the lack of expressiveness. This lack of expressiveness may be felt, by the other, as intentional and designed to prevent any deeper contact; or it may be felt as basically friendly and unintentional (as in the example from Wharton's novel about Ethan Frome). Our earlier discussions can help us to see that in these two cases, although there is a common thread of reserve (and presumably one type of distance), another type of distance is not equally implicated. That is, the first example, of a person who is trying to control the relationships and to prevent any further development of a more personal relation, the reserve may create one type of distance and help to maintain another second kind as well. The type which is created by reserve involves the dimension we have been calling understanding, which is related with what we have called a point of view. A reserved person keeps his point of view out of sight and prevents the other from understanding him better. This is what Ethan Frome does. But Ethan is felt as friendly and he is not opposed to all further contact. He does, briefly, open up as we might say, and though he does not reveal much, nor for very long, his having done so at all makes clear his orientation towards his listener. That is, he

is not distant in this other way which involves
orientation or the directedness of our behavior.
He does direct behavior towards his companion: he
talks to him briefly. But the other example involves
a person who may be reserved as a way of inhibiting
more extensive contact with others. Thus he may be
keeping others at a distance, as we say, not just by
making himself less accessible, but by making clear
to others that they should not themselves get too
involved with him. They should, in short, leave
him alone (and not, as we have been putting it,
direct behavior towards him).

Our next example, shyness, is similar to those
we just considered. Like the reserved person, the
shy person stints on free and easy communication,
but his motive is more lack of confidence than
anything else; he fears other people, what they will
think of him or do to him. Although the end result
of shyness often resembles reserve -- in both cases,
the person may not let the other become interested
in him or interact with him -- the shy person is not
so much refusing to let the other person become
interested as he is exhibiting his unsureness about
and incapacity for letting others include him in
their behavior. He is unsure of how to approach
others, of how to integrate others into his activity, of what to do when others attempt to approach
him. He is wary and cautious in his dealings with
others because to him other people are strange, not
like him, perhaps better than he.

The notion of modesty, which is linked with
shyness (as Roget's, 1965, Thesaurus testifies, for
example) makes clearer the connection between shyness
and being reserved. The modest person is concealing
himself, he is avoiding exhibiting himself before
others, and preventing others from seeing one is a
way of staying distant from them.

The shy person lacks the courage and confidence
required to express himself freely before others,
requisite to getting in contact and dealing with
others, as the following example illustrates:

The mind of the country girl became filled with
the idea of drawing close to the young man.
She thought that in him might be found the
qualities she had all her life been seeking in
people. It seemed to her that between herself
and all the other people in the world, a wall
had been built up and that she was living just
on the edge of some warm inner circle of life
that must be quite open and understandable to
others. She became obsessed with the thought
that it wanted but a courageous act on her
part to make all of her associations with
people something quite different and that it
was possible by such an act to pass into a
new life as one opens a door and goes into a
room. (Anderson, 1919, p. 91)

Here it is made quite clear the way in which the
girl lacks the capacity to create certain acts
which would bring her into warmer association with
others; she hangs back to such an extent that it
seems as though there is a wall between her and
others (and this notion of a wall appears frequently in descriptions which evoke distance).

The wall in this case is created by the shy
person. A person's shyness is accompanied by a lack
of expressiveness (similar to that exhibited by the
reserved person); and by a fearfulness which prevents him or her from moving into closer contact
with others. Here again are combined what appear
to be two kinds of distance. That is, the lack of
expressiveness inhibits understanding (one type of
distance); and the lack of courage to direct
behavior towards others creates another type of
distance. The "understanding" distance is connected
with point of view; when one does not understand
another, one does not see his point of view; and
the shy person prevents others (unwittingly perhaps)
from seeing his point of view by being shy and
unexpressive. The "directed behavior" type of
distance arises when one does not make the other the
focus of behavior, either because (as in ritual) one
has his eyes focussed on something else (the
ceremony of the ritual), or because (as in shy

behavior) one is fearful of this kind of more intimate engagement with others.

Another set of distance examples involve respect. Respect is often connected with distance; for example, in Stendhal's novel, The Red and the Black, Julien in his relationship with some people is described as "keeping them at a respectful distance" (p. 325). Or in another example, a research partner told me of a professor whom he respects and whom he has difficulty in approaching for conversation, no matter what the topic.

Respect is commonly used with at least two meanings, one of which is not relevant for us. Respect can mean an ordinary granting of basic rights to the other person and we are not interested in this sense of respect. The respect we are interested in is a more unusual way of treating someone, making him special, setting him apart from other people. The process of respect which we are interested in may be similar to making a hero out of someone and it may involve placing someone on a pedestal above other people (we say that we look "up" to someone we respect). The saying "no man is a hero to his own valet" emphasizes the way in which respect involves seeing the other person as unusual, not like ordinary men; a valet must see to the ordinary human needs of his master. The valet presumably is privy to all the man's secrets and thus cannot respect him; respect seems, according to this saying, to depend somewhat on not knowing every little detail about the man's private life. Staying at a distance would seem, in this connection, to be related to not seeing much of a man, not getting to know him very well, not knowing a variety of intimate details about his living habits and character.

Insofar as respect involves looking up to someone, it seems to involve considering oneself less than the other person; being with the respected person makes one constrained, out of a fear (perhaps) of appearing foolish. Thus the student interviewed felt constrained in the presence of the respected professor and his conversational powers were hampered.

Admiration is not entirely similar in this regard (according to the information provided by my research partners); there are interesting examples in which P, because he admires O, pursues O and does not feel any hesitancy in going up to O and asking for an autograph (for example), or following O around and trying to imitate him or trying to share O's life with him.

Another example from a novel indicates the way in which respect involves a kind of separation of one's own status from that of the respected person:

> (Richards is a Jew from around Boston who is going to Harvard, who has social ambitions. Richard meets another boy named Drury, who) was born to a very snob-worthy pedigree and had prepared for college at St. Paul's School, but nevertheless...had refused bids to all of Harvard's social clubs, because he opposed snobbery on moral grounds and wanted to protest the clubs' exclusiveness. Richard was awed both by the pedigree and by this tale of hot egalitarianism and after hearing it he tendered Drury a kind of fond respect...
> (Kaufman, 1957, p. 80)

Richard looked up to Drury and found Drury a rather special kind of person, altogether more worthy than Richard himself.

In some ways, respect is connected with ritual. Sacred objects which are used in rituals often must not be approached casually or not approached at all. People are urged to respect these objects or sacred people who carry out rituals, by bowing before them or by kneeling in their presence or by addressing them with head averted.

Another common way of speaking which illustrates some connections between respect and distance describes insults, which damage one's respect or honor,

300

as "coming too close." Honor is connected with one's self and is felt as being "here" (near us, wherever we are); thus, insults which are aimed at our honor may come too close to us.

Respect is often connected with avoidance; for example, a child who is required to show respect to his elders may be told not to initiate conversation but to speak only when spoken to; he is supposed to avoid talking on his own. Or in certain gatherings, jokes are tacitly forbidden; people avoid joking in order to show respect for the occasion. Communication and talking are ways of approaching people; thus insofar as respect involves avoiding certain types of talk, it preserves a certain distance between people.

Our comments about respect make clear that several distance processes may be occurring in respect. First of all, respect can involve avoidance. That is, one stays away from the other and does not direct behavior towards the other or expect the other to direct behavior towards oneself. Secondly, one does not reveal oneself so openly when one is with a respected person; thus something of one's point of view remains hidden and concealed. These are two types of distance we have already discussed. But in addition, there is possibly a third type of distance involved. Our remarks about placing someone on a pedestal seems to imply a setting apart of the other. When P respects O, he may be seeing O as a special person, almost in a separate class of beings from himself. This placing apart of another in a separate group may involve a third type of distance. We cannot be very certain of this on the basis of our analysis of respect, but the next group of examples will give us further evidence that some such third type of distance may exist.

Exclusion and rejection examples involve a process of keeping the other person out of one's own group. P can exclude O by keeping O out of a conversation or a gathering; or simply by failing to welcome O to a situation. For example, if P is

301

talking with his friend X and P's acquaintance O
happens to come along, P can exclude O simply by
neglecting to introduce O to X, by failing to
include O in his conversation with X. In such a
situation, P may not even know fully that he is
excluding O, much less why he is excluding O.
That is, the factors influencing P in his action
of excluding O may be very unclear to P himself.
But in other situations, the factors responsible
for the exclusion of a person from a gathering can
be much more explicit; for example, in certain
restaurants, a man who is not wearing a tie and a
jacket will not be admitted; or similarly, some
parks are open only to residents of a specifically
circumscribed area surrounding the park.

Sometimes it is not clear that the rejection
differs from exclusion, but the term seems to imply
something more than merely a shut door (as it were);
the term implies a more actively opposing force.
When P simply fails to include O in his conversation
with X, P may be said to be excluding O, but if O
explicitly tries to enter the conversation and P
repeatedly rebuffs O, then P is said to be reject-
ing O. Rejection involves a more active opposition
on the part of P.

The groups that a person belongs to -- whether
formal or informal -- often become the sources of
exclusion actions. That is, people see belonging
to their own groups as an important source of their
own security; and P will often try to exclude others
from groups which P already is part of, whether a
country club or a simple conversation between himself and a friend on a street-corner.

Extreme examples of exclusion (including for
example discrimination) impress all of us in everyday life; a more subtle example of exclusion is
contained in the following:

> (A young girl is talking with an older foreign
> man whom she likes very much.) "I didn't like
> your friend at all," she remarked. "He looks
> as if he's plotting to blow up the Houses of

302

Parliament," she said, and at this he suddenly
laughed -- but it was at her and remarked,
"He'll be dead in a year, poor devil." The
way he said it -- for to her it sounded indifferent, gave her what she had been wanting;
"the poor devil" had been pushed outside the
circle of intimacy they sat in, the two of
them. (Lessing, 1956, p. 33)

When $\underline{P}$ wants to be with $\underline{O}$, small variations in the
inflections of $\underline{O}$'s voice can indicate to $\underline{P}$ that $\underline{O}$
is welcoming him or excluding him, or excluding
someone else; here the young girl wants to be with
the older man and eagerly seeks for hints in what
the older man says that she is more important to
him than his other friends.

Thus, exclusion and rejection have as central
elements the fact of group formation; one excludes
an other from a group, even if it is just a small
group of two people. As we pointed out in discussing respect, the process of putting someone in
another group may involve a third type of distance
and this third type is most vividly portrayed in
these exclusion and rejection examples. Respect
of course implies a more honorific setting apart
of another, but whether the setting apart of another
outside one's own group is intended to be a compli-
ment or a degradation, either way it implies a
distance which is connected with the setting apart
process. We will call this type of distance "unit"
distance, and refer to being in a unit (or group)
with another as a form of closeness; and feeling
outside a unit (or group) with another, or wishing
to keep the other outside one's own group, as a form
of distance.

Contempt is another psychological process which
creates distance; the distance created appears to
be the same sort as is created by exclusion and
rejection. Contempt is often explicitly connected
in speech with a sense of looking down on someone,
as from a height. Another way in which the relation
between distance and contempt can be seen is in the
fact that $\underline{P}$ sometimes conveys contempt of $\underline{O}$ by

303

refusing to meet O's eyes and looking away from O when O is in the same region. The following example was given to me by a research partner.

> I was walking to school with an acquaintance and as we approached Third Avenue we saw 2-3 derelicts on the sidewalk. The person I was walking with wanted to cross the street, to avoid walking near them; I asked her why and she said that she knew they were going to ask for money and then she went on about what worthless people they are. They never work for anything, she said; they are lazy and good for nothing except bothering us as we walk alone here.

This example reveals the way in which contempt is connected with rejection so far as distance is concerned.

Another closely related set of examples involves cases in which P does not belong to some group to which other people belong; when P wants to belong to that group, he may feel on the outside, left out of the group. In an example from a novel:

> (The narrator has met a woman at a bar, and is now helping her walk her inebriated male companion home; he thinks they are husband and wife.) I heard her say, "It'll be nice to get to bed, won't it, Colin?" "Hit the hay," he nodded, very serious. His feet lapsed sideways and we all three seemed to traverse the pavement like a chorus line, and laughed -- but through it, I remember a sore little jolt of envy. The two together? I alone left out? (Sansom, 1958, p. 13)

The narrator wants to belong somewhere with someone; he sees these two as belonging together; and he wishes he were in a similar situation; he feels on the outside, he feels alone.

Envy can establish this feeling that one is separated from what one wants; envy sees other

people as having desirable things which one cannot
obtain easily; and it only flourishes where there
is some important separation between oneself and
what one wants.

Envy is explicitly connected with distance in
the psychological literature by Heider (1958); he
discusses envy as a relation between a person and
some goal object he desires. When P wants something which O has and envies O for its possession,
P is expressing his own feeling of being distant
from that object (of not being likely to get it in
the near future; of not being able to obtain it).
Our analysis here of the relation between distance
and envy differs slightly from that of Heider, since
we conceive that relation as expressing not so much
the lack of some desired goal object, as a person
feeling that he is outside of some group to which
he would like to belong. When P envies O, he is
expressing his feeling of not belonging; the
popular expression refers to not being "in" or to
wanting to join the "in people." This expression
implies that the use of certain clothing or possessions, or recreation, can lead to one's being
"in;" in what is never specified, but the implicit
notion is that one will belong to some important
coterie if one has a sailboat for instance or goes
to Switzerland to ski.

The examples we have been considering, of
exclusion and rejection, contempt, respect and envy
all seem to be best understood as having to do with
units or groups. These psychological processes
create distance in that they help to create, or
maintain, or emphasize the importance of units. A
person who is in a unit may keep someone else out
who wants in; or he may see someone else as being
outside, or he may want to see someone else as
being outside; or a person may want to get into a
unit or group that other people are in; but all of
these processes can be understood as involving a
similar type of distance which we are calling
"unit distance," different from the other two types
we discussed earlier. As we continue to discuss
our groups of examples, we will continue to refer

305

to these types of distance in order to see whether they help us make sense of the examples.

What Bales (1950) calls instrumental behavior is similar to impersonal behavior. Instrumental behavior is oriented towards a goal and people are dealt with as means to the fulfillment of that goal. Impersonal behavior occurs when P disregards the particular O before him and instead acts according to some set of rules (for example) or in such a way as to pursue some goal he has set for himself to which the nature of the particular O before him is not relevant. There are very clear affinities between impersonal behavior and ritualistic behavior in that both impersonal behavior and ritualistic behavior involve minimizing the specific individuality of the person in front of us, in favor of an emphasis on rules, or decorum, or ceremony. Both, in short, involve the same type of distance.

An example of impersonal behavior may occur when a person checks a book out of the library; he has a goal and his behavior with the librarian may well be impersonal, disregarding the librarian as a unique person and treating him just the way he would treat any other librarian who happened to appear before him. Behaving impersonally means making no distinction based on the particular person being dealt with. The particularity or specificity of our behavior is important. That is, if we take particular notice of the specific person in front of us, then we are not distant on the dimension which we have referred to earlier as directed behavior. Taking particular and special notice of a person is the opposite, on this dimension, of being impersonal, or engaging in ritualistic behavior where the form of the behavior has less to do with the particular person one is engaging than with social rules or social norms.

In interviews, impersonal behavior is often mentioned, with examples given of the research partner confronting some bureaucracy and pleading for individual consideration and getting nowhere. A student tells of a time when he was unable to get

his paper in on time and he went to the instructor
and asked for permission to hand it in late, because
of personal problems. The instructor applied the
rules and did not grant an extension; the instructor
is being impersonal and characteristically the
student reports feeling distant from the instructor
in such situations.

There are any number of phrases which people
use to describe the impersonal mode of behavior
which we are discussing; one appears in the following example:

> (A man is asking a woman whom he is having an
> affair with about her former lovers. His tone
> of voice alters.) She thought that whereas a
> moment ago he was asking on his account, as a
> man, now he was again talking like a man
> behind a desk. (Lessing, 1962, p. 169)

The phrase "like a man behind a desk" aptly expresses
what is happening in impersonal behavior, because
so often the P who is being impersonal is in actuality sitting behind a desk; he is an official in
some bureaucratic capacity. An interesting feature
of this example is that the woman was not expecting
impersonal behavior from the man. The man's
impersonality surprises her; it is not called for
in this intimate situation and in fact seems
inappropriate. But in daily life we all are
impersonal sometimes, regardless whether or not we
hold positions in a bureaucracy; given this fact
and the generally recognized appropriateness of
impersonal behavior in some situations, the curious
result is that sometimes, when a person is expected
to behave impersonally and fails to do so, his
failure -- which may involve an attempt to behave
in a personal manner -- may create greater distance.
Imagine a man O who employs a person P; one evening
O and P have a few drinks together, and talk about
matters which they had never discussed in the office
before. The next day at an office meeting, O is
startled when P adopts the same personal manner
towards him which they had used towards one another
the previous evening; O would prefer that in the

office, P maintain the usual impersonal relationship. O may well react to this breach of propriety by not again seeing P after work for friendly drinks.

The phenomenon of special recognition which is perhaps the opposite of impersonal behavior deserves separate discussion here. Why special recognition should be so important is on the face of it somewhat mysterious, but the "special" hello or gift or gesture are mentioned again and again by subjects as helping to decrease distance, so frequently that we came to give it a name of its own, namely specialization. Specialization is the process of making someone special and of course many different overt deeds can convey specialization. We can say that when O's behavior seems impersonal to P, what is lacking in O is any kind of special recognition of P.

We have discussed the behavior of people who have feelings but who prefer not to reveal them; such reserved behavior differs from the behavior of people who cover up their real feelings with a layer of pretense. People who ignore their real feelings in favor of expressing feelings which they think they ought to have, who deceive themselves as well as others, we sometimes call phony. Phoniness involves putting on an act not only for the benefit of others but also for the benefit of oneself. This is happening in the following example:

> (Daisy is talking to Nick.) "You see I think everything's terrible anyhow," she went on in a convinced way. "Everybody thinks so -- the most advanced people. And I know. I've been everywhere and seen everything and done everything."..."Sophisticated -- God, I'm sophisticated." The instant her voice broke off, ceasing to compel my attention, my belief, I felt the basic insincerity of what she had said. It made me uneasy, as though the whole evening had been a trick of some sort to exact a contributary emotion from me. I waited and sure enough, in a moment she looked at me with an absolute smirk on her lovely face, as

308

if she had asserted her membership in a rather
distinguished secret society to which she and
Tom belonged. (Fitzgerald, 1934, pp. 21-22)

Daisy here is putting on an act to please herself
and to encourage Nick (her listener) to regard her
in a flattering way. She is trying to place herself
in a certain light; but what she is doing is very
different from lying (which we will discuss next);
for she herself is taken in by her own act to a
certain extent. The descriptive phrase "putting
on an act" often seems very opposite in such situations, as in the following example:

(A supermarket executive talking about his
relationships with women after his divorce.)
For a while I enjoyed the mutual confession
sessions with each new girl. But after a
while it got to seem to me that I had developed an act -- I knew just what stories to
tell about myself, how to say who I am and
what things matter to me, what questions to
ask that would make her do the same. But how
many times can you go through all that and
still care? Or still believe in yourself?
(Hunt, 1966, p. 120)

Here the man who is talking makes explicit the fact
that when one comes to feel that he is putting on
an act, large questions loom about who one really
is; phoniness and insincerity clearly have something to do with how one's identity is created,
maintained, or eroded. One last example which
illustrates the same themes:

(A young psychologist on a field research
project with an older more experienced
psychologist is trying to learn how to behave
with the research subjects; he tries to
imitate the older man.) I watched him with
a respect which was beginning to be overcast
by some doubt I couldn't put a name to, and
tried to imitate his technique. Whatever was
said to me, I repeated it, or exclaimed over
it: "Oh, really?" "How interesting!" "Gee,

that's too bad." It worked all right; they smiled, relaxed, leaned closer and spoke with a more affectionate, confidential intensity. The disconcerting thing was that none of them seemed to notice that they were no longer talking to another human individual, but to a mechanical echo. (Lurie, 1967, p. 53)

Here also the narrator feels a "doubt" which he cannot "put a name to;" he also feels some vague uneasiness about what is occurring. He is aware that his expressions ("Oh really" and "How interesting") are not really his; they are not accurate reflections of his feelings; they are rather "mechanical" (as he says), having been programmed beforehand. What does distance have to do with such mechanical repetition of prearranged exclamations? When we think about our discussion of ritual and of impersonal behavior, we can see a pattern in which distance is related to a lack of spontaneity, in which distance is a function of mechanization of interaction. In all of these processes, there appears behavior dominated by rules and mechanical formulas.

In the last example given, we actually see insincerity rather than phoniness; the insincere person does not believe what he is saying as fully as does the phony person. The insincere person is not completely taken in by his own act (as the phony person is). Insincerity verges on out-and-out deception, which we will turn to next.

An explicit statement of the relation between deception and distance exists in the psychological literature, in the formulation of Joe Adams (1964). His discussion of deception focuses on situations which arise in mental hospitals, for example when a patient is deceived in the process of involuntary commitment, or in the treatment process by the doctor (e.g., the doctor gives placebos).

Adams first differentiates between intended and unintended deception. Then he isolates spontaneous deception in a separate category (for

310

example, a person lies in order to impress someone
else; he lies without thinking about it beforehand,
sometimes even without consciously wanting to lie).
This seems more like what we have called insincerity
or phoniness than out-and-out deception. Adams'
main concern is with intended deception; he states
that "intended deception of another person Y by a
given person X increases X's distance from that
person in important and identifiable respects"
(p. 31). He does not say what distance means, but
rather seems to take it for granted that there are
"common sense" meanings of distance with which
people are generally familiar.

He specifically points to guardedness as one
consequence of lying; that is, if X is lying, X may
exhibit a mechanical manner of speaking and in
addition eliminate certain feelings which ordinarily (were he not lying) would occur. Adams also
indicates that the fact that X is deceiving Y means
that X feels he cannot trust Y with the truth; the
breaking of this bond of trust is in Adams' view
intimately connected with the increase of distance.

Interviews with my research partners indicate
that out-and-out deception with no extenuating
motive is much harder to sustain than deception
which seems to have some rationale. Iago was
unusually lucid in his own self-appraisal; he knew
he was lying. For this reason -- because daily
deception usually is based on some extenuating
excuse -- such deception becomes difficult to
distinguish from phoniness and insincerity. The
person who is lying will probably not consider his
actions a deception (since he will have a "good
reason" for his deceiving words); however, we are
justified in separating deception from phoniness so
long as the actor can admit that what he is saying
is not true. The following example illustrates
the kind of deception which is most common in daily
life:

(A student reported the following to me.) I
went to the first meeting of a course in
sensory processes in graduate school and the

311

teacher asked each member of the class if he
or she had had the background in physiology
which would be necessary for this course. I
nodded yes when he came to me, even though I
have never taken a course in physiology,
because I thought that physiology probably
was not so necessary for the course as he
imagined, and that if it were, I could learn
what I needed by reading a book outside class.

The student sees the teacher as exaggerating the
importance of physiology for his course, and says
he knows physiology when in fact he does not.

The examples we have just been considering of
phoniness and deception have implications for
identity formation and self-awareness, but we are
more interested in how they are related to distance.
We can see, in light of our earlier discussions,
that the phony person and the deceiving person
both are making any accurate understanding of themselves difficult, by not revealing themselves.
They are hiding themselves just as surely as the
reserved person, although with different motives
and different effects perhaps. But with regard to
distance, they all have something in common; they
all imply that one type of distance, the type that
involves expressing what one feels, and thus making
oneself available for being understood by the other,
is increasing.

Other types of distance may be involved as
well, depending on the examples. For instance,
some people who engage in deception do so with a
great contempt for others; in this case, the
deception mingles with the contempt and the deceiving person is not only making himself inaccessible
to accurate understanding (creating one type of
distance), but he is placing others in a different
unit or group by being contemptuous of them, thus
creating another type of distance.

There are other examples which appear related
to phoniness and deception, in which P perceives the
overt content of what O is saying as untrue or mis-

312

leading. Sometimes this happens when P thinks he knows what O is "really" saying; P is then engaged in an act of what I call translation. P translates O's overt explicit statements in order to emphasize some implicit meaning which P thinks he discerns. Sometimes this act on P's part involves a thorough contempt for O, as when P hears O talking about some exploit in a way that seems to give O the major credit for the achievement and P reinterprets or translates O's statements in such a way as to deny the real importance of what O was doing. At other times, P's feelings may be sympathetic and kindly; he may see O as confused and want to try to help O straighten things out for himself. Two examples from the same novel follow which illustrate translation:

> (Peter and his father are at home, his father telling about a meeting of a local club in which he had played an important role, according to his own account.) His father paused and Peter realized it was the end and said "Huh." He could not help half believing. He instinctively interpreted a different meaning into every sentence, trying to distinguish what had happened from what his father said.

> (Peter has retreated to his room after a quarrel with his father; his father follows him there.) "We can't go on like this, old boy." His voice was hoarse with genuine emotion. "No." Peter was so angry that his eyes wanted to water. "What's it all about?" "I don't know." "Why can't we get on as we used to? I can remember a year ago you and I walking up and down the lawn discussing things together, and everything was pleasant and friendly. Can't you?" "Yes." Peter could. It was useless to explain who had done the discussing. (Hinde, 1953, pp. 17 and 22)

What is crucial in translation is that P does not make explicit to O his translation or reinterpretation of O's acts and words; notice that in these examples, Peter does not tell his father what he

313

is thinking. If P makes the translation explicit,
then he is trying to convey to him what he sees in
his father; there is still an attempt at communication, at bridging the gap between himself and O.
When P does not make his translation explicit, P⁻
is indicating that he considers O unreceptive to
the truth of the translation; this in turn usually
implies that P considers O hopelessly confused, or
neurotic, even crazy.

This is an important distinction relevant to
our attempt to achieve a theoretical understanding
of psychological distance. When P is trying to
make explicit to O his translation, then he is
revealing his point of view to O, and in terms of
our earlier discussions, he is trying to reduce
distance on this dimension. When he does not make
his translation explicit, then he is creating or
maintaining distance on this dimension, and in
addition, he may be creating another type of distance, the one we have called unit distance. That
is, P may be placing O in another group from himself, in considering O crazy. This issue is inherent in the next set of examples, which involve
seeing the other as irresponsible.

Seeing the other as irresponsible is a complex
act in which one says to the other person (in effect,
if not explicitly): You do not have the same rights
I do. P sees O as having fewer rights than himself
because he sees O as acting in an irresponsible
way. Many superiors see their subordinates in this
way; many adults see children in this way; many
teachers see students in this way; most people see
those who are labeled "insane" or "crazy" in this
way. Subordinates, children, students, crazy people:
they all seem in the eyes of some others to be
incapable of dealing with life or of taking care of
themselves in some respects.

Responsibility is what gives a person's acts
legitimacy, not in a legal sense, but in a psychological sense; when a person is responsible, he has
a right to behave as he does. Denying that the
other person is responsible is a psychological act

314

which has profound implications for how one behaves with him; for example, in doing this, one is liable to take responsibility for the other (often without being asked to do so). For example, a parent may decide for his child, in the belief that the child is not capable of reaching a responsible decision on his own. In this society, parents are expected to make decisions for their children when their children are young; but this process of taking responsibility for the other person is often extended inappropriately, in which case I call it seeing the other as irresponsible.

Seeing the other as crazy is one way of denying that the other is responsible. When P is seeing the other as crazy, he is denying the other a fundamental legitimacy as a human being; for example, seeing the other as crazy disburdens one of what may seem the complicated task of trying to understand him of declaring him beyond understanding with the usual concepts; he must be shoved out of the human community into the group of those who are strange and alien. One refuses to make a serious effort at confronting the other person when one starts seeing him as crazy. One no longer has to try to piece together his various acts, his ideas and feelings; one can instead stop listening, and dismiss him.

In order to illustrate what has just been said, let me cite a comment made by the literary critic Blackmur (1964) in a discussion of the main character in a novel by Conrad Aiken, King Coffin (1964). The character's name is Jasper Ammen; the story reveals how Jasper picks out a man on the street and follows him with the intention of murdering him, even though Jasper never saw the man before in his life. Jasper is simply exercising his power over the strange man for the delight of it. The author at the end of the novel makes explicit the fact that he considers Jasper crazy and Blackmur comments as follows:

> I am rather sorry that Jasper Ammen should be explicitly insane, for it impairs the credi-

bility of his thoughts and acts. I would,
for the joy of reading, take him as one of
the condottieri of the Psyche, a good companion on the domestic scene for Gide's
Lafcadio, Dostoevsky's Stavrogin, Balzac's
Vautrin, or even Mann's Felix Krull, with
all of whom I feel much personal sympathy.
(p. 11)

Blackmur observes that making Jasper explicitly
insane places him in another category, separate
from the rest of us, so that any sympathy we may
have for him is destroyed, so that we no longer
try to see his acts as part of the human scene.[3]

These examples bear an obvious affinity, in
terms of distance, with other examples of placing
or keeping people outside one's own group. Seeing
someone as crazy or irresponsible places him or
her outside the group of sane and responsible
people. But there may possibly be another distance
process involved, treating people as particular
persons. Whether or not this other distance
dimension is involved depends on the example used.
Examples involving P's seeing O as irresponsible
where P continues to have considerable attachment
to O, considerable involvement with O, as a parent
ordinarily has with a young infant is different
from P treating O as irresponsible where O is seen
as totally different, unsympathetic, not worth
paying attention to, not worth helping. Thus
whether or not another distance dimension is involved
as well will depend on the nature of the specific
example used.

Another psychological process which involves
seeing the other as irresponsible is humoring. The
act of humoring someone means that P is treating O
as eccentric in some particular way; P sees O as
being incomprehensibly set on carrying out some
peculiar activity and P decides to tolerate that
activity even though it is bizarre. For example:

I'm with an elderly lady, eating in a restaur-
ant; she begins to complain about the draft on

316

her legs. I feel nothing. She tells me with
great detail to go find the manager and complain, but complain nicely; she tells me
exactly what to say and makes me repeat it
after her, all the time unsure whether I'll
have to go find the manager and complain.
I hope that she will forget about the draft
after a few minutes; if she does not, perhaps
I'll ask the waiter if we can move to another
table.

Here the narrator is not taking her request completely seriously, yet he is not arguing with her
or trying to force her to drop it.

In another example:

I recently saw a man and his wife together
with their small child. The child was playing
unhappily on the floor, crying and complaining,
while the couple were trying to eat. The man
offered to help the wife by taking care of
the child while she did the dishes, the woman
said in a somewhat distraught voice that that
would be nice, except that if he was to help
by playing with the child, he must walk the
child; nothing else would do. She explained
that the child wanted to practice walking,
since she was just learning to walk. The
husband agreed, saying "yes dear," although
indicating in his tone of voice that he
thought this was a strange imposition his wife
was placing on him. He proceeded to walk the
baby around.

The husband clearly regarded his wife's insistence
as a whim and he humored her.

This humoring process is related to what we
earlier called translation. As we pointed out
earlier, the translating process varies depending
on whether one attempts to convey one's translation directly to the other. Similarly, the humoring process varies depending on whether one is
fundamentally sympathetic with the other or not.

Humoring can be hostile or friendly and the variation in tone is accompanied by a variation in distance implications. Humoring always involves an increase in one type of distance, that involving what we call units; that is, in humoring others, we are seeing them as fundamentally different from ourselves. But we may or may not be oriented towards them and trying to treat them as particular individuals; and we may or may not be trying to understand their point of view. The examples we just reviewed do not seem to involve any attempt to understand the other's point of view, but in both there is an acceptance of that point of view and an attempt to behave so as to take it into account. Thus in both cases, there is apparently distance on one dimension (the unit dimension) and closeness on another (orienting oneself towards the particular other one).

Another set of examples which may be related to alienation is seeing the other as a robot. Sometimes while looking at the other person you begin to see him or her as a robot or a machine. Your capacity to see and understand the other person's covert behaviors -- his feelings, his thoughts, his intentions -- disappears, perhaps because you are under stress, or in great fear; or perhaps because the other person has rigidly excluded from his behavior all indication of or allusion to any fluctuating feelings and is behaving very mechanically.

The category of impersonal behavior which we already discussed is related to this process of seeing the other as a robot; for when P and O are interacting and O is being impersonal, P may see O as relentlessly carrying out a pre-written program, much the way a machine would, with no allowance being made for the particular nature of P's presence.

When P sees O as a robot (or a machine, or a wind-up doll), not only has P's capacity for visualizing and understanding O's covert behaviors vanished, but P is often seeing O as a more powerful being who cannot be entirely ignored or dismissed. P feels that there is no appeal; he feels that O would not understand anything that he might say and has entirely given up all efforts at communicating with O.

This way of experiencing others is sometimes described as characteristic of the experience of schizophrenics; and yet I have found that it is not an uncommon feature of daily experience for many people. Charles Dickens in his novels portrays many of his characters as automatons who can only be described externally; that is, his characters are described from the outside, in their movements and external gestures, and are explicitly compared with machines and animals.[4] The effect of Dickens' characterization of such people is often comic; missing from his descriptions is that kind of fear which often accompanies this experience in daily life.

John Holt, in his book, How Children Fail (1964), devotes a whole section to "Fear and Failure;" in this section, he gives many examples of what happens when children are placed under great pressure in classroom situations. He is trying to explain why many children, although intelligent in a great variety of daily situations, become stupid in classroom situations. The following example is illustrative; it comes from his own experiences of learning to play a musical instrument. He reports that after a very difficult day of teaching and meetings, he went for a music lesson; his teacher was particularly exasperated because Holt had made so little progress.

The pace was much too fast; I began to make mistakes; I wanted to stop, but, cowed by his determination, hesitated to make the suggestion. A feeling of physical pressure built up in my head. It felt as if something inside were trying to burst it open, but also as if something outside were pressing in it. Some kind of noise, other than my miserable playing, was in my ears. Suddenly I became totally note-blind. The written music before me lost all meaning. (pp. 65-66)

319

The written music became mere black marks on the
page; their associations with each other vanished;
and in the experience of seeing someone as robot-
like, the same kind of dissolution of internal
cohesiveness occurs. P no longer can see O as a
coherent person, but can only see external movements.

Another example from a student:

I'm taking an oral exam and what the teacher
is saying gradually begins to lose all its
meaning; I see only the mouth opening and
closing and hear sounds coming out, and
individual words, but I cannot make sense
of them; I cannot figure out what he is
saying.

Fragments of what is being perceived seem separated
from each other and do not fit together; the purpose of the movements is invisible. This experience
is somewhat like seeing a familiar street corner
from a fairly high building, from the top of which
all the movements on the street corner seem part of
a gigantic mechanical toy; or like watching a
familiar person in a movie which has been speeded
up with the sound turned off, so that the familiar
person is making jerky movements which seem to have
no meaning.

This evaporation of meaning also sounds very
similar to what we observed in the example from
Sartre's novel Nausea, where the narrator experienced events as not fitting together but simply
coming, one after another, in a monotonous succession. Deciding how these processes -- alienation
and seeing the other as a robot -- are related to
distance is difficult. In all probability, all
three types of distance are often involved, though
in which ways and what proportions would depend on
the particular example. Alienation certainly
involves being outside of social groups. The
alienated person typically lacks any shared positions with others; he is not caught up in social
movements or in any form of social organization.

Of course he may appear to belong to some social groups but he is not really concerned with the group. Therein lies one distance aspect of his situation.

In addition the other two types of distance may be created as well, both in alienation and in seeing the other as a robot. In both cases there seems to be a disappearance of the personal quality from the interaction. One does not try to see the other's point of view, nor does one really act as though there is any point of view to be understood.

Our last group of examples involves devaluing others, dehumanization, treating others as objects. This process is one of ceasing so entirely to see another person as human that he becomes in your eyes equivalent to and no better than other objects, which you can manipulate at will without concern for feelings or reactions. Exactly what is involved in this process is not clear; but somehow one manages to ignore the human aspects of the other person. What makes a person seem human is not clear. It seems to have something to do with a capacity for feeling, but in addition to that, a capacity for self-consciousness, for knowing what is felt; a capacity for symbolic communication (for making clear what is felt); and some kind of dignity or worthiness.

George Orwell was very concerned with this psychological process and the following examples come from two of his essays:

In a tropical landscape one's eye takes in everything except the human beings. It takes in the dried-up soil, the prickly pear, the palm tree and the distant mountain, but it always misses the peasant hoeing at his patch. He is the same colour as the earth, and a great deal less interesting to look at (1954a, p. 190)

He is talking about the situation of the white man in Africa; he observes that while men do not see the brown or black men who are natives in the country. Such natives do not count, for the white man, as human beings. And in another example:

> (Orwell is fighting in the Spanish War; he is out about one hundred yards from the Fascist trenches, sniping at the enemy soldiers.) At this moment, a man, presumably carrying a message to an officer, jumped out of the trench and ran along the top of the parapet in full view. He was half-dressed and was holding up his trousers with both hands as he ran. I refrained from shooting at him...I did not shoot partly because of that detail about the trousers. I had come here to shoot at "Fascists;" but a man who is holding up his trousers isn't a "Fascist," he is visibly a fellow-creature, similar to yourself, and you don't feel like shooting at him. (1954b, p. 199)

Here Orwell's label for the enemy ("Fascist") is not adequate; Orwell cannot sustain the illusion that the enemy is different, and not a human being like himself; and so he finds that he cannot shoot at him. Labels often serve this function, of enabling someone to diminish another human being, to make another person less than human, to make him into an object which can be manipulated as one desires.

A Theory of Distance

We have completed our analysis of the eight groups of examples of interpersonal distance. These examples constitute the basic data to which a theory of distance is accountable; they provide the phenomena which the theory must explain.

Even though there is a variety of material, we have seen that there are various kinds of similarities among the examples. First of all, the examples for any one psychological process -- such as impersonal behavior -- are similar to each other; and secondly, the examples contained within different psychological categories have some resemblances to each other. For instance, in several processes --

ritual, alienation, exclusion and not belonging --
there exists an emphasis on units which people form
together, or on the presence or absence of a social
position which serves as a basis for one's interaction with others. In other processes -- deception,
shyness, reserved, and closed-off -- there exists
some impairment of full and open communication. The
sources of the impairment vary to be sure, but
throughout these various processes is a general
similarity.

We have tried, as we analyzed and discussed
the groups of examples, to show that three types of
distance are needed to account for the variations
in the examples. One of them requires some degree
of orientation towards a particular other; the
second, some degree of communication of one's own
point of view and striving to understand the other's;
the third involves unit-formation.

Type I exists when P is not behaving towards O
as a person; when P is behaving towards O as a person,
no Type I distance can exist. For P to behave
towards O as a person, he cannot treat him as an
object or see him as a robot. In addition P must
see O as having a point of view, a unique way of
organizing events, a personality of his own.

Our examples have made clear that a variety of
processes can create this first type of distance;
that no one event necessarily leads to this type of
distance; and that a relation between two people
must be considered from both sides. Whether or not
distance is felt will depend on what each person is
looking for in the relation; and further, P may feel
and be more distant on this first dimension than O,
and vice versa. Ordinarily, we might suspect, this
imbalance will lead to P's changing his behavior
towards O, but there is nothing in the distance
phenomenon to necessitate this change.

A more technical way of putting this last
point is to say that distance is not a transitive
relation; P can be close to O in this first dimension without O necessarily being close to P.

Further, whatever the distance relation of P and O, it is dynamic; that is, it will change from moment to moment, depending on what each person is doing in the relation.

Note that when P is close to O in this first sense, and is behaving towards O as a particular person, there is an element of what we are calling "specialization" in his treatment of O. That is, P is making O special by treating O as a particular individual. When P notices what O's particular tastes are, then O feels that P is taking special notice of him (though of course he need not necessarily enjoy this). Some of the psychological processes already discussed, such as behaving impersonally, lack just this quality of specialization.

The second type of distance is intimately connected with the first. The second type arises when one does not take the point of view of the other person, or does not help the other person take one's own point of view. Both sides of the process are important: communicating openly and trying to understand the other and helping the other understand oneself.

What specifically is occurring when P tries to take O's point of view? Many of the psychological processes connected with distance revolve about P's inability to gain a view of O, whether because O is hiding himself, or because O is not like anyone P has met before, or because O is not behaving in a human way but impersonally or like a robot. When one tries to take the point of view of the other, he must first understand him, get some coherent view of him. Usually one tries to piece together the varied bits of information or clues which the other person exudes. This of course is not like a detective working on a case, or someone working at a jigsaw; it is complex and intuitive.

Every person interacting with another gives the other some opportunity to figure him out; this is true even when P does not want O to understand him for O can see, if he is alert, that P is trying to hide himself. When O cannot figure P out, this in itself becomes a topic for comment; in general, people expect to be able to figure out others while talking with them. This figuring out process, this activity of piecing together the other person out of the clues he gives about himself, is precisely what underlies the activity of taking the other's point of view. If P cannot figure O out, then P cannot take O's point of view.

How does a person go about trying to understand the other person? Which aspects of his behavior are useful? Primarily his feelings, we think; and any-thing else that makes him distinguishable from everyone else. Understanding requires knowing his individuality; you want to see how the traits we all have in common fit together to form a partic-ular whole.

Certain aspects of a person's activity are less subject to his control than others, and thus are used as pointers to personality. For example, all aspects of what is called expression are somewhat involuntary and therefore convey intimations of the real you. Your hidden intentions will more likely be revealed by expressive gestures than by your actual words.

Anyone can either be relatively frank, open, sincere, and honest in his behavior -- revealing his own self with candor -- or can be relatively re-served, insincere, and even dishonest, refusing to give out accurate information about himself. Frank, open behavior can easily convey understanding to the other person; expressive gestures must be relied on in its absence.

This entire process of trying to make sense of the other, of trying to take his point of view and understand him, is only possible if he is regarded as "responsible" for what is happening with his body, for what "he" is doing. By the concept of respon-sibility we mean a direct link between a person and his behavior.[5]

325

We want to stress the relation between comprehension and seeing; one can only comprehend the other when the other is visible and the other makes himself visible by expressing himself, through what we call spontaneity, through frankness, through any kind of behavior which makes clear what he as a person is like. Communication is the generic word which covers all this expressiveness, through which P makes himself clear to others; and the importance of communication in this consideration of distance is evident in the psychological processes in which a failure to communicate often plays a part. For example, in a shy person there is a lack of full communication; similarly when P is deceiving O, P is failing to communicate fully (although here his motives are of course different). Thus, although shyness and deception are clearly different psychological processes, they both become connected with distance through analysis of the notion of communication and its relation to comprehension of a person's self.

There are obviously other possible sources of a failure on P's part to take the point of view of O, besides O's lack of communicativeness. P may fail to take O's point of view because he is not interested in O; or because, even though he is interested, he lacks the kind of experience which would enable him to do so. That is, P may be a young man and O an older one, and P may fail to take O's point of view because P cannot grasp the nature of O's experience. P may be totally unfamiliar with the type of person he is confronting.

The third and last type of distance which is inherent in the distance examples we have discussed we have been calling unit distance, when people are not in a unit. Conversely, being in a unit makes people close. A unit is possible, in the first place, only because people have presence. Presence is the embodiment of a person; it indicates a person's whereabouts, physical and psychological. Most obviously, presence is conveyed by one's body; less obviously, by gestures, expression, and symbolic representations. Being in a unit involves shared

326

presence.

However, shared presence is not sufficient in itself to create a unit. Two people can be sitting next to each other on a subway and aware of each other's presence without necessarily being in a unit. Or two people can be talking on the telephone and thus sharing presence, and still not be in a unit with each other.

The best illustrative example of unit closeness is a situation in which P and O are working together on a joint task and report that they feel they are "together." Part of what is happening in such situations is that P and O have the same object for their behavior (some object outside them); they are behaving with reference to the same goal or purpose and in so doing they have in addition some kind of subsidiary awareness of each other's presence in the situation. Although the behavior involved in such an example is often quite obvious -- e.g., P and O are working together building a boat; or are helping in a political campaign, stuffing letters -- sometimes it can be less overt. For example, P and O may be stuck in some situation, for example a subway car which is stalled, in which the behavior is made up of feelings about the situation, or worries and thoughts about what will happen next. Or P and O may be in a foreign country and run into each other and find out that they are both from the same home town; this accentuates their togetherness in this foreign situation. Often out of these rudimentary unit situations arise the other kinds of closeness, but that need not inevitably happen; this kind of unit closeness can exist independently of any other. An example is the kind of relationship that exists between military men who live in the same barracks. One man may not know the other at all, save as a familiar face with which he exchanges greetings; but if one of the men gets into a fight, the other may come to his aid, simply on the basis of the solidarity which arises from the fact of their sharing the same living-quarters.

In addition to shared presence, being in a unit

with someone involves the following three characteristics: (a) dependence; (b) commitment; and (c)
acceptance. Dependence exists when P relies on the
unit for support, for the unit arises out of a
desire for support, for some ground on which one's
self may rest and find leverage for confident action.
A person in a unit is able to act confidently; and
this is the function belonging to the unit has for
him. Insofar as actions are behavior, they proceed
from the self towards objects; and the self is only
able to create such behavior if it has the kind of
strength (called confidence here) which derives
from being supported in a unit. Examples of factors
which can contribute to creating a unit (and thus
contribute to a person's strength or confidence) are
numerous: certain important types of similarity
(such as agreement on a matter of opinion); some
kinds of shared activity (taking part in some group
activity); and many kinds of emergency situations or
disasters (the electricity blackout in New York; the
death of John Kennedy).

Related to this characteristic of a unit is the
fact that psychological forces exist within the unit.
For example, people in a unit can ask favors of each
other, or make requests of various sorts. This is
not to say that whenever P asks a favor of O, that
P and O are in a unit; but within any unit, P and O
take each other for granted to the extent of being
able to rely on one another for help in cases of
need, and an example of that kind of reliance is
asking a favor. However, this reliance of P and O
on each other cannot become too explicit, cannot
become linked to demands, without danger to the unit.
As soon as demands and threats are being made by
either P or O, then the unit is dissolving or has
dissolved.

Commitment is the second of the caracteristics
important in a unit and exists when P dedicates
himself to the maintenance of the unit with O. This
is the factor which most clearly differentiates the
unit from more casual groups of people.

Acceptance is the third characteristic and means

328

that $\underline{P}$ admits $\underline{O}$ to the unit. Acceptance is basic to the formation of a unit and rejection of course leads to the dissolution of a unit (or prevents a unit from forming). Acceptance is linked most immediately to the idea of equality of worthiness. If $\underline{P}$ and $\underline{O}$ regard one another as equally worthy, then they accept each other. Any kind of inequality in this respect -- whenever $\underline{P}$ feels more or less worthy than $\underline{O}$ -- works against the formation or endurance of a unit.

Similarity sometimes seems to be related to the formation of units, but on analysis it seems important only as a contributory factor; for example, a superficial similarity -- in appearance -- can lead two people to consider each other equally worthy, and thus facilitate the formation of a unit. Bogardus' research (1949) is concerned with the kind of dissimilarities -- in nationality or skin color -- which lead sometimes to the supposition that another person is not as worthy as oneself; and thus distance is created.

There is also some tendency for units to spread and irradiate; that is, if $\underline{P}$ and $\underline{O}$ are in a unit at work, there seems some expectation on their part that outside of work they will also be a unit. Now actually many unit formations are bound very tightly to particular situations and linked to very specific factors; but most people in units do not seem to appreciate this. The reason there is this generalizing tendency, this expectation that what is a unit in one situation will be a unit in another, is that people -- who make up the units -- are seen as having identities which are inherent "in" them, which they carry around with them. Given this perception, $\underline{P}$ and $\underline{O}$ who form a unit at work naturally tend to expect a unit elsewhere when they meet, since they perceive each other as still being the "same" as earlier.

Let me make clear that $\underline{P}$ and $\underline{O}$ can coordinate their activities without necessarily being in a unit; that is, a unit is a psychological creation which consists of this relation of dependence on the other's presence, commitment, and acceptance, the factors just discussed. An example of coordination which would not seem to be accompanied by any of the three types of psychological closeness is two people walking down a street who manage not to bump into each other; there is a rudimentary kind of coordination in this situation; each person must be -- however dimly -- aware that another body is approaching. However there is not necessarily any closeness. At the same time, it is obvious, from numerous daily examples, that such situations of coordination -- especially when they involve more extensive collaboration on the part of P and O -- provide a fertile breeding ground for the creation of the kind of psychological units we have been talking about.

In general there are a number of factors providing a situation favorable to the creation of units, but none of these inevitably creates a psychological unit. In addition to similarity, there is the well-recognized role which proximity plays (see Festinger, Schachter, and Back, 1950); other factors whose importance has been recognized are those of sex, length of acquaintance, race, and place of origin (hometown or country). A factor which has received little attention in the published literature but is important in my examples is that of synchronization. When two people must synchronize their movements with one another, this can be a potent factor leading to the development of the psychological processes crucial to unit formation. Dancing, for example, involves more or less intricate synchronization of movements; and so do many jobs done in cooperation with others. But all of these factors are important only insofar as they lead to the creation of the psychological processes which are crucial.

We have now considered both the distance examples, organized into various groups, and a theory of distance which specifies three types of distance. Some of the distance examples appear to be connected with one or another specific type of distance; other distance examples seem more complex and involve more than one type of distance. An example of the former is rejection, which may involve only one type of distance, the third type. When P rejects O, he places O outside his unit. A more complicated example is that inherent in ritual where the first type of distance is certainly created but where the third type of distance may not exist; that is, two people engaging in a ritual may be distant in one sense, but close in another sense.

We must recognize that any given instance of distance may involve only one type, or all three. There is no way to know a priori what is the case; to find out, one must examine the particularity of the phenomenon one wants to understand, and then think about it. For example, any given instance of ritual does not necessarily create Type I distance and simultaneously create Type III closeness. To know what is happening, the phenomenon itself must be examined and as full an account obtained as possible of what is happening with the two people involved.

Another kind of complexity is inherent in the fact that distance is not transitive or reflexive. P can be distant from O on one dimension, and yet O be close to P on that dimension. Further, P can, as in the case of some instances of shyness, be close to O on the first dimension -- have feelings towards O, be involved with O -- and yet, by his behavior, prevent O from becoming close on either that same dimension, or on another dimension (for example, the second). P may be concealing himself from O, because he is too shy to talk to O, and thus make less likely the possibility of O's becoming close on the second dimension.

Another type of complexity is made clear in the examples of reserved behavior. When P is being reserved, he is keeping himself partly concealed and thus creating the second type of distance; he does not give a full detailed picture of his life to O. But more importantly, P in being reserved is trying to prevent O from becoming attached to him, and thus is trying to ensure that O remains at a distance -- Type I distance -- from P. This is a level of complexity which we have not hitherto considered; P may want to direct his behavior to O, but he does not want O to direct his behavior to P̄. The person who is beīng reserved typically retreāts from O when O shows signs of becoming particularly atten- tive, when O shows signs of finding P particularly interesting.

Some processes appear to create distance because there is closeness; this paradoxical situation will become clear in looking at an example of deception. When P deceives O, the deception occurs because therē is some form of con- nection between P and O. This connection may involve closeness̄, eithēr between P and O or simply in O's relation to P. That is, P may be in a unit witȟ O (close in thāt sense) and then deceive O (creāte distance in the Type II sense); or P may be able to deceive successfully only because O is very attentive to P, listening carefully, involved in the Type I sense. To some degree, in fact, all distance phenomena arise in experience out of close- ness; one will only notice distance being created if one has been or expected to become close.

A problem which has not been solved is that inherent in trying to ascertain whether a given psychological process such as contempt occurs because distance of some sort already exists, or whether contempt creates the distance. A third possibility is that contempt helps to perpetuate a type of distance which already existed. Contempt of course involves placing the other person on a lower level; one looks down on the other and P's contempt functions to separate himself from O and arises out of an inequality which P perceives. The contempt may be created because of a prior closeness; for example, in the familiar valet example, if P and O are together in a unit P may come to feel contempt for O and thus destroy thē existing unit, psycho- logically speaking. Or in some cases, P and O may already be separated by one psychological process (such as exclusion or rejection); there is no unit to begin with and this may make contempt more likely to occur. In this situation, contempt of course would not alter the distance situation at all, since Type III distance would already exist; but contempts may help to perpetuate this type of distance and make less likely any future decrease in this type of distance.

A very real question exists as to whether or not some type of closeness is necessary for any form of human interaction. Our distance examples and our analysis of them does not address this question, but the question arises when one considers such processes as treating the other as an object. That process appears to involve all three types of distance. But the impersonal behavior we discussed elsewhere appears to involve only one type of distance, the first. If impersonal behavior involves only one type of distance, does this mean that closeness exists on one or the other of the other two dimensions? Not necessarily. In some cases, one or another of the dimensions may be irrelevant. Thus, one process -- seeing the other as an object -- may implicate all three dimensions; and another process -- impersonal -- may implicate only one dimension. But the general question of whether each of our psychological processes can be labeled in terms of a position on each of the three distance dimensions -- this question remains unanswered. The data of the examples appear to indicate that all three dimensions are not always relevant, but why?

Another general issue which pertains to the theory as a whole is that of the function of distance. All three types of distance are related in the way they function; they all prevent danger to the person. This function has both positive and negative aspects.

The first kind of distance prevents the development of feelings which, if they occurred, would link P and O together. P may go to a party and meet someone he likes; and consequently, he may try to see more of that person. As P directs activity towards this person, P to some extent (however slight) is changing. Furthermore when P is close to O in this first sense, he is increasing the

333

chances of becoming close in the second and third senses; thus maintaining this first type of distance guards against the kinds of increased involvement which are made more likely (but not of course necessitated by) becoming close in this first sense.

The positive aspect of this first type of distance is clearly its protective function; such distance enables a person to preserve himself from certain kinds of changes which, were they to occur, might make difficult the carrying out of tasks he has already committed himself to. A woman who is married may endanger her ability to preserve a perhaps precarious balance in her marital relationship if she either gets interested in another man, or becomes involved in a woman's liberation movement which might lead her to change in ways not functional for her existing marriage. Given a commitment to a particular marriage, certain changes might not be beneficial. The negative aspect of this kind of distance is of course part and parcel of the positive aspect: just as avoiding change is functional in some situations, it is clearly dysfunctional in others.

The second kind of distance wards off any chance of change of a person's point of view or self. This can occur in two ways. $\underline{P}$ may ward off possible change of his own point of view by concealing his point of view from the other person. This concealment helps preserve his own point of view in that it preserves it from attack. If no one else knows what you think, they cannot try to change your opinion. Telling someone may leave you open to arguments. R.D. Laing (1960) touches on this topic in discussing engulfment (a form of anxiety an insecure person is liable to). In his words,

> This anxiety accounts for one form of so-called "negative therapeutic reaction" to apparently correct interpretation in psychotherapy. To be understood correctly is to be engulfed, to be enclosed, swallowed up, drowned, eaten up, smothered, stifled, in or by another person's supposed all embracing comprehension. It is lonely and painful to be always misunderstood,

334

but there is at least from this point of view a measure of safety in isolation. (p. 45)

But as Laing points out, it is also lonely and painful not to be understood and this is one of the negative aspects of the second kind of distance.

Another way in which this type of distance may reduce the chance of change in the self is by avoiding taking the other person's point of view, by avoiding understanding of the other person. This helps preserve one's own point of view in a more direct way, for of course whenever you take someone else's point of view (by understanding it) your own point of view alters slightly. Clearly this could be either negative or positive. Depending on the situation, maintaining one's point can be either vital to survival, or disastrous.

The third type of distance prevents commitment and thus prevents the kind of interdependence and responsibilities which such commitment entails. In staying out of a unit, P avoids the intricate interdependence that being in a unit with someone else creates, and thus keeps himself free of the burdens of such interpersonal ties. To give a small but revealing example, other people cannot so easily ask him favors and he need not feel obliged to do them if he is not in a unit. Obviously the third type of distance can arise in two ways: either because P is staying out of a unit, or because P is being kept out of a unit by O. And again, this third type of distance can be either positive or negative in its function. In some cases, one already has enough interdependency and the concomitant responsibilities, and wants to use distance to avoid any further ones. In other situations -- imagine an alienated person -- one may be lacking the kind of responsibilities which would make life interesting or even tolerable, and in this situation distance is clearly not adaptive or positive in its function.

Although closeness is not the main topic of this study, we can say a word about the functions of

335

the three kinds of closeness as well. The first
kind of closeness, by enhancing the development of
feelings, keeps the person psychologically alive;
it prevents apathy, boredom, alienation, and other
related psychological processes from arising. The
second kind of closeness leads to recognition of
the self, which in turn creates some kind of
security; when one is known for what one is, security in some manner is created. The third kind of
closeness promotes confidence or the ability to act.
Exactly how security (created by the second type of
closeness) and confidence (created by the third)
differ is not clear, but the difference is related
to the distinction between resting calmly (security)
and being able to engage in activity (confidence).

Distance then functions to prevent the dangers
inherent in closeness, and closeness functions to
prevent the dangers inherent in distance. The enigma
here of course is why people ever bother to become
close to others, if such closeness always entails
risk; but this is one of the central enigmas in
human relations.[6] We must strive to maintain some
kind of equilibrium between too much closeness and
too much distance. They both entail risks. But
people who pursue perfect security through isolation
from others (through minimizing all chance of danger
to themselves) achieve less security than those who
seek it through connections with others.

Reference Notes
for Chapter VI

1. See Deutsch and Isard's paper (1961) and Matore's work (1962).

2. Because of space limitations, this chapter will focus on the examples of distance which were collected and on the theory which accounts for them, rather than on the psychological literature about distance (which is not very substantial anyway). For more detail on the psychological literature, see Kreilkamp, 1970.

3. Michel Foucault, in _Madness and Civilization_, 1965, discusses this point at length.

4. For example, see Mrs. Pardiggle or Mr. Turveydrop in _Bleak House_ (1853).

5. Of course, as Kenneth Burke or Goffman might point out, often there is an exhortative component in talk which attempts to assign responsibility. That is, often in pointing out responsibilities, one is trying to establish connections or persuade others to see connections, where there may in fact be none at all, or only very tenuous ones. See Burke, 1950, for examples.

6. For example, Freud comments: "...we may even venture to touch on the question: whence does that necessity arise that urges our mental life to pass on beyond the limits of narcissism and to attach the libido to objects?" (1914, p. 66).

337

References
for Chapter VI

Adams, J. K.   Deception and intrigue in so-called
     mental illness.   Journal of Humanistic Psychology,
     1964, 4, 27-38.

Aiken, C.   The collected novels.   New York: Holt,
     Rinehart and Winston, 1964.

Anderson, S.   Winesburg, Ohio.   New York: Modern
     Library, 1919.

Bales, R. F.   Interaction process analysis.
     Cambridge, Massachusetts: Addison-Wesley Co.,
     Inc., 1950.

Bettelheim, B.   The empty fortress.   New York: The
     Free Press, 1967.

Blackmur, R. P.   Introduction to King Coffin.   In
     Aiken, C.   The collected novels.   New York:
     Holt, Rinehart, and Winston, 1964.

Bogardus, E.   Social distance in poetry.   Sociology
     and Social Research, 1951, 36, 41-47.

Bogardus, E.   Changes in racial distance.   Inter-
     national Journal of Opinion and Attitude Research,
     1949, 1, 55-62.

Bogardus, E.   Social distance in Shakespeare.
     Sociology and Social Research, 1933, 18, 67-73.

Boll, H.   Billiards at half-past nine.   New York:
     McGraw-Hill, 1962.

Brod, M.   Franz Kafka.   New York: Schocken Books,
     1960 (originally 1937).

Bronte, E.   Wuthering heights.   New York: Modern
     Library, 19-- (originally 1847).

338

Burke, K. A grammar of motives. New York: Prentice-Hall, 1950.

Deutsch, K. and Isard, W. A note on the generalized concept of effective distance. Behavioral Science, 1961, 6, 308-311.

Dickens, C. Bleak house. London: Bradbury and Evans, 1853.

Fitzgerald, F. S. The great Gatsby. New York: Modern Library, 1934.

Foucault, M. Madness and civilization. New York: Pantheon Books, 1965.

Freud, S. On narcissism, 1914. In Riviere, J. and Strachey, J. (Eds.) The collected papers of Sigmund Freud. New York: The International Psycho-Analytical Press, 1924-1950. Volume IV, pp. 30-59. Reference here is to the paperback edition, Rieff, P. (Ed.) General psychological theory. New York: Collier Books, 1963, pp. 56-82.

Goffman, E. Behavior in public places. Glencoe, Illinois: The Free Press, 1963.

Heider, F. The psychology of interpersonal relations. New York: John Wiley and Sons, 1958.

Hinde, T. Mr. Nicholas. New York: Farrar, Straus and Young, Inc., 1953.

Holt, J. How children fail. New York: Pitman Publishing Corporation, 1964.

Hunt, M. The world of the formerly married. New York: Mcgraw-Hill, 1966.

Jones, E. The life and work of Sigmund Freud. New York: Basic Books, Inc., 1955, Volume II.

Kaufman, M. Remember me to God. Philadelphia: J.P. Lippincott, 1957.

Kreilkamp, T. The dimensions of psychological distance. Ph.D. Dissertation, New York University, 1970.

Laing, R. D. The divided self. Chicago: Quadrangle Books, 1960.

Lessing, D. Retreat to innocence. London: Michael Joseph, 1956.

Lessing, D. The golden notebook. New York: Simon and Schuster, 1962.

Lurie, A. Imaginary friends. New York: Coward-McCann, 1967.

Matore, G. L'espace humain. Paris: Le Colombe, 1962.

Melville, H. Bartleby the scrivener. In Standard Edition of the works of Herman Melville. New York: Russell, 1963. (Originally in 1853).

O'Neill, E. Long day's journey into night. New Haven: Yale University Press, 1956.

Orwell, G. Marrakech. In A collection of essays. New York: Doubleday, 1954a.

Orwell, G. Looking back on the Spanish war. In A collection of essays. Doubleday, 1954b.

Roget, P. M. Thesaurus. New York: St. Martin's Press, 1965.

Samuels, G. The people vs. Baby. New York: Doubleday, 1967.

Sansom, W. The cautious heart. New York: Reynal, 1958.

Sartre, J. P. Nausea. Norfolk, Connecticut:

Shute, N. On the beach. New York: William Morrow and Company, 1957.

340

Stendhal, (Marie-Henri Beyle). *The red and the black*. New York: Modern Library, 1926.

Tomkins, C. *The bride and the bachelors*. New York: Viking Press, 1965.

Wharton, E. *Ethan Frome*. New York: Charles Scribner's Sons, 1911.

VII

OVERVIEW

Joseph de Rivera

It might seem that a handful of investigations, the exploration of a few emotions, would not tell us much about the vast complexity and range of human experience. However, each particular emotion involves important dimensions of experience and these may be related to the work of other investigators so that even a few sample studies suggest the outlines of a much larger mass of experience. While I shall not attempt to render a detailed picture of this mass, a picture that would be comprehensible to readers who were unacquainted with the preceding pages, the following abstract sketch may convey the richness of the territory which may be opened by future exploration.

The lifting quality of elation implies a vertical dimension which is characterized by a sense of freedom and an absence of contact with the reality of others. Lindsay-Hartz relates this to the realm of fantasy characterized by Dembo (1976) as a dream-like region of free movement where wishes can come true because no barriers stand between a person and his or her goal. Termed the "region of unreality" it may be represented topologically as a plane which is above the region of reality. A person may retreat to this plane of fantasy as a way of escaping tension in the region of reality. However, assent also serves a more positive function, for this "upper" region provides the opportunity for greater vision and is the realm of ideals as well as fantasy. It permits the imagination which is so necessary if planning is to rise above the dulling concerns of present reality to guide movement towards the ideal.

343

Lewin (1935) noted that the boundary between this region and the region of reality became more differentiated in conditions of high tension (when a person may confuse fantasy with reality).

The investigation of elation suggests that when events make a wish come true, a person must go "up" to the level of unreality in order to believe in the reality of the event. It is from this raised position (out of contact with others) that the person announces the new reality until it becomes part of social reality and the person can return to being grounded.

At first glance, the lifting of elation appears related to the "levitation" described as an aspect of laughter. However, Funk notes that levitation does not involve going up to a region of fantasy but going out of the situation to a region of experience where things are not serious. Elsewhere (de Rivera, 1976) I have pointed out that Lewin and his students used the concept of unreality in two different ways: 1) to refer to a realm of fantasy where a person can move without constraint above the region of reality, and 2) to refer to sub-regions of reality where events were not serious because they involved pretending (as in taking a practice test rather than a real test, or pretending that a doll is alive). It would seem that laughter is a non-intentional way of entering such a sub-region of reality (see Figure 2).

If this view is correct then the lightness of levity is not achieved by the person going up along a vertical dimension but by the maintenance of a personal world within the horizontal dimensions of ordinary reality. Rather than the lift of elation, the person might experience the private world of euphoria. Behind the autonomous boundaries of such sub-regions the "work" of play or laughter can proceed without being encroached upon by the heaviness of serious reality.

The drawback of such privately maintained sub-regions of reality is that they prevent a meeting

FIG. 2

SOME REGIONS OF EXPERIENCE

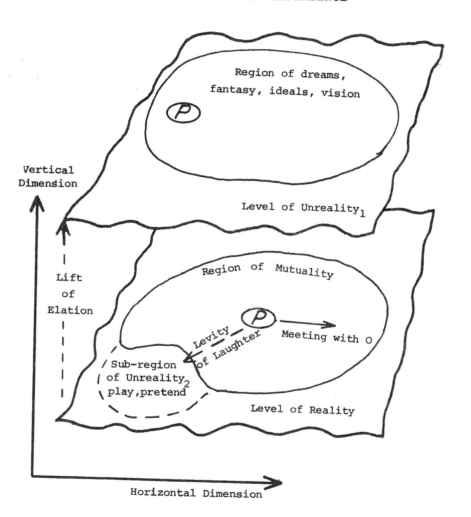

with the reality of others. That such meetings are possible is evidenced by emotions such as joy. When joy is experienced it is clear that the person has stopped autonomous willing and has opened the boundary of the privately maintained world (sub-region of reality) so that he or she can meet the presence of an other. Such a meeting completely grounds the person in a reality that is larger than that maintained by the personal will so that the person experiences the self as part of a larger whole and is connected to the other in a way that abolishes the first type of distance deliniated by Kreilkamp.

This meeting with an other has taken place along the horizontal dimension of reality and the contrast between the grounding of joy and the lifting quality of elation may be related to Jaeger's (1971) analysis of the difference between the horizontal and vertical dimensions of experience. In Jaeger's articulation, the horizontal is the dimension where persons can meet each other, where a person can feel "backed" by supportive figures and can "face" others in mutual exchange. By contrast, the vertical often involves a loss of this mutuality, as when a person rises to private heights and looks down on those beneath, or falls to the depths of despair (as an addict rises and falls in an isolated world).

While Jaeger stresses the deficits of the vertical mode, it is clear that its assent may provide a person with vision and does not neces-sarily involve a loss of mutuality. In fact, recent work suggests that at least two emotions involve an integration of the vertical and horizontal. In exaltation the person is raised to heights but re-mains grounded, either through communication with others who are also raised or through an audience's recognition of the self's triumph (cf. Kahn, 1980). In the latter case, the group often places its hero on an elevated platform and the hero walks out to accept honors with a measured stride that serves to ground the self and prevent the private bubble-like lift of elation. In hope the person is buoyed up and moves freely with a general body tonicity in spite of an obvious gap between ideal and present

346

reality. This is achieved, not by denying the
gravity of the current situation, but by relying on
the reality of an other's caring (cf. Brown, 1979),
and the discussion of hope and gladness in Chapter
IV).

The integration of vertical and horizontal
dimensions is also achieved whenever anger is
successfully expressed. We have seen that anger
occurs when a meeting (on the horizontal dimension)
challenges a person's sense of what ought to exist
(on the plane of ideality). Anger "instructs" us to
remove this challenge to what ought to exist. If
the anger is shared then mutuality is achieved, the
other may assume a responsibility that was previously neglected, or the person may achieve a more
separate identity. In any case the person publicly
asserts his or her position, maintains ideals, and
influences social reality. Of course, if the anger
is not shared, it only affects the person's private
reality -- it maintains what ought to be in a limited
sub-region of reality. And if the person "distances"
the other by putting the other down on the vertical
dimension, an alienation is created which weakens
the unity of the human community.

The "distancing" which may occur as an
alternative to anger, as when someone says, "he's
a jerk, so why care what he does?," appears to
involve all three of the types of distance articulated by Kreilkamp. Conversely, the experience of
anger seems to presuppose a lack of any of the
different types. The analysis of distance allows us
to make a more refined analysis of the alternatives
to anger. Ideally, it should be possible to state
these alternatives in a way that shows the relationship between the different types of distance and the
horizontal and vertical dimensions of experience.
At present, we must be satisfied with the following
observations:

1. A person may avoid anger by using only the
third type of distance, creating a boundary between
the other and the self on the plane of reality by
making a distinction that places the other outside

one's unit so that he or she is no longer seen as
responsible, yet is still attended to personally
and still openly communicated with (hence, avoiding
the first and second types of distance). For example,
a father might avoid anger by concluding that his
son was still too much of a child to be held responsible for some failure, yet continue responding to him
as a person and communicating with him.

2. A person may avoid the full experience of
anger by failing to express it, thus establishing
the second type of distance by not communicating and
hence, creating a lack of understanding between the
friend and the self. We may also note that if a
person cannot at all comprehend why the other acts in
a disagreeable way the person may find it difficult
to become fully angry.

3. A person may avoid anger by using only the
first type of distance as when a person "withdraws"
from a friend in order to avoid feelings of hurt or
anger but, consequently, fails to respond to the
friend with any personal feeling.

As Kreilkamp notes, there is an interesting
theoretical problem posed by such experiences: while
the person is withdrawn (thus creating the first
type of distance), the withdrawal itself is based
on feelings of anger or hurt which the person is
reluctant to experience and express because of a
fear of being rejected by the other. This implies
the existence of the very same personal relationship
which the first type of distance negates. Of course,
if the person experiences too much hurt, the relationship may be seriously altered, either by a severing
or withering of the personal connection (thereby
creating a permanent distance of the first type),
or by an altering of the boundaries of the unit
which formerly included the person and the other (as
when lovers become friends, or children grow up, and
a distance of the third type is created). However,
at the time of the hurt the person is obviously still
affected by some personal aspect of the relationship
and must be unwilling to face whether or not the
other really cares about the self. Evidently, the

person is only withdrawing into a sub-region of reality, thus interupting the mutuality of the relationship and creating the first type of distance, but only within the sub-region. Of course, this creates communication problems, thereby establishing the second type of distance. However, an illusion of worth is maintained on the fantasy level and the person successfully defends against the anxiety that is inherent in facing whether or not he or she is really loved. To the person it must appear that his or her worth depends on being attended to and accepted by the other. If this conviction is tested and the other lacks the interest or stamina to really care for the self, then, the person fears, he or she would really become worthless.

When a person does experience anxiety it would seem that he or she is emerging from the relatively deprived reality of either a sub-region of pretense or a vertical position of fantasy, and is on the verge of claiming a position of worth within his or her community. The person must attain this ideal position if he or she is to reach full selfhood. But the actual position achieved, the socially real position, must be mutually determined. Hence, others and not simply the self are involved in the determination of who one is, the person lacks complete control and a risk is involved. Either success or failure may occur and since one's desired identity appears to be at stake, success is required, a "must" is experienced, and the person becomes anxious. Since the very notion of self identity implies a continuity with the past, and since becoming whom we must become implies the future, we must add a temporal dimension to the spatial aspects of experience we have been discussing until now.

Goodman notes a paradox that exists in the experience of anxiety: while the person appears to confront a risk to self identity, the anxiety seems to vanish as soon as a decision is taken to face the risk, before either success or failure is experienced. This may possibly be explained by the fact that when we accept "reality," the nature of the reality we experience changes, so that the "reality" we confront

349

after acceptance is different from the "reality" we experience before acceptance. It seems possible that when an anxious person is in a position to accept risk and fully face reality, this acceptance changes the nature of the reality involved so that one sees that one's essential identity is not really at risk and a particular outcome is no longer required.

How we experience reality appears to depend on the fundamental choices we make. If we allow the experience of anger we do not experience distance. If we use the third type of distance and differentiate the other from our self we experience separation but may preserve our special feeling for the other, thus avoiding the first type of distance. If we allow ourselves to laugh we can risk entering situations which would otherwise overwhelm us. If we open the boundaries of sub-regions that enclose us, we establish the possibility of a meting with the presence of others. This may lead to an experience of joy, a grounding of the self and the requirement of celebration. On the other hand, we may open ourselves to anxiety and the choice of whether or not to accept the risk of developing our identity.

The explorations in this book are investigations of such choices and their consequences, an attempt to begin maping the ways a human soul may take. While we have confined most of our investigations to which anyone may have experiences, it seems clear that rarer experiences may be described quite accurately, as some aspects of schizophrenia have been described by Laing (1960) and by Green (1964). And more basic choices may be deliniated as Macmurray (1961) has done in his description of the alternative ways in which a child may cope with being weaned, and the resultant consequences for how he or she perceives both the badness of the world and what social institutions are needed to insure goodness.

Perhaps a knowledge of our human choices and their consequences will enable us to make the decisions we must make if we and our human community are to continue to develop. In any case, we hope others will join us in exploring these largely uncharted realms.

References
for Chapter VII

Brown, F. The experience of hope. Unpublished
    paper for Research on Emotion and Motivation,
    1979, Clark University.

Dembo, T. The dynamics of anger. In J. de Rivera
    (Ed.) Field theory as human science. New York:
    Gardner Press, 1976.

de Rivera, J. The nature of unreality. In J. de
    Rivera (Ed.) Field theory as human science.
    New York: Gardner Press, 1976.

Green, H. I never promised you a rose garden.
    New York: Holt, Rinehart and Winston, 1964.

Jaeger, B. Horizontality and verticality: A
    phenomenological exploration into lived space.
    In A. Giorgi, W.F. Fischer, and R. Von
    Eckartsberg Duquesne Studies in Phenomenological
    Psychology: Volume I. Duquesne: Duquesne
    University Press, 1971.

Kahn, W. The structure of exaltation. Unpublished
    paper for Research on Emotion and Motivation,
    1980, Clark University.

Laing, R. D. The divided self. Chicago: Quadrangle,
    1960.

Lewin, K. A dynamic theory of personality. New York:
    McGraw-Hill, 1935.

Macmurray, J. Persons in relation. New York:
    Harper, 1961.

SUBJECT INDEX

dependence on investigation, 8, 13-14, 85, 87, 145
description of, 4-8, 38, 274
description of interview in, 86-88, 163-164, 213
development of a, 4-8, 38, 274
examples of, 52-54, 55-57, 57-60, 322-324
focused on one personal example, 226
formulating the conceptualization, 15
as an inner dialogue, 226
insuring exciting encounters, 51
limitations of, 26, 28, 143-145
with non-verbal material, 226
method for testing, 211-214, 222
and modifying conceptualizations, 55, 57, 63, 69, 71-73
realism vs. idealism in, 29
results of, 55
role of language in, 16-20, 163
role of research partner, 3, 8
role of sensitive listening, 14-15
tested against categories, 226, 244-245
testing of, 165
use of map construction in, 76

use of written encounters, 51
used with other methods, 27
validity of, 28-29, 211
Confident state, 99, 101, 111, 181, 328, 336
Conflict, 49
Confusion, 105-109
Connection, 279, 289, 332, 336, 346, 348,
lack of, 279, 284
Consciousness, 70
not allowed, 141
Consumatory behavior, 240
Contempt, 303, 304, 313, 332
Contest, 42, 44
Control, 42, 100, 240, 294, 325
lack of, 104, 135, 181, 349
loss of, 250
Critical listening, 88
Crying, 230, 260-262, 267
Cynicism, 285
Culture, 121
cross-cultural research, 19, 31
differences in, 144-145, 209

Danger, 73, 108, 134, 137-138
Deception, 310-312, 326, 332
Decision, 109, 112, 121-122, 143, 153, 315, 349
Defence, 243, 255, 333, 349
Defensive, 193, 282, 334
Dehumanization, 231, 321-322
Dependency, 181, 182, 184, 185, 186, 187, 188, 191,

179
structure of, 179
transformation of,
  172-177, 179
Embodiment, 47, 48,
  49, 326
Embarrassment, 254
Emotion, 240, 262
  expression of, 72-75
  intensity of, 187,
    208, 209
  mixed, 182
  positive, 163
  related to
    laughter, 260, 261
  structure of, 48,
    50, 51, 165
  as a way of being, 51
Empathic listening, 88
Energy, 74, 94, 237,
  257
  flooding, 126-128, 130
Environment, 165
Envy, 304
Essence, 35, 78
Eternity, 238
Ethno-methodology, 25
Euphoria, 344
Exaltation, 346
Exclusion, 278, 301-304,
  316
  contempt, 303
Existential perspective,
  55
Expectancy, 183
  negative, 191
Experience, personal,
  3, 4, 11, 21
  "An experience," 21
  and art, 27
  concrete, 10
  as created, 21
  defined, 1, 5, 20
  developmental dynamics
    of, 22

dimensions of, 343
intensity of, 113
as interpretation, 30, 32
language and, 16-20
and laughter, 258
meaning of, 22-23
as narrative, 10-12
as an objective event, 22
regions of, 344-345
structure of, 18, 55,
  209, 263
of wholeness, 197, 202
Experimental approach,
  22-23, 24, 27
Experimental phenomenology,
  26, 65
Explicit understanding, 17,
  19-20
Exploration, 1, 76, 343,
  350, 351
Expressiveness, 296, 298
Expression, 325, 326
  of anger, 48
  of elation, 177-179
  of emotion, 70-75
  of gladness, 190-192
  of joy, 206-207

Faith, 267
"Family resemblance," 78
Fantasy, 118, 171, 174,
  183, 343, 344, 349
  enjoyment of, 209
  fear of, 210
  realized, 178
  see also Dream
Fear, 36, 37, 38, 41, 47,
  59, 66, 73, 75, 137,
  155, 210, 348
Feelings, 281, 284, 286,
  288, 294, 308, 321, 325,
  333, 336,
  lack of, 286
Field, 66
Field-theory, 24

361

see also Unreality
"Real me," 111, 122
Recognition, of
  experience, 2, 107, 149
Region of low gravity,
  234, 242, 243, 247, 249,
  250, 263, 265
  see also Reality,
  sub-regions of
Rejection, 302, 303, 304
Repression, 90, 91, 145
Requiredness, 113
Research partner, 9, 11,
  13, 22, 26, 27, 30, 163
  definition of, 3
  described, 83, 89, 143,
  212
  individual differences,
  in, 53, 139, 209-210
  relationship to, 8
  selection of, 89
Reserve, 293-297, 308,
  331, 332
Respect, 299-301
Response, 50, 261, 263,
  284
Responsibility, 39, 40,
  41, 43, 52, 75, 99, 102,
  110, 113, 114, 122, 128,
  132, 139, 142, 325, 337,
  348
  lack of, 314-316
Responsiveness, lack of,
  278-279
Restructuring, 66, 70,
  73, 240
Results, of matching
  study, 214-220
Rights, 122, 314
Risk, 60, 108, 109,
  122, 336, 349, 350
  criteria for meeting,
  116-118
  situations of, 115-116
Ritual, 275-281, 300,

306, 331
  as creating distance, 276
  as holding unit together,
  278
  and obsessive acts, 280
  and politeness, 279-280
Robot, 318-321
Roles, 110

Sad, 230
Satori, 225, 229, 265
Schemata, 233
Schizophrenia, 225, 230,
  243, 265, 319, 350
Security, 302, 336
Self,
  actualizing, 90
  boundaries, 56, 203
  confusion about, 105-108
  criticism, 102-105, 119
  definition of, 78
  as origin of space-time,
  98, 141
  disintegration, 91, 131-
  136
  experience of, 98, 99,
  346
  in anxiety, 101-102
  "being myself," 99-101,
  111
  as insubstantial, 103,
  111
  in panic, 131-132
  involvement, 170
  one must not become, 141
  and others, 240-242
  respect, 104
  responsibility, 132, 141,
  142
  revelation, 296, 312, 325
  survival of, 136
  and time, 237-238
  and world, 232-237
  see also Identity